LEAVING THE NEST

LEAVING the NEST

THE COMPLETE GUIDE TO LIVING ON YOUR OWN

by
Dorinne Armstrong
and
(her loving son)
Richard

Illustrations by Doris Reich

BⱵB
BEECH TREE BOOKS
A QUILL EDITION
New York

Library of Congress Cataloging-in-Publication Data

Armstrong, Dorinne.
  Leaving the nest.

  Bibliography: p.
  Includes index.
    1. Young adults—United States—Life skills guides.
  2. Home economics. I. Armstrong, Richard, 1952–
  II. Title.
  HQ799.7.A76   1986   640   85-28102
  ISBN 0-688-05260-6   (pbk.)

Printed in the United States of America

2 3 4 5 6 7 8 9 10

BOOK DESIGN BY LINEY LI

BⅠB

The word "book" is said to derive from *boka,* or beech.
The beech tree has been the patron tree of writers since ancient times and represents the flowering of literature and knowledge.

To Dick,
*who taught me there was life
after the tuna fish casserole.*

—DSA

To Sharon,
*who begged me to
put her name in this book.*

—RAA

Preface:
Don't Pour the
Grease Down
the Drain

Richard

In Shakespeare's *Hamlet*, Polonius sends his son Laertes into the world with a wise and gentle speech that includes some of the Bard's most memorable lines: "Neither a borrower nor a lender be . . . give every man thy ear, but few thy voice . . . to thine own self be true."

When, after four years and thirty thousand dollars of higher education, I bid my parents goodbye and set off into what we college students had always naïvely referred to as "the real world," my mother looked into my eyes and uttered a piece of advice as sound as any I had ever heard:

"Don't pour the grease down the drain."

I was immediately struck by the beauty and simplicity of her words. But the wisdom of them did not fully dawn on me until several months later, when, after blithely pouring the drippings of hundreds of fried hamburgers down my sink, the dishwater began to back up. And up. And up . . . until it flowed over the countertop, leaked onto the floor, seeped into the dining room, cascaded through the bedroom, flooded the bathroom, and finally drowned my cat.

There's nothing like the sound of a wet, angry, dying cat to remind a guy of the fact that his mother was sometimes, maybe even frequently, right.

And it was that realization, plus the realization that I was not alone—that there were millions of highly educated morons out there just like me—that germinated the idea for this book.

This is a book for people like me. It is a book for kids who get out into the real world and suddenly discover four years of college taught them a lot about Plato but nothing about Drano; a lot about Yeats, but nothing about yeast; a lot about the tide of man's history, but nothing about the history of man's Tide.

It is for young people who live in squalid apartments not because they hate to clean, but because they don't know how . . .

For kids who spend hundreds of dollars a month in restaurants eating food less than half as good as what they could prepare at home if only they had the barest instruction and advice . . .

For people who live in apartments that look like they just moved in the day before, when, with a little ingenuity and advice, they could decorate a home worthy of a full-color spread in *Better Homes and Gardens*.

Of course, not all of these young men and women have their mothers handy when they need them. And that's why this book is a mother and son collaboration. Here is the book that says, "If you don't have your mother around to help you, take *my* mother."

Please.

RAA
New York City, 1985

Dorinne

Many years ago, when my father threatened to lock me in my room until I cleaned up what he referred to as the potato patch growing underneath my bed, I vowed that I would never be so mean to any children of mine. They could live in squalor if that's what made them happy.

Guess what?

I spent twenty years yelling and threatening, but all I ever accomplished was what came to be known as the "green plastic bag." That's where my daughter put everything that was supposed to be carefully folded, sorted, or put away. It didn't leave her bedroom until the day she left for college.

As I look back on my mistakes, it occurs to me that few parents—even those with the best intentions—actually give their offspring much on-the-job training. It was easier to "do it myself."

True, there are a few conscientious mothers who recognize what the future holds in store. One of my closest friends has four daughters who, as children, were numbered one through four. Household chores were posted by number, and some-how—through some fantastic planning that was beyond my comprehension—Number Three always managed to get the table cleared just as Number One was filling the dishpan. It worked. And today, those little girls are four competent and, as far as I know, perfectly happy young women.

But let's face it. Most parents aren't that well organized. We have more of an "I had to learn it the hard way and you should too" attitude. We comfort ourselves with the thought that while Number Four was learning how to scrape a carrot, *our* kids were learning the lyrics to the theme song of the Flintstones.

At least, we are comforted until that untrained young adult sets out to conquer the world. At that point, I for one developed a great sympathy for the world—or at least that part of it that would be cashing his personal checks, sharing his living quarters, and—God forbid—eating his cooking. All of a sudden I realized this kid didn't even know enough not to pour the grease down the drain!

This, then, is an attempt to rectify my mistakes, fill in my omissions, and say for all parents to all kids: We're really glad you had a carefree childhood, but here's a book full of things we probably should have mentioned.

DSA
Potomac, Maryland, 1985

ACKNOWLEDGMENTS

When I telephoned my mother to tell her the William Morrow publishing company liked her idea for a survival manual for young adults and wanted to see it fleshed out into an entire book, she said:

"Oh my God, Ricky, don't they realize it was just a joke?"

To get this idea from the just-a-joke stage to the stage where it does indeed look something like a book required the help of many people. Foremost among them were the wonderful folks at Quill:

Our publisher Jim Landis, who had the courage, insight, and—let's face it—sheer brilliance to buy this book.

Our editor, Jane Meara who, lucky for us, turned out to be the only person in America who knew less about living in the real world than we did. (In the course of working with Jane, we discovered she had never defrosted her refrigerator, balanced her checkbook, or in fact, done anything that could be construed as adult behavior without first calling her parents in California. And we realized, to our delight, that yes, there *is* a need for such a book.)

And Jim's crack assistant, Ginny Richards, who took our manuscript out of the "slush pile," wiped the slush off it, and gave us much needed encouragement and advice every step of the way.

We must also thank the two literary agents who worked on this project: Ruth Aley, who believed in the book when no one else did; and Richard Pine, who didn't believe in it until *everyone* else did (but we like him anyway).

Thanks also to Bobby Haft and Ann Liski, who acted as the small hinges on which huge doors were finally opened.

Four people made up our editorial advisory board, or as we lovingly called them, "the gang of idiots." Each of them gave up many hours of time to pore over our manuscript and offer hundreds of valuable comments and suggestions. They are: Bob Bly, John Bullion, Kevin Kinley, and Roann Rubin.

From this group, we must single out Bob Bly, without whose knowledgeable advice at several crucial junctures this book surely would not have been published.

The following individuals served on our distinguished panel of self-appointed experts. We've listed their areas of "expertise" in parenthesis:

Lydia Armstrong (being young, single, and a willing guinea pig)

Richard Armstrong, Sr. (cooking, insurance)

Sharon Armstrong (everything)

Blanche Brixey (cleaning)

Catherine Foti (being young and single)

Elina Korney (cooking, home repair)

Gilla McCarriston (cooking)

Stan Scott (home repair)

Alex Semple (furniture)

Carol Williams (cooking)

In addition to these characters, we also had a distinguished panel of *real* experts:

Dr. Mark Finger, MD (health)

Dr. James Sipkins, MD (health)

Holly Slocum (financial planning)

Dr. Brian Weiss, DDS (health)

Any errors, mistakes, typos, libelous statements, poor grammar, and in fact, anything at all wrong in this book may be blamed directly on these people. All the good parts are our own.

Wait a second. We meant the opposite, of course.

Finally, to all the publishers, literary agents, and assorted know-it-alls who rejected the idea for this book, we'd like to say,

"Hi."

Contents

Preface: Don't Pour the Grease Down the Drain   7

Acknowledgments   11

1. All I Need Is a Room Somewhere—How to Find an
   Apartment   19

2. Not by Bread Alone—Stocking the Essentials   43

3. Feathering Your Nest—Furnishing and Decorating Your
   Home   63

4. Cooking 101—An Idiot's Guide to the Art of Cooking   95

5. Spit and Polish . . . Mostly Spit—How to Clean Your Home
   Quickly and Easily   169

6. The Trickle-Out Theory—Managing Your Money   199

7. Tell Mommy Where It Hurts—Health and Hygiene   229

8. Mother, Please! I'd Rather Do It Myself—Home Repair   255

9. How to Become a Decent Human in 7 Days or Less—

   Commonsense Etiquette   283

Epilogue: The Secret of Life   305

Bibliography and Sources   307

Index   311

CHAPTER ONE

All I Need Is a Room Somewhere—

How to Find an Apartment

DORINNE: On the day my daughter moved into her first apartment, she ran into a drunk sitting on the sidewalk in front of her building.

"Moving in?" he asked.

"Yes," she said. "Is this a good neighborhood?"

He took a long drink from a bottle hidden in a brown paper bag and wiped his mouth with the back of his hand.

"I wouldn't live here," he replied.

Looking for an apartment is like looking for a job. You spend a lot of time filling out applications. You pound the pavement until your feet hurt. And you tend to get more disappointments than results. Like looking for a job, there are two ways to go about it. You can follow a systematic and conscientious plan, or you can lie in bed watching TV, waiting for the phone to ring. The difference in the success of these methods is startling.

The first step in finding anything, of course, is to know what you're looking for. That's why we've begun this chapter with an overview of the most important qualities to consider when choosing an apartment. Once you can picture your dream house in your mind, we'll show you how to go out and find it. And we'll also give you some tips on signing a lease.

Choosing an Apartment

Although choosing an apartment is one of life's major decisions—almost as important as finding a mate or selecting a career—most people approach the task in a surprisingly haphazard way. They grab the nearest edition of the classifieds, circle several likely prospects, spend a hurried Saturday morning looking at a few of them, and sign the lease for the first one that seems barely habitable. No wonder they are disappointed when, a week or so later, they discover a leaky toilet, loud neighbors, and hot and cold running mice.

Fortunately, there's a better way. Apartments can be evaluated by four major characteristics: neighborhood, size, price, and amenities, or "style." As you learn to judge these characteristics, you will develop a picture of what kind of apartment would be right for you. Later, when you go out to look for it, you can use the chart at the end of this chapter to rate the apartments against each other and against your ideal. That way, you'll avoid the two most common mistakes in choosing an apartment: accepting one that's not as good as what you might be able to find; or committing yourself to one that's better than you can afford.

NEIGHBORHOOD

Responding to the charge that he could never become a great philosopher without traveling, Henry David Thoreau once said, "I've traveled a good deal around Concord." But how many of us can say we've traveled a good deal around our city?

So why not begin your apartment hunt by taking a tour. Stay away from familiar paths and concentrate on areas you've never seen before, even the so-called "bad" areas your aunt warned you not to go near. What's bad for your aunt and what's bad for you may be two different things. Check out the ritzy neighborhoods, too. Perhaps one of those mansions you thought were only for millionaires is actually divided into dozens of apartments for poor folks like you. In short, put aside your preconceived ideas and look at your city with the fresh eyes of a tourist.

Then ask yourself one simple question: "Where would I most like to live?"

Once you've narrowed your search down to three or four areas, plan another tour. Only this time, do it on foot. And as you leisurely walk around each neighborhood, rate it for the following qualities:

SAFETY   The safety of a neighborhood can be a little hard to judge on a casual visit, so ask around. Ask a policeman for his expert advice or any local person for a firsthand opinion. Your own instincts are valuable, too. Walk the streets. Do you *feel* safe here? Would you feel safe staggering home from a party at 3:00 A.M.? In most large American cities, crime can occur anywhere, so the quality of the neighborhood doesn't always make as much difference as we'd like. But if you're constantly looking over your shoulder, you've chosen the wrong place to live.

CONVENIENCE   If you lived in this neighborhood, would your commute to work include three bus rides, one subway trip, and a quick whitewater raft shoot? Or would it be relatively simple? What about its convenience to the other places you visit regularly: Mom and Dad's house, your lover's place, your karate class, and so on. Don't forget about rating how convenient it will be for people who want to visit *you*. You shouldn't be forced into the life of a hermit by your address.

ATTRACTIVENESS   Living in an ugly neighborhood takes a heavy psychological toll, but living in a charming one will lift your spirits even in the worst of times. Bills may be adding up, your health may be failing, your sweetheart may have left you, but when you walk out that door and see those tree-lined streets and picturesque townhouses, you'll feel like the romantically suffering young genius you really are.

SHOPPING   There's nothing worse than walking out the door of your new apartment after a hard day of moving and discovering that the nearest grocery store is five miles east of Minsk. Good supermarkets *must* be handy. The same goes for drug stores, laundromats, and dry cleaners. On the second rung of importance you can put restaurants, newsstands, stationery shops, hair salons, liquor stores, hardware stores, and late-night or all-night convenience stores.

PUBLIC SERVICES   If you don't own a car, you must check a neighborhood carefully for its access to public transportation. Buy a transit map and keep it with you on your apartment hunt. Always make sure you know where the nearest bus and subway stops are and how many transfers will be required to get to work. Never take a landlord's word that "the bus stops just up the street," or "the subway's only a few blocks away." Instead, use public transportation as you explore new neighborhoods, so you'll always know exactly how well each area is served by public transportation.

If you do own a car, check carefully for the availability of parking. Read the signs to learn exactly when and where you can park free. Don't be fooled if the streets look empty: You may have arrived moments after the cops towed everyone else away.

A nearby post office is important, not only for stamps and such, but if you tend to get large packages in the mail, you'll welcome not having to travel too far to pick them up.

Convenient banks won't hurt either, since you'll soon learn the life of an adult is a drama played out mostly in arguments with low-level bank officers.

Finally, if this is an urban area, you'll appreciate the presence of a nice park. And if you have a dog, he'll appreciate it even more than you.

APARTMENT SIZE

Apartments come in all different shapes and sizes, and—as when picking mushrooms in the forest—it's a good idea to know the standard varieties before you take a bite.

THE TWO-BEDROOM A two-bedroom is probably the largest apartment a single person would ever consider. Even if you can afford it, it's apt to have more space than you'll ever need. If you're planning to add a roommate to the picture or to convert the extra room into an office, it may be worth the extra expense. But please don't sign a lease for a two-bedroom apartment just because you like the spacious feeling. Chances are you'll wind up living in one room anyway, and the rest of it will always look like a ghost town.

THE ONE-BEDROOM If it fits your budget, a one-bedroom apartment is the ideal size for a single person. Even well-adjusted roommates can survive in a one-bedroom and save enough money to smooth any ruffled feathers that may occur. This apartment typically consists of a large separate kitchen, a combination living/dining area, and a separate bedroom. Don't be too concerned about the overall size when you look at one-bedrooms. Since you probably don't own much furniture, you'll be glad the bedroom is compact. A room big enough for a bed, a chest of drawers, and a nightstand is all you need.

THE EFFICIENCY How can you help but love that name? Don't ask your efficiency to be honest, courageous, or warmly self-effacing. Being efficient is about all it can handle, but that it can be—both in terms of offering a livable space and an affordable price. The typical efficiency consists of a separate kitchen, separate bathroom, and one large room that serves as dining room, living room, and bedroom. Unlike the one-bedroom apartment, size *is* an important consideration here, so look for the biggest one you can find. Even more important, look for an efficiency where the main room is L-shaped, or any shape other than square. An unusual floorplan creates an illusionary division of space that allows you to suggest the presence of different rooms. The sensation of walking from one room to another is an important psychological lift to efficiency dwellers, who otherwise start to think of themselves as prison inmates.

Studios   Scientists have not yet determined the exact distinction between a studio and an efficiency. Modern apartment buildings tend to call their one-room units efficiencies; older buildings tend to call them studios. (Perhaps they hope the name will conjure up images of artists' garrets and thereby blind you to the cracked plaster.) For our purposes, we'll consider them virtually the same.

Miscellaneous   In addition to the major types of apartments listed above, here are some other common varieties you are likely to encounter.

• Garden apartment: This sounds a lot prettier than it usually is. It means the apartment is on the ground floor and has a back door. Does the back door lead to a garden? Well, yes, if your idea of a garden is a slab of cement, three beer cans, an old tire rim, and a family of dead rats.

• Basement apartment: This one is actually not as bad as it sounds. A basement apartment is usually the renovated basement of a townhouse, with a separate entrance and a ½ address, such as 1600½ Pennsylvania Avenue (where Billy Carter used to live). The quality of basement apartments depends almost entirely on how well they've been renovated. One major drawback they all suffer, however, is a lack of natural light. Of course if you have a pet mole, this will be ideal.

• Loft apartment: Like the studio, the loft apartment is an example of how landlords enjoy playing to your artistic soul. Doesn't the word *loft* conjure images of painters' studios and renovated warehouses in Greenwich Village? What does it really mean? It means your bed is on stilts. In a desperate attempt to create extra space in a tiny apartment, the landlord has built a ledge for your bed. The place where artists live and work, by the way, is called a loft, not a loft apartment.

PRICE

No, we mustn't forget about the rent because your landlord seldom will. Perhaps the most important and difficult aspect of looking for an apartment is to find a rent that is perfectly suited to your income and your needs. For years, the 25 percent rule was a handy standard for judging the amount of money you could afford to spend on housing. Simply stated, you should not spend more than 25 percent of your take-home income on rent. But in many cities today, the price of real estate has risen out of proportion to the overall cost of living. In such areas, you may have to spend 30, 35, even 40 percent or more on rent.

So let this be your new guideline. Never pay more than 50 percent of your income on rent, and strive toward the goal of 25 percent. If living in a nice apartment is more important to you than owning a car or going out on the town, it's possible you could handle 40 percent with no sweat. If, on the other hand, you're just looking for a place to hang your hat, you could get by with 25 percent or less. Whatever guideline you choose, though, please spend a few minutes of your life thinking about it. Don't fall in love with an apartment and sign the lease in the heat of passion, putting off until later any sober thoughts about how you're going to pay for it. Personal emotion and gut feelings *do* have a role to play in the process of choosing an apartment, but only after the other "little" details are out of the way.

STYLE

We've saved this category for last because we're not sure whether it's the most important or the least, and we've called it style simply for lack of a better word. What we're talking about

here is like what Supreme Court Justice Potter Stewart said about
pornography: "I can't define it, but I know it when I see it."

We trust you'll know you've found the right style of apartment when you see it. But to increase your chances of seeing it,
you should spend a few moments picturing what it might look
like.

Apartment dwellers can be divided into two groups: the
moderns and the primitives. In which do you belong? Are you
the kind of person who can't sleep at night unless you know
your refrigerator is automatically defrosting itself? Or are you
the type who likes to put a six-pack of beer on the window
ledge overnight to get 'em nice and cold for breakfast? Is an
automatic dishwasher important to you? Or are you the type
who's willing to bite the bullet and do the dishes by hand every
three months or so, whenever they get piled up too high?

Yes, apartments and apartment buildings come in many different styles, with many different appointments. Check the list
of amenities in the chart at the end of this chapter and decide
for yourself what's important to you and what isn't.

How to Find an Apartment

By now you should have found one or two neighborhoods in
which you'd like to live; you should know the size of the apartment best for you; you have a range of prices that are roughly
in line with your income; and you know enough about the style
of apartment you want to be able to judge—let's say from the
outside of the building—whether or not you're on the right
track. Now that you know what kind of apartment you want, all
you have to do is find it.

There are several ways to find an apartment, none of them
easy, none of them foolproof. So let's start with the worst and
move up to the tolerable.

THE RENTAL AGENT

In cities where housing, while not cheap, is still somewhat plentiful, the rental agent (or broker) exists primarily as a servant of the businessman on temporary assignment. In cities where apartment hunting has ceased being an adventure and become something more like a life-and-death struggle, the rental agent has arrived on the scene like an angel of death. In very tight real estate markets, he is a morbid fact of life, almost—but not quite—a necessity.

What does a rental agent do? Basically, he keeps a listing of nice apartments, and for a financial consideration he lets you take a peek at them. But the better agents do somewhat more. They actually *show* you some apartments, and if you decide to take one of them, they charge you a fee.

Is it worth it? No, not usually. Not unless you're in a dreadful hurry to find a place or you have unusually demanding specifications for one. Even then, the agent could not honestly be called a bargain.

By listing available apartments with a rental agent, landlords avoid advertising costs and spare themselves the hassle of interviewing and investigating prospective tenants. This, in turn, provides the agent with a wide range of apartments to show you when you straggle through his door after a long day of apartment hunting. All he asks in return for his helpfulness is a little piece of the action.

How little?

It varies from agent to agent, but the range is generally from 12 to 20 percent of a year's rent. Notice we said a *year's* rent, not a month's. A $250-a-month apartment, for example, would (at 15 percent) go for a $450 fee to the agent:

$250 $\times$ 12 (months/yr.) = $3,000 $\times$ .15 (15% fee) = $450

Some agents charge exactly one month's rent, which, by comparison, is a good deal.

If you can afford to spend this kind of money and it's worth it to find a good apartment fast, by all means check out the agents in your city. To say a word in their favor, you can often walk into an agency and say, "I want an apartment of *this* size, in *this* neighborhood, at *this* price," and chances are he'll have it.

But here are a few things to be aware of in dealing with rental agents:

• The forehead slap: After you've visited a few, you will come to recognize the following ritual. At some point, as you sit at the agent's desk and start to tell him what you're looking for, a flash of memory will sparkle in his eyes, an exaggerated expression of regret will form on his face, and he'll slap his forehead with the palm of his hand. "I wish you'd walked in here *five minutes earlier*," he will exclaim. Then he will tell you about a ten-room triplex with sunken bath, indoor swimming pool, private handball court, and three-directional window exposure renting for $52 a month that he just gave to the guy who walked in before you.

Why does he perform this elaborate incantation? Students of unethical advertising may recognize it as a variation on the old bait and switch. Presumably, it's supposed to set the hook in the customer and keep him interested even if the agency has nothing worthwhile to offer. But the agents enact these fictions with such relish, we think they just like to make their customers feel unlucky.

• Shop around: Here's a little-known fact about rental agents: Landlords often use several different brokers to represent the same apartment. So it pays to shop around and look for the lowest fee, even if you see what you want at the first agency you visit. It's quite possible another broker will offer you the same apartment, or a different apartment in the same building, at a lower fee.

• Contracts: At some point during your struggle with rental agents, a devilish thought will occur to you. "Why can't I just look at the apartments the agent shows me," you say to yourself with a mischievous grin, "and then go rent the one I like directly from the landlord." Beautiful idea. Unfortunately, the agent has been in this business a long time, and he had a hunch it would take a bright guy like you only a few hours to come up with a clever notion like that one. That's why he shoved a paper in your face the moment you walked in the door and asked you to sign it before you could even say hello. He may have led you to believe you were signing a guest register or an autograph book. Actually, what you were signing was a contract, stating explicitly that you would not do what it would eventually occur to you to do.

In fact, the agent may take some other measures to make sure you don't get too smart or creative. He may ask you to pay a registration fee of anywhere from 1 to 100 dollars. This is to guarantee he will give you "exclusive representation," making you feel something like a movie star and, more important from his standpoint, making it unlikely you'll sign with another agency. Don't pay it; go somewhere else.

• Think small: Even though large agencies carry more apartment listings, you'll often have your best results with the smaller ones. Most brokers promise to call you as soon as a listing for your ideal apartment comes in. The little agency might actually do so; the big one will simply give it to the next guy who walks in the door.

THE CLASSIFIEDS

Studying the classifieds is how 90 percent of all Americans look for a place to live and a place to work. There, in a nutshell, is the reason for both unemployment and homelessness.

"Everybody uses the classifieds," you say. "What could be wrong with them?" What's wrong with them is simply that everyone uses them. Let's face it. The apartment listing in the paper that looks good to you is going to look good to a hundred other people, too. And some of those people are bound to make a more favorable impression on the landlord than you will. They might make a little more money, have a better credit rating, wear a better-looking suit, or have whatever else landlords consider important. So when you look for an apartment in the classifieds, you're apt to invest a lot of time, effort, and emotion in a losing cause.

No, the classifieds aren't the whole answer, but like rental agents, they can be useful if you proceed with caution. Study the classifieds for an overall picture of the rental market in your city. They will give you a general feel for the availability of apartments in certain neighborhoods, as well as the going price for apartments of various sizes. Even though we've been careful to point out the negative aspects of the classifieds, many people actually *do* find their home this way, and you could be one of them. In short, it certainly won't hurt to try them; just make sure you try other ways too.

Here are a few important things to know about the classifieds:

• Minesweeping: We've been in too many apartment wars not to know this sickening scenario by heart.

A young man prepares to study the classifieds in search of his first apartment. It is 0700 hours of a gray, drizzly morning. He is finishing the last of his K-ration breakfast of powdered eggs and Spam. He sips from a tin cup of hot java. The classifieds are spread out in front of him like a topographical map. His eyes scan the terrain. Suddenly, they alight upon something interesting, something unusual, something unique:

15 rooms. 3 and ½ baths. Excellent area. Luxury high rise. High security. No deposit. $100 per month. Call Phillipshead Realty. 751-4628. Fee.

The man explodes from his breakfast table and lands on his field telephone in one sickening heap. His fingers twitching, he convulsively dials the number.

"Good morning, Phillipshead Realty."

"Apartment . . . paper . . . I . . . saw ad . . . you got it?"

(Mysterious slapping sound)

"Oh, I wish you'd called *five minutes earlier.* We just let it go to someone else. But we have others you'll be interested in. When can you come in?"

"Soon as I can get an ambulance."

This man is the victim of a classified ad land mine. Who set it? The clue lies in the mysterious slapping sound. Did you recognize it? Yes, it was set by a rental agent! In fact, about a third of the ads in any classified section are put there by agents; two-thirds of the good ads are; and virtually all of the fantastic ones.

That's why the reader of the classifieds has to do a little minesweeping before he begins to make calls.

Most agency mines can be disarmed by looking for the word *fee* at the end of the ad. Also look for corporate names that have the suspicious ring of a rental agency. Most landlords do not use their corporate names in the classifieds, and if they do, they usually put "no fee" to indicate they aren't an agency.

• The early bird: Given what we said earlier about the number of people who respond to a good classified ad, you can see the advantage of "gittin' thar firstest with the mostest." In other words, you can beat the system if you act before it has a chance to go into effect.

Find out when the earliest edition of the Sunday classifieds is ready and where you can get it. Go to the newspaper office itself if you must. Sometimes it will be available as early as Thursday afternoon, and that gives you almost three days to make your calls and see some apartments.

When looking for an apartment in this fashion, remember the motto of every used car salesman: "Close that deal fast." If you see an apartment that meets your specifications, compares well with the others you've seen, and gives you a good gut feeling, don't hesitate. Take it. Remember, Sunday morning six hundred people are showing up here, armed with high credit ratings and good jobs. You can head them off at the pass by grabbing the apartment now.

The landlord may resist and ask you to fill out an application, so take out your checkbook and offer him the first month's rent (plus security) right away. Deep down inside, he wants to lease the apartment as fast as possible, even though his better judgment may be telling him to pick the best applicant. The offer of ready money, however, will topple his resolve in a hurry.

A GLOSSARY OF CLASSIFIED-ADVERTISING JARGON

Before you dig into the newspaper, take a moment to familiarize yourself with some of the most common abbreviations and phrases.

A/C: It means air conditioning. But be sure to find out whether this is central air or room-to-room. Central air conditioning is more efficient, has total coverage, and sometimes comes free. Room air conditioners usually only cover the room in which they are located, and they can put your electricity bill into orbit.

AVL IMMED: The apartment is vacant, and the landlord may be getting desperate. If you have good negotiating skills, you might get a bargain.

BKR: Beware. This ad is a land mine set by a real estate agent, or broker.

CONCIERGE: A word borrowed from the hotel business, a concierge is someone who is always nearby to satisfy your every little whim. In an apartment building, however, it simply means there is a staffed front desk for receiving and handing out mail, taking messages and announcing visitors.

CUTE: Minuscule.

DNG L: The dining room extends off the living room like the lower leg of an L. Usually a plus.

DUPLEX: Sounds like a form of herpes, doesn't it? Actually, it's an apartment on two floors.

EXPSD BRK WLS: Exposed brick walls. An asset, we think.

FLOOR-THRU: Sometimes it means an apartment on two floors (like a duplex); sometimes it means an apartment that takes up an entire floor. You're just going to have to see it to find out which meaning the landlord intended. One way or the other, though, it's probably a very big apartment.

FROM: As in, "Studios available *from* $300." Watch out! The price quoted is the absolute rock-bottom worst apartment in the building. (Don't even bother to ask to see this apartment, it's long gone . . . that is, if it ever existed.)

KITTE: Short for *kitchenette,* this means the landlord is giving you something less than a full kitchen. Also called a pullman.

PERFECT FOR EXECUTIVE: If you're not Lee Iacocca, you can't afford it.

PRESTIGE: Deliberately overpriced.

PREWAR: Be sure to ask which war. Anything prior to the Norman Conquest usually spells trouble. Actually, this means the apartment building was built before 1941. Ironically enough, prewar buildings are in demand because construction standards have declined since then.

RLRD: Railroad. The rooms are arranged in a row, like a train, so you may have to walk through the bedroom to get to the caboose . . . er, living room.

RENOVATED: Take this with a grain of salt until you see what kind of work has been done. Sometimes they've only changed the grease stains on the walls from black to dark brown.

SO EXP: So expensive? Close, but no cigar. Actually, it means southern exposure, usually the sunniest side.

WALK UP: Looking for a good aerobics regimen? You'll love this building. It has no elevator. If your apartment is on the fifth floor, you're going to be the healthiest thing this side of NASA.

wBF: White Bohemian Female in search of swinging male . . . no, wait a second, wrong section. In real estate, this stands for wood-burning fireplace.

FRIENDS

This may be both the easiest and most effective step you can take toward finding an apartment. Just make sure everyone in your life knows you're looking. You'll be surprised how many leads will turn up, how many friends of friends happen to be moving next month. Again, when you get a lead in this fashion and like what you see, act fast. Go directly to the landlord and take your checkbook with you.

THE ROUNDS

You've heard it said a million times. To get the starring role in the movie, to be hired for the big job, to strike it rich in business . . . *you've got to be in the right place at the right time.* The same applies to finding the perfect apartment. But as any struggling actor will tell you, the only way to make sure you're in the right place at the right time is to be in *all* places at *all* times. In other words, you've got to do everything we've discussed already and one more thing: You've got to make the rounds.

In a way, making the rounds is the best way to find an apartment because: a) it doesn't cost anything; b) it pinpoints only the areas where you'd most like to live; c) it puts you ahead of the pack of other apartment hunters. You'll be independent and in control of your own destiny, and these things— like virtue—are their own reward.

How do you do it?

Simple. Buy a pair of very comfortable shoes and hit the

streets. Go directly to the neighborhood in which you'd most like to live and start looking.

Here's what you're looking for:

• Front desks: If the apartment building has a staffed front desk, you're in luck. Just march up to the staff and tell them you're looking for an apartment. It's not as improbable as it sounds. They may just have one, right price and all.

• Doorman: If there is no front desk but there is a doorman, ask *him*. A good doorman not only knows how many apartments are available, he knows how often Mrs. Jones in 3-C cleans her dentures. Of course, you can't close the deal with the doorman, but ask him whom to see after you've learned if there's a vacancy.

• Superintendent: If there is no desk and no doorman, look at the mailboxes inside the front door until you find one that looks something like this: "J. Doe—Super" or "J. Doe—Mngr." Push the button and get ready for a treat. You're about to meet your first live-in superintendent.

Part confidence man, part handyman, part bag-man, the live-in super is one of God's most imaginative creations. Of course he'll know if there's an apartment available. In many cases, he'll be delighted to meet you because it's often his duty to find a tenant for that empty apartment, and like all of his other duties, he hasn't quite gotten around to it yet.

In dealing with the live-in super, remember this is a man who has taken on various tasks in exchange for a free apartment. He doesn't have a job in the conventional sense of the word. As a result, his sense of economics is—how shall we say?—fluid. He usually needs money and is not above certain unorthodox means of acquiring it. In short, here is a man who can . . . and who, in fact, expects to be . . . dealt with.

• Signs: You seldom notice apartment-for-rent signs until you start looking for them. Once you do, however, you'll notice they come in two basic varieties: the obvious "Apartment for Rent" and the more subtle "Managed by Fill-in-the-Blank Realty

Company." Take down the phone number and call from the nearest phone booth. The managing agent might send someone over right away to show it to you.

REWARDS

The latest technique in the hunt for the ultimate apartment is to offer a reward. We're not kidding! In cities with very tight real estate markets, it's become common to see hand-lettered signs posted around town saying something like this:

> *** $500 REWARD ***
> WANTED: A one-bedroom apartment for under $400 a month. We will pay $500 for information leading to the capture of such an apartment. Call (523) 334-2212.

It sounds ridiculous, but when you stop and think about it, it's more honest than offering a bribe to a superintendent and probably cheaper than hiring a broker. We don't recommend it unless you're desperate, though, because it's bound to send you on many wild-goose chases and put you in touch with some unsavory people. But if you do try it, make sure your informant understands he won't be paid until *after* you sign the lease.

Before You Sign on the Dotted Line

You've found the perfect apartment at the right price in a beautiful neighborhood. You're home free, right?

Wrong.

There's more excitement yet to come. Give the landlord a little credit; he hasn't yet begun to fight.

SECURITY DEPOSIT

After carefully budgeting how much to spend on an apartment, you may be upset to learn that in addition to the first month's rent paid in advance, your landlord wants a large sum for "security." Unfortunately, this is a standard practice and a perfectly legal one. The security deposit, which usually equals one month's rent, is designed to compensate the landlord in case you damage his property or move out before your lease has expired. Ideally, he should keep the security deposit in an interest-bearing bank account and return it to you (with interest) when you move out. In practice, many landlords consider security deposits part of their profit, and if they think they can get away with it, they'll withhold it for a variety of real and imagined damages.

Although there's usually no way to avoid paying a security deposit, there are several ways to make sure you get it back:

First, make a list of all the damages you find in your apartment on the day you move in. Send the list to your landlord with a note explaining (in a nonthreatening way) that these are *preexisting* conditions and that you won't be held responsible for them. Send it by registered, return-receipt mail and save copies for yourself. You might even ask the landlord to sign and return the list to you, but don't hold your breath.

Second, if your landlord refuses to return your security deposit, demand an itemized invoice for the damages. If the invoice is false or exaggerated, drag him into small claims court and have him explain it to the judge. Some states allow courts to assess a punitive judgment against landlords who fail to return a security deposit without cause, so you may collect two or three times what you originally paid!

Third, you might consider using your security deposit as your last month's rent. In some cities, this practice is so common that landlords themselves refer to the initial rent payment and the security deposit as "first and last month's rent." Check with a lawyer before you try this, though, because technically

you are breaking the terms of the lease, and you could be liable
for damages or unpaid rent or both.

UTILITIES

Sometimes the landlord pays for your gas and electricity; sometimes he doesn't. If you have to pay utilities yourself, you can
add that cost to your rent and it may change your mind about
the whole deal. Ask the landlord to estimate the average
monthly cost of utilities for an apartment similar to yours. Then,
if you get a chance, double-check his figure by calling the utility
company.

LEASES

When your landlord is ready to have you sign the lease, he will
hand you a pen, wave his hand over the papers, and say
something like, "It's the standard form."

Before you sign, ask yourself the following question: The
standard form of what?

Standard contract selling your soul to the devil? Standard
surgical release for a frontal lobotomy? Standard death warrant
on your mother?

No, you needn't drag it to a lawyer, who will probably say,
"it's the standard form." But it is a good idea to spend some
time reading it. Remember, leases can be changed. If there's a
provision you can't abide, ask the landlord to change it. Usually,
all it takes is crossing out and initialing the offending clause or
adding a typewritten line at the bottom. No big deal. So test
your skills as a negotiator; you may turn out to be the next
Henry Kissinger.

Here are some important issues to consider as you read
your lease:

• Length: Essentially, the question of length is one of flex-
ibility versus security. The short lease of one year or month-

to-month is flexible. The long lease of two or more years is secure.

Among the advantages of the short lease is your ability to move out at any time with little or no obligation. Among the disadvantages is the landlord's right to move *you* out on short notice and to raise your rent at will.

Advantages of a long lease include protection against rent increases and sudden eviction. A disadvantage, however, is the fact that you may be legally obligated for the entire length of the lease even if you want to move out.

As a general rule, the short-term lease is best in healthy real estate markets, where prices are good, competition between landlords is strong, and availability is high. In poor real estate markets, on the other hand, where prices are rising and vacancies are scarce, get a long-term lease.

• Renewals and sublets: Although the end of your lease may seem far in the future, find out the procedures for renewal before you sign. Unless you have an automatic renewal, you may find yourself out in the cold on the day your lease expires. And if you do have an automatic renewal, you may be obligated for another full term (and a rent increase) unless you give adequate notice. Check the clause on subletting too, because if you're stuck in a long-term lease and suddenly need to move, you could become a prisoner in your own apartment.

• Pets: Don't wait to find out about this until it's too late, and don't try to pull a fast one by sneaking your puppy through the front door in a suitcase. Make sure your landlord knows beforehand that you have a pet, or you and Fangs may find yourselves on the street. And if you sign a no-pet lease, be sure you're not going to want one later.

• Rent control: Many cities have laws to protect apartment dwellers from unfair increases in their monthly rent. Rent control, as it's commonly known, sounds great, but it can be a double-edged sword. If you already have an apartment, you'll love it. But if you're still looking for one, you may discover that vacancies are scarce because tenants hesitate to leave apartments with extremely low rents.

If your city has rent-control laws, investigate the rental history of your building by contacting the local housing authority. Find out exactly how much your landlord can raise the rent and how often. If possible, ask what the previous tenant paid for the same apartment. There may be laws regarding how much the landlord can jack up the rent between tenants. Be discreet. You don't want a reputation as a troublemaker before you move in, but don't let yourself be duped either. [TIP: When the landlord charges an even dollar amount—$500, for example—for a previously occupied apartment, it may be a sign he's violating the rent control laws.]

The Five Point Chart

Here's a handy chart to help you assess the relative merits of the apartments you'll see on your search. By rating a few, you'll begin to know a good deal when you see one and know when to act fast. Rate each apartment vertically down the line for the characteristic or quality listed on the left. Use a five-point scale, in which 5 is the best and 1 is the worst. This will not only help you compare different places, but it will also force you to think about every major consideration before you make a decision.

APARTMENT COMPARISON CHART

Rate each apartment on a five-point scale (where 5 is the best and 1 is the worst) for the characteristics listed down the left-hand column. Use the chart as a handy checklist or to compare two or more apartments against each other.

	Apt. #1	Apt. #2	Apt. #3
Address	_____	_____	_____
	_____	_____	_____

Size	___	___	___
Rent	$___	$___	$___
Length of lease	___	___	___
Safety (of neighborhood)	☐	☐	☐
Convenience to work	☐	☐	☐
Convenience to friends and relatives	☐	☐	☐
Attractiveness of neighborhood	☐	☐	☐
Attractiveness of building and apartment	☐	☐	☐
Shopping	☐	☐	☐
Convenience to public transportation	☐	☐	☐
Public services	☐	☐	☐
Parking on street	☐	☐	☐
Bathroom fixtures (rate for quality and looks)	☐	☐	☐
Kitchen fixtures and appliances (rate for quality and looks)	☐	☐	☐
Spaciousness	☐	☐	☐
Utilities (5 if paid, 1 if not)	☐	☐	☐
Style/amenities (overall rating)	☐	☐	☐

AMENITIES CHECKLIST
(circle yes or no)

Air-conditioning (central)	Yes/No	Yes/No	Yes/No
Air-conditioning (window)	Yes/No	Yes/No	Yes/No
Bike room	Yes/No	Yes/No	Yes/No
Cable TV	Yes/No	Yes/No	Yes/No
Carpeting	Yes/No	Yes/No	Yes/No
Community antenna TV	Yes/No	Yes/No	Yes/No
Dead storage space	Yes/No	Yes/No	Yes/No
Dishwasher	Yes/No	Yes/No	Yes/No
Doorman	Yes/No	Yes/No	Yes/No
Elevator	Yes/No	Yes/No	Yes/No
Extra closet space	Yes/No	Yes/No	Yes/No
Extra door locks	Yes/No	Yes/No	Yes/No

Extermination	Yes/No	Yes/No	Yes/No
Fireplace (working)	Yes/No	Yes/No	Yes/No
Fireplace (non-working)	Yes/No	Yes/No	Yes/No
Freight elevator	Yes/No	Yes/No	Yes/No
Front desk or package room	Yes/No	Yes/No	Yes/No
High floor	Yes/No	Yes/No	Yes/No
High-security building	Yes/No	Yes/No	Yes/No
Incinerator chute	Yes/No	Yes/No	Yes/No
Individually controlled thermostat	Yes/No	Yes/No	Yes/No
Laundry in apartment	Yes/No	Yes/No	Yes/No
Laundry in building	Yes/No	Yes/No	Yes/No
Maintenance and cleaning crew	Yes/No	Yes/No	Yes/No
Parking in building	Yes/No	Yes/No	Yes/No
Plentiful electrical outlets	Yes/No	Yes/No	Yes/No
Pool/Health club	Yes/No	Yes/No	Yes/No
Secretarial (answering) service	Yes/No	Yes/No	Yes/No
Superintendent on premises	Yes/No	Yes/No	Yes/No
Tennis courts	Yes/No	Yes/No	Yes/No
Thick walls and sound insulation	Yes/No	Yes/No	Yes/No
Terrace	Yes/No	Yes/No	Yes/No
View	Yes/No	Yes/No	Yes/No

CHAPTER TWO

Not by Bread Alone—

Stocking the Essentials

By now you may have noticed something unusual about your new apartment, something different from all your friends' apartments, all the apartments you've ever seen before.

It's empty.

Well, maybe not completely empty. You probably have a few cardboard boxes lying on the floor. If you're lucky, you might have a stick or two of furniture, and the refrigerator may contain a carton of milk. But basically, the place is empty . . . so empty, in fact, that when you speak, you can almost hear an echo.

Believe it or not, some people are content to live like this for years. They have a high tolerance for the "beach cottage effect"—the feeling of living in a place that isn't quite their own. Somewhere in their ancestry they must have nomadic blood, because most of us can't bear to live this way for more than a week. We're eager to make our house a home as quickly as we can.

If you find yourself confronted with an empty apartment,

think of this brief chapter as a sort of written CARE package—emergency relief for the barren-apartment dweller. Use it as an extended shopping list to start buying and borrowing all the things you need to make yourself at home. The sooner you do it, the better. So plan a frontal attack on the grocery store, dime store, and thrift shop in the next few days to buy anything you can't get by more devious means. We've tried to focus on the most important items because after all, you've got an entire lifetime to acquire luxuries and junk. At the end of the chapter, we'll give you a few tips on how to acquire these things at little or no cost.

The Kitchen

The mark of a good kitchen is one that can yield a decent meal on a moment's notice. To do that, you need basic equipment, basic foods and a basic knowledge of how to cook. We'll take care of the latter in another chapter. But for now, here's a simple shopping list to get your kitchen up to speed.

EATING UTENSILS

• Dinnerware: Let's correct an important misconception right now. Using paper plates for every meal does not save money. After a month or so of buying paper plates, you'll have spent enough money to buy yourself a set of permanent dinnerware.

On the other hand, don't go overboard and buy eight settings of fine china. Acquiring good china is what the institution of marriage is for. Until that blessed day arrives (the day you receive your wedding presents, we mean, not the wedding itself), buy yourself some decent everyday dinnerware. If money is a problem, plastic plates may be your best bet. If not, look for "stoneware" or pottery-type dinnerware. And if you don't care whether your plates match, auctions, garage sales, and thrift shops are also good places to look for inexpensive plates.

How many do you need?

Six to eight dinner plates, six salad bowls, six small salad or dessert plates, six cups and saucers, and four soup bowls.

• Flatware: Again, good silverware is not something you buy for yourself, it's something you receive at your wedding. You probably don't want real silver anyway. It's hard to keep clean and easy to steal. Even stainless can be quite expensive these days, so buy it second-hand if you must. Better yet, go to the dime store and buy stamped-steel flatware. It's cheap, easy to clean, and works just as well as the others. What's more, you can buy it by the piece.

A single person needs at least six place settings of flatware. [A basic setting consists of a fork, a teaspoon, and a knife.] Then buy about three additional forks and teaspoons and six steak knives. While you're at the dime store, pick up a rubber bin in which to put your silverware; it's more sanitary and convenient than tossing silverware into a drawer.

• Glassware: Six 10-ounce tumblers, two or three small glasses (for orange juice and such), and four coffee mugs should meet your needs. All of this can be found at the dime store.

• Table linen: How much you spend on table linen depends on how much you plan to entertain. If you and a few close friends are the only people who will ever eat at your dinner table, you need never buy anything other than paper napkins and a few inexpensive placemats. If, however, you expect to give a dinner party and invite people you want to impress, go to your favorite department store and buy a tablecloth, or six placemats, and six matching linen napkins.

COOKING UTENSILS

You could spend the rest of your life acquiring fancy cooking utensils (and if you become a good cook, you probably will), so we've tried to rank this list in order of importance. A well-stocked kitchen, however, should contain everything listed here, because we've completely left out items that we consider frivolous or luxurious.

VITAL

- Aluminum foil: Buy the heaviest kind you can find.
- Can opener: Find one that doubles as a bottle opener.
- Chopping board: Never chop food on easily damaged countertops.
- Colander: The plastic kind is cheaper, but a metal one will last longer.

- Garbage bags: Buy a box of heavy plastic garbage bags to line the inside of your garbage can.
- Garbage can: Get one with a tight-fitting lid to keep out roaches and mice.
- Grease can: An empty peanut butter jar or coffee can will do. Pour cooking grease here (not down the drain), keep it in the refrigerator so the grease will congeal, but when it's full, throw it out.
- Ice cube trays: The plastic kind is better, because metal sticks.
- Knives: Start with three: a small paring knife, a large chef's knife, and a medium-size serrated knife. Don't skimp on quality when it comes to cooking knives; buy the best you can afford. One sign of a good knife is when the blade extends all the way through to the end of the handle, so the entire knife is, in effect, one solid piece of steel. Stainless steel knives are good-looking, but carbon steel can be sharpened to a razor edge.
- Measuring cup: We find the large two-cup measuring cup

with amounts printed on the side more handy than the set of separate cups in different sizes, but you may disagree.

• Measuring spoons: Look for the kind that are held together on a single ring.

• Paper towels: We're addicted to these for both cooking and cleaning. They will be even more handy if you take a moment to install a simple paper towel dispenser in the kitchen.

• Potholders: Buy at least three: a glove-type potholder for handling hot pans while you're cooking, and two or more flat ones. Look for the most heavily padded potholders you can

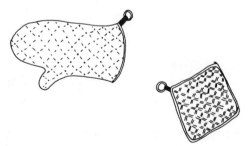

find. Also buy some "trivets," or hotpads, to protect your dinner table when serving.

• Salt and pepper shakers: Buy a pepper *mill* if you can,

because freshly ground pepper tastes much better than the processed kind.

• Spatula or pancake turner: Look for the kind with slots to allow grease to fall back into the frying pan.

• Slotted spoon: The slots let you remove food from boiling liquid without removing the liquid.

• Sugar bowl: Get one with a lid if possible, or ants will colonize it.

• Timer: Not a luxury at all, but an indispensable tool that will make cooking many times easier.

• Vegetable peeler: For peeling carrots, potatoes, and other vegetables.

IMPORTANT

• Apron: An underrated cooking tool, the apron protects both you and your clothing from hot and messy spills.

• Cheese grater: The cheese grater shaped like a box gives you four different grains.

• Egg beater: Not just for eggs, but for a variety of mixing and blending tasks.

• Knife sharpener: The little round ones are the easiest to work with. Just stick your knife in the slot and roll it back and forth.

• Mixing bowl: If you have some extra money to spend,

buy a *set* of mixing bowls in three different sizes (when stored, they fit inside each other). If you can afford only one, buy a big one.

• Plastic wrap: You can buy several different kinds of plastic wrap for leftover foods, including flat, all-purpose wrap like Saran Wrap or handy plastic bags, like Baggies.

• Potato masher: Less expensive than a hand mixer and almost as good for mashing potatoes.

• Tea kettle: Buy one with a whistle top to let you know when the water is ready.

• Wooden spoons: This is perhaps the only item on this list that we'd rather have you buy new than used, because they absorb food odors after a while. Wooden spoons are useful for stirring foods while they cook. You can leave them standing in the pot because they don't conduct heat.

USEFUL

As you become more skilled at cooking and learn to enjoy it, you'll probably want some of these items:

• Apple corer: Most recipes calling for apples ask you to remove the core first, a tedious job unless you have one of these.

• Pastry brush: Allows you to "paint" a piece of meat with its own juices, a process known as basting.

• Canisters: Three or four large containers will be very handy for storing flour, sugar, coffee, and tea.

• Cooking fork: Larger, longer, and sharper than a regular fork, it helps you reach into deep pots and spear foods.

• Corkscrew: And you thought all wine came in bottles with screw-off tops!

• Rolling pin: If you come to enjoy baking homemade pies

and cookies, you'll need one of these. Traditionally used by housewives for beating their husbands, too.

• Rubber spatula: Useful for baking cakes [and other somewhat sophisticated projects].

• Salad spinner: Lettuce and other fresh vegetables are notoriously dirty. Washing and drying them is a tiresome job unless you have one of these.

• Scissors: Handier than a knife for snipping certain vegetables, scissors are useful for many household tasks.

• Tongs: Grabs hot food that you can't spear with a fork.

• Wire whisk: You'll really look like a pro when you own one of these. It's used for whipping food to a fluffy consistency.

POTS AND PANS

Unless you're hard pressed for cash, don't skimp on quality when you buy pots and pans. Good cookware should last the rest of your life, so get the best pots and pans you can afford. Generally speaking, the thicker and heavier the metal, the better the pot. Steer away from thin "tinny" pots, and look for heavy-gauge aluminum or stainless steel. Cast-iron pots and pans with an enameled surface probably represent the best combination of price, durability, and good looks. But we also like no-stick Teflon™ pans, because they're inexpensive and easy to clean.

Here are the most important types of pots and pans. You need *all* of them.

• Broiling pan/Roasting pan: A broiling pan contains a rack or slotted sheet that holds the food near the flame and allows the grease to drip down into the pan below. When you remove the rack, you have an ordinary roasting pan. Look for one about 9″ × 13″ × 2″.

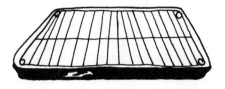

• Casserole dish: These are usually ceramic and have a volume of about 2 quarts. They must be able to withstand high temperatures in the oven. Corningware makes excellent ones.

• Cookie sheet: A flat, wide pan used for baking cookies and many other foods.

• Disposable aluminum pans: Buy these on an as-needed basis at the grocery store. Among the most useful are pie tins for pies and a variety of other tasks, and large roasting pans for turkeys and roast chicken.

• Frying pans: You need two: an 8-inch diameter and a 10-inch diameter. They should each have lids. (You can also buy a single frying pan lid that fits all sizes.)

• Loaf pan: Used for making meat loaf, look for one about 9″ × 5″ × 3″.

• Pot: For cooking spaghetti, stews, and shellfish, you need

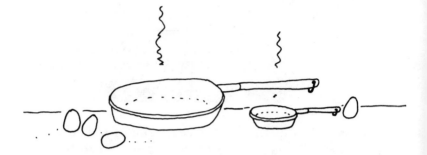

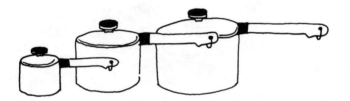

a large 6-quart pot. Look for one with a cover and a built-in colander.

• Saucepans: You need three: a daddy saucepan (3 qts.), a mommy saucepan (2 qts.), and a baby saucepan (1 qt.). Each one should have a lid.

CLEANING UTENSILS

See Chapter 6 for more than you ever wanted to know about cleaning tools and detergents.

STAPLE FOODS

Shortly after you move into your new apartment, you should plan one major trip to the grocery store to stock your cupboard and refrigerator with staple foods. You may spend a lot of money on this trip, but don't worry. Most of this stuff will last a long time. Here's a shopping list:

FOR THE CUPBOARD

baking soda

bread

cereal

coffee/tea

flour

oil

pasta (you'll never starve if your cupboard has spaghetti in it)

peanut butter

pepper

rice (have some on hand at all times in case you need a last-minute side dish)

salt

shortening (unless you prefer oil)

soup (two or three cans of your favorite kind)

No storage space for all your new pots and pans?
Try hanging them on the wall.

soy sauce

sugar (brown *and* white)

vinegar (Buy one bottle of each: red wine, cider, and white.)

FOR THE FRIDGE

butter

catsup

cheese (Sharp cheddar is a good all-around cheese, useful for cooking and snacks.)

eggs

jelly

mayonnaise

milk

mustard (both yellow and dijon)

USEFUL VEGGIES AND FRUITS   The following vegetables and fruits will be in almost constant use in your kitchen (especially if you intend to follow the meal plans in Chapter 4), so it's a good idea to keep them in stock.

garlic

lemons

onions

parsley

potatoes

tomatoes

SPICES   If you plan to follow the meal plans in Chapter 4, you will buy spices as you need them. If not, stock your shelf with these major spices:

basil

cinnamon

garlic salt

oregano

paprika

rosemary

sage

thyme

APPLIANCES

We'll assume you have a working refrigerator and stove, because in most states landlords are required by law to provide apartment tenants with those major appliances. But what about the little appliances, the so-called labor-saving devices that have supposedly revolutionized the American kitchen?

Well, you can get by with amazingly few of them.

Think how few your great-grandmother managed to survive on, and she was probably a better cook than you'll ever be.

But if you have the money, you will probably want to own one or more of the following:

• Blender: Buy one if you wish, but we'll bet you find yourself using it less for cooking than you do for making fancy drinks and milkshakes.

• Electric can opener: A pure luxury. If you use canned pet food, don't be surprised if your dog or cat develops a Pavlovian response to the sound of this machine.

• Electric frying pan: A very handy item, especially if you have a small stove. When cleaning, be careful not to submerge the entire pan or scratch the no-stick surface with an abrasive soap pad.

• Electric hand mixer: If you come to enjoy baking, an electric mixer will be indispensable.

• Electric knife: Not as frivolous as it sounds, an electric knife is great for carving roast chicken or turkey, roast beef, london broil, and for other difficult slicing jobs.

• Food processor: Quickly becoming the hula hoop of the

1980s. Everybody has one. Scarcely anyone knows how to use it . . . or cares.

• Microwave oven: If you understand its limitations and don't expect too much of it, a microwave oven can be a useful addition to your kitchen. It's a whiz at frozen vegetables, baked potatoes, and bacon. It's great for heating up leftovers, thawing frozen food in a hurry, or warming a meal before you bring it to the table. But major cooking jobs—like roasting a chicken, for example, or frying a hamburger—are still best when they're done the old-fashioned way.

• Toaster: The kind with a little oven is great for making open-face sandwiches and other quick snacks, but in Chapter 4, we're going to wean you from that kind of meal.

The Bathroom

One quick trip to the dime store will take the "just-moved-in" look out of your bathroom. If, however, you want finer quality items, go to the bath section of your favorite department store.

SHOWER CURTAIN We recommend buying a fabric shower curtain and a cheap vinyl liner. The liner will protect the expensive outer one and make it last longer. We've found that shower curtains that hang by rings last longer than those that hang by hooks. The hooks tend to pull and tear at the plastic until it finally rips through.

TOWELS You'll need two large bath towels, two hand towels, and two washcloths. Alternate and launder them once a week.

MATS A few well-placed bath mats help make a bathroom look warm and cozy. Bath mats are like ordinary throw rugs except they have a rubber matting at the bottom to help grip slippery bathroom floors. Because of that, they also add an extra measure of safety to your bathroom. You can buy one that is specially designed to fit around the perimeter of your toilet. If possible, choose a color that matches or complements your linen.

Tub mats are rubber mats with suction cups underneath that stick to the bottom of your bathtub. Tub mats prevent the bathtub pratfalls that are among the most common and serious household accidents.

SOAP DISH You probably have built-in soap dishes by your bathtub and sink. Even so, it wouldn't hurt to buy an extra soap dish or two, especially the kind that are designed to let the soapy water drain into a container, from where it can be easily cleaned later. The problem with built-in soap dishes, as you will soon discover, is that they have no such draining capacity. As a result, they quickly become caked with a thick layer of gunk.

SHOWER CADDY Some shower stalls are messy and dangerous because the occupant has no place to put her soap, shampoo, conditioner, creme rinse, styling mousse, and "Dippity-do." A shower caddy is an inexpensive plastic tray that hangs from the shower head and keeps all of these important items neatly in place and within easy reach.

GLASSES OR CUPS As you've heard a million times by now, bathroom glasses are notorious for passing germs from one person to the next. Even if you live alone and no one ever drinks out of the bathroom glass but you, it may still be unsanitary because you probably won't clean it as often as you should. Instead, we recommend you buy a Dixie cup dispenser and attach it to the wall.

LAUNDRY HAMPER This doesn't necessarily have to go in the bathroom, but you should have a permanent place to store your dirty clothes. You can buy a good-looking wicker laundry hamper at your local department store.

AND DON'T FORGET Bar soap, shampoo, toilet paper, facial tissue, and whatever health and beauty aids you prefer. [See Chapter 7 for a list of items that should be in a well-stocked medicine cabinet.]

Elsewhere Around the Apartment

Once you've stocked your kitchen and bathroom, you've made your new apartment livable. But there are a few more odds and ends to gather.

BEDROOM LINEN

If you can't borrow bedroom linen from Mom, go to the linen section of your favorite department store. You need two sets of sheets, matching pillowcases, and at least one pillow. (A set of sheets consists of a contour sheet, called a fitted sheet, which fits tightly around the mattress, and a second sheet, called a flat sheet, which goes loosely on top.) Alternate your sheets and launder them once a week. You'll also want two blankets and a bedspread . . . or perhaps one blanket (maybe an electric blanket) or a comforter (which looks good enough to serve as a bedspread). Make sure your bedding fits your bed. Beds come in four standard sizes: twin, double (or full), queen, and king.

TURNING ON YOUR UTILITIES

If you're lucky, you'll be moving into an apartment where the landlord pays the gas and electricity. If not, you'll not only have to pay for them, you'll also have to take charge of getting them turned on—and putting the account in your name.

Call the gas company and the electric company (sometimes they are the same) about two weeks before you move. If you're opening your first account, you may have to go to their office, fill out some credit information, and show them a copy of your lease. You may even be required to pay a small, refundable deposit. Be very clear about when you plan to move in and when the old tenant is moving out. Otherwise, you may pay for some of *his* electricity.

With the recent break-up of AT&T, getting a telephone is not as simple as it used to be. Your first step is to call your local telephone company and set a time for them to come to your apartment and install a phone line. (Try to get an appointment for moving day or the day after, if possible.) You will be asked whether you want a touch-tone or a rotary-dial line and if you want a few other costly options (call waiting, for example). Most important, you will be asked if you want to supply your own telephone or rent one from the phone company. We suggest you buy your own, because in the long run it's much cheaper. Look in the Yellow Pages under "Telephone Equipment," and you'll find dozens of stores that sell them. Buy your phone *before* the phone company arrives to install the line.

A few weeks before you move into your new apartment, go to the post office and pick up a few dozen change-of-address notification forms. Fill them out and mail them to all the people and businesses who frequently write to you. If you are moving from one apartment to another, make sure your old post office and former building superintendent have a record of the new address, so they can forward your mail. On the day you move in, clearly mark your mailbox with your last name, and if you get a chance, introduce yourself to the mailman. He's a good person to know.

A Shopping Strategy

Even if money isn't a problem, you'd be silly to run out and buy all the things mentioned in this chapter at your local department store or kitchen boutique. Instead, follow this simple six-step strategy, crossing off each item in this chapter as you acquire it in the following order:

BORROW FROM YOUR MOM AND HER FRIENDS   About a month before you plan to move, have your mother put out the word at her weekly coffee klatch that you could use any spare pots, pans, cooking tools, and dinnerware. In thirty years of marriage and homemaking, most people acquire more of this junk than they really need and are usually thrilled to give some of it away.

GIVE YOURSELF A HOUSEWARMING PARTY   Invite all your friends to come see your new apartment by hosting a cocktail party. If you discreetly mention the word *housewarming* in the invitation, guess what? Many of them will show up bearing little packages containing some of the very things we've discussed in this chapter. Act surprised.

GO TO GARAGE SALES   Check the Sunday classifieds for garage sales, tag sales, and apartment sales. They're good places to pick up used dinnerware, flatware, glassware, pots and pans (to tide you over until you buy permanent ones), and cooking utensils. Arrive early, bring cash, and never pay the listed price for anything.

GO TO THRIFT SHOPS   Go to Goodwill Industries, the Salvation Army, or other non-profit thrift shops to buy anything you haven't found so far.

GO TO A DIME STORE OR DISCOUNT STORE   These stores are especially good for drinking glasses, inexpensive silverware, inexpensive dinnerware, cheap linen, bathroom supplies, and whatever cooking tools you haven't already found.

GO TO DEPARTMENT STORES, RESTAURANT-SUPPLY HOUSES, KITCHEN BOUTIQUES Use these expensive stores to buy permanent dinnerware, permanent pots and pans, fine linen, good knives, and new appliances.

CHAPTER THREE

Feathering Your Nest—
Furnishing and Decorating Your Home

RICHARD: *For reasons I can't entirely recall, when I decorated my first apartment, I shoved all the furniture over to one side of the room and left the other side completely empty. The first time I showed it to my mother, I had to bring her in blindfolded and point her in the right direction before I let her look at it. If the way you decorate your home does indeed express your personality, mine is clearly unbalanced.*

DORINNE: *I wound up decorating the first apartments of both my kids, and I'll help you decorate yours, too. It's easy. And it can be a lot of fun. You'll have to spend some money, sure. But not as much as you might think. And once you've learned how to furnish and decorate, you'll use these skills again and again throughout your life.*

Do you remember Superman's Fortress of Solitude near the North Pole? The Fortress of Solitude was where the Man of

Steel went when fighting for truth, justice, and the American way got to be too much of a pain in the neck. When he was in his fortress, he didn't have to pretend he was Clark Kent. He didn't have to worry about Lois's nosy questions or Perry White's temper tantrums. It was his place to be alone . . . and to be himself.

Of course, Superman had very unusual taste when it came to furnishing the fortress. He kept a miniature version of a city from his native Krypton in a bottle on his fireplace mantel (a real conversation piece), and the whole place was decorated in an icicle motif.

Not *our* taste, certainly, but it doesn't matter. Whatever Superman had in his fortress was what *he* wanted, what made him happy, relaxed, and secure.

And that's what your apartment should be, too. After all, an apartment is more than just a resting place for your body; it's a resting place for your soul. You don't have all the resources Superman had to furnish *your* home, but look at it this way: You've got a much better location than he did. With a little money, a little effort, and a lot of ingenuity, you can have a fortress of solitude of your very own.

Your apartment doesn't look very promising right now, though, does it? Like most young people, you've probably just moved into a building that twenty years ago was considered a slum. And you probably feel lucky to have it—cracked plaster, warped linoleum, and all. The changing real estate market caused by the gentrification of inner-city areas around the country has forced people like yourself to seek apartments in buildings that a few years ago a self-respecting roach would not consider. Even if you've moved into a so-called luxury apartment or a suburban garden apartment, you may be alarmed to learn what an immensely boring space you have to work with.

As you stand in the center of your new apartment and gaze at the bare walls, cold floors, and gaping spaces between the few sticks of furniture you already own, the day when you'll come home to a completely furnished and lavishly decorated apartment may seem far in the future. But it doesn't have to be.

Although decorating your home is one of those jobs that is never quite done, you can have a beautiful apartment in less time than you think.

Let's begin with a little advice on how to develop a furnishing plan to meet both your immediate needs and your long-term goals. We'll show you how to buy fine furniture, how to buy serviceable furniture, and how to acquire decent furnishings without spending any money at all. Once you've managed to get a few nice pieces, we'll show you how to place them in your apartment to make the most functional and attractive use of space. Of course it takes more than furniture to make a house a home; it takes decoration. So we'll talk about what to do with your walls, windows, and floors. We'll show you how to use lighting in both a functional and a decorative way, and we'll talk about the two best ways to give life to an apartment: pictures and plants.

The Five-Year Plan

Next to a house or a car, furniture is probably the most expensive thing you'll ever buy in life, and just as with those two things, buying furniture requires a great deal of planning. Unless you're very rich, you probably can't run out and buy a houseful of furniture for your new apartment. Yet if you wait until you can afford good furniture before you buy anything, you may sleep on the floor and eat on a packing crate for much longer than you'd like. If you buy furniture haphazardly, as you can afford it, you may wake up one morning five years from now to find yourself living in an apartment that looks like it was decorated by someone on LSD. Each piece will reflect whatever style happened to be in fashion or whatever mood you were in when you bought it. Meanwhile, you might also find yourself in the awkward position of owning a gorgeous antique dining room table, for example, and no bed.

Obviously, you need a plan. So why not follow the example

of our friends in the Soviet Union and use a five-year plan? Just picture what you want your apartment to look like five years from now and put together a gradual program for getting there.

Start by making a list of all the pieces of furniture you'd like to have: bed, sofa, dining table, coffee table, chairs, and so on. Don't worry about money for the time being, because you're not going to buy it all at once. Just write down what you'd like to own and think about how the pieces will go together—both stylistically and functionally. Now, rank the items on your list in order of urgency. A bed, for example, is much more urgent than a loveseat. Next to each item, jot down a little note about what you intend to do on a short-term basis and what you plan to do in the long run.

Suppose you can afford to buy a good piece of furniture every six months or so (a piece worth $500, for example). You should buy these pieces in the order you ranked them, and after five years have elapsed, you will own ten pieces of expensive furniture—a heck of a lot. Meanwhile, you can furnish the rest of your apartment with inexpensive or even free furniture of lesser quality by following the advice later in this chapter. When the time comes to replace a stop-gap piece of furniture with a long-term piece, you can "trade up" by selling the old piece and using the money to help you buy a new one.

When you're ready to buy a long-term piece, you should buy the best one you can possibly afford. That way you'll never make the mistake of trying to survive for twenty years with a piece of furniture too cheap to last that long. That's why it's a good idea to rank a bed and a sofa at the top of your list of things to buy: not just because they are important furnishings, but because it's a waste of money to buy cheap ones, which will disintegrate after a few months of use.

Good furniture (and by that we mean—unfortunately—expensive furniture) is built to last a long time. [*Dorinne:* We still have furniture we bought thirty-five years ago.] Keep that in mind when you buy it: first, so you will buy furniture that will fit in with your long-range plans (especially if you intend to live in a house someday); and second, so you will understand its true cost. A $1,000 couch, for example, may seem expensive today, but when you "amortize" that cost over 35 years, it comes to only $2.38 a month!

Of course, don't expect to be finished in five years. By then your taste will have changed, your budget will be fatter, you might be in a different place, you may even have a new addition to the household. In short, the process of furnishing and decorating your home will continue. When five years is up, do what the Russians do: attribute your successes to the purity of your ideology, ascribe your failures to bad weather, and sit down to write *another* five-year plan.

How to Acquire Furniture at High Cost, Low Cost, and No Cost

A good five-year plan for acquiring furniture should include a few long-term pieces for which quality is more important than price and several short-term pieces for which price is more important than quality. If you're moving into a completely empty apartment, you may want to put both price and quality aside for a moment and try to acquire a few pieces by hook or by crook. As a result, you need at least three strategies for buying furniture: buying it at high prices, buying it at low prices, and not buying it at all.

BUYING FURNITURE AT HIGH PRICE

As we mentioned before, when the time comes to buy a good piece of furniture, don't skimp on quality. Buy the best piece you can possibly afford, but don't pay top dollar for it if you can get the same thing for less money by shopping smart. Window-shop among some of the better furniture stores in town to get an idea of what's available and what you like. Look for stores that have good locations, that have been in business for a while, and that have a good reputation among your friends and acquaintances.

Don't buy impulsively. Wait for one of these stores to have a sale. Furniture stores have excellent sales at least twice a year. (After Christmas and August are the most common times.) Unlike clothing stores, which often bring in a load of inferior clothes for their sales and put phony "mark down" tags on them, furniture sales tend to give genuine discounts on current inventory, so it pays to wait until the piece you've been admiring goes on sale. On the other hand, don't let the existence of a sale pressure you into buying something you're not completely happy with. There will always be another sale.

Here are some of the places where you can buy high-quality furniture:

INDEPENDENT FURNITURE STORES   These stores tend to serve either the very rich or the very poor, and you can usually tell them apart by their location. The one with the fashionable address caters to the well-to-do, while the one in the seamier section of town specializes in flimsy furniture at low prices. Stay away from the latter altogether, and use the former primarily as a way to establish a base price for the furniture you want. If you see a piece you really like at one of these stores and you can't find anything comparable at a better price elsewhere, wait for it to go on sale before you pounce.

CHAIN AND SPECIALTY STORES   These stores specialize either in a certain kind of furniture (convertible couches, for example) or a certain style (Scandinavian, for instance). If you are in the market for what they have to offer, by all means check them out. Again, wait for the inevitable sale before you buy.

DEPARTMENT STORES   Discount department stores sell furniture that is only slightly better than what you'll find in the cut-rate independents, so stay away from them. Good department stores, however, are an excellent place to buy high-quality furniture. The prices are high, but fair, and the sales are genuine.

UNPAINTED-FURNITURE STORES   If you're good with your hands and don't mind a little extra work, check out the unfinished-furniture stores in your area. They sell well-designed, well-built furniture in a variety of woods (ranging from the cheap to the luxurious) that haven't been painted or stained. You can do the work yourself and own a piece of furniture that would have cost substantially more elsewhere.

FACTORY OUTLETS AND WAREHOUSE SALES   If you find a genuine factory outlet or warehouse sale, you're in luck. You will get good furniture at dramatic savings. The problem is, many of these places aren't really what they pretend to be.

To find out if you're dealing with a legitimate warehouse sale, know your prices before you go in. If the price of a couch is, let's say, 50 percent less than what you'd pay at a department store, you've found the real McCoy. Go ahead and buy furniture until you drop dead. But if the discount is more like 5 to 10 percent, you're at a retail store *posing* as a factory outlet. This kind of store will give you the worst of both worlds: high prices, no delivery, limited choice, and no guarantee.

ANTIQUE SHOPS   If you don't know anything about antiques, stay away from them. Your chances of stumbling on a good deal in an antique shop are roughly the same as winning the Irish Sweepstakes. Only people with a trained eye will spot the bargains. The rest of us are apt to pay *more* than something is really worth when we venture into an antique shop.

If you like visiting antique shops, however, here's a tip. Sometimes antique dealers have to buy an entire estate full of furniture just to get the one or two valuable items they want. When this happens, they will unload the ordinary furniture at fabulous prices. When your favorite antique dealer suddenly seems overstocked with a lot of non-antique furniture, he may be in this situation and ripe for a deal.

MAIL ORDER   As far as price, quality, and value go, mail-order furniture is comparable to department-store furniture—which, as we've said, is pretty good. But there's one disadvantage: You can't see it in person. If you're the type who kicks the tires on a used car, you may not be comfortable with mail order. If so, try taking the catalog with you around town to see if you can find the same pieces in stores.

Incidentally, don't avoid mail order because you don't want to wait a long time for the furniture to arrive. You'll find no matter where you buy it, furniture has the longest delivery time of anything you've ever bought before.

RENTING FURNITURE   Another way to acquire decent furniture is to rent it, but don't rent unless there's a compelling reason to do so—if, for example, you plan to move soon.

You might consider a lease-purchase plan. In such an arrangement, you have the option to purchase the furniture after the rental period expires and have your rental payments applied to the purchase price. Don't be surprised, however, if this winds up costing you more than buying the same furniture outright.

BUYING FURNITURE AT LOW PRICE

If you're following a five-year plan similar to the one we outlined earlier, you can afford to buy an expensive piece of furniture only about one or two times a year. Does that mean you have to spend the rest of your time watching TV from the floor and eating dinner on a cardboard box? Of course not. You can furnish an entire apartment with temporary or stop-gap furniture for less than what it might cost to buy one very nice couch. Then, as the months go by, you will replace your temporary pieces, one by one, with furniture designed to last the rest of your life. Out with the bad stuff, in with the good!

Here are some places to buy furniture at low prices:

GARAGE AND HOUSE SALES   We mentioned these briefly in the last chapter because they are a wonderful way to get inexpensive kitchen supplies. But they are equally good for certain kinds of furniture.

When it comes to beds and sofas, we'd rather you put them at the top of your list of things to buy at high price, because buying them second-hand will often mean getting a piece with exposed springs, "leaking" stuffing, even insects and mice. But when it comes to buying a hardwood piece—a dining room table, a coffee table, a chest of drawers—garage sales can't be beat.

Get to the sale early, if possible *before* it begins, and be prepared to act quickly on something you like. If the seller resists because he thinks he'll get a better price later in the day, write down your "bid" on a card with your name and address and tell him to call you if it doesn't sell. Always carry cash, and never pay the listed price for anything. Nor should you make a blind offer until you've heard how much the owner wants to charge. If you say, "I'll give you fifty dollars for this" and the owner really only wanted ten dollars, you've made a horrible blunder. Keep in mind, the owner organized this sale because he wanted to get rid of all the junk in his house and garage. In most cases, he's more interested in *clearance* than income, and you should negotiate accordingly.

FLEA MARKETS, CHURCH BAZAARS, ETC.   Flea markets are similar to garage sales, except they're slightly more organized and sometimes more permanent. It's sort of like the difference between a floating crap game and a casino. The permanent flea markets (and by permanent we mean those that are held every day or every week in the same location) are less likely to contain huge bargains because they've already been picked over by hundreds of people. Again, arrive as early in the day as possible to get first dibs on whatever happens to be new. Special flea markets—those held occasionally by churches and other non-profit groups—are like giant garage sales in which you can pore over items from not just one household, but many. We highly recommend them.

Here's a tip for succeeding at garage sales and flea markets: Try to come up with unusual uses for familiar items. Will that old trunk serve as a coffee table? Can that strange piece of scrap-iron be made into a lamp? Use your imagination, and you will turn an ordinary item into an extraordinary find.

AUCTIONS You'll find great bargains at auctions, but to do so you must exercise both care and restraint. Arrive at the auction *before* it begins and study the merchandise up close. If you find a piece that interests you, decide how much you would pay for it and make a mental note (or better yet, an actual note) of the figure. Promise yourself you won't exceed this figure in the heat of the bidding. Participating in an auction is fun, but not if you let yourself pay more for an item than you can afford or, worse yet, more than it's worth. It's a good idea to attend a few auctions strictly as an observer before you join in.

CLASSIFIED ADS The main advantage of buying from a classified ad is that you can see what kind of home the furniture had before you showed up. You can tell if it has been cared for properly, how old it is, and—if you ask a few well-chosen questions—*why* it's being sold. The classifieds are an acceptable way to find a temporary bed or couch, because you can judge for yourself if the previous owners were sanitary enough to meet your standards.

Incidentally, the classifieds are usually where you find out about the other things we've mentioned: auctions, garage sales, and flea markets. Poring over the classified ads should therefore be a regular part of your weekend routine until such time, if ever, as you're "finished" decorating your apartment.

APARTMENT SALES Similar to a classified ad is a 3 × 5 card announcing an apartment sale. Look for such notices near the check-out lines at your grocery store, at the bus stop, the laundromat, or wherever folks in the neighborhood congregate. People selling furniture because they have to move suddenly often use such community bulletin boards to advertise their goods.

SECOND-HAND SHOPS AND CHARITY THRIFT SHOPS Although the furniture in these stores is used, it has been restored (with varying degrees of skill) to the point where it can be sold for somewhat more than what you'd pay for the same thing at a garage sale or flea market. Goodwill Industries and the Salvation Army run two of the best known second-hand furniture operations, so look for them in the Yellow Pages. You're not going to find a tremendous bargain in these stores, but you could buy an acceptable piece of temporary furniture at a reasonable price. Be sure to check out the section of the store reserved for items that have not yet been "improved." The prices will be lower, and you can decide for yourself what kind of paint or finish to use on them. As with all the strategies for buying cheap furniture we've discussed, you're going to have to arrange your own delivery. So if you have to rent a truck, for example, be sure to factor its price into the total cost of the furniture.

WRECKING-BALL SALES As wonderful as they are rare, a wrecking-ball sale takes place when a building is about to be destroyed—especially a hotel building. On these occasions, anything and everything that can be picked up and carried away is for sale. Wrecking-ball sales are great for air conditioners, chests, nighttables, lamps, pictures, credenzas, desks, and office furniture.

HOMEMADE If you're reasonably handy, there's a wide range of simple, inexpensive furniture you can make at home. Brick-

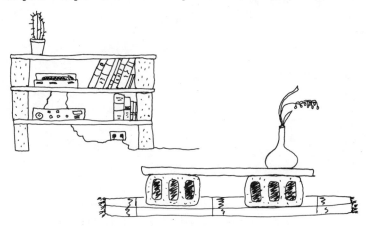

and-board construction offers many possiblities, from simple bookcases to serviceable bedframes. Buy the materials at your local plywood dealer, hardware store, or homeowner's store. You can also buy the materials for simple wall bookcases, kitchen shelves, and lamps.

ACQUIRING FURNITURE FREE!

Free furniture comes in two different varieties: the hand-me-down and the pick-me-up.

To acquire hand-me-down furniture, simply let everyone in your life know that you would welcome gifts of used furniture. If you live in the same town as Mom and Dad, make sure they pass the word among their friends, too. Before long, your most difficult problem will be deciding what to accept and what to decline.

And that raises a serious point: Don't be afraid to say no. If someone says, "Would you like a handsome aluminum sofa in

The ultimate furniture sale. But stay away from
the upholstered stuff. It may contain some
four-legged roommates.

the shape of a blue whale?" decline the offer. When it comes to furniture, beggars can and should be choosers.

Pick-me-up furniture is even easier to acquire. Just keep your eyes open. You can find discarded furniture in junk yards, city dumps, dumpster bins, or even on the street.

Plan your scavenging hunts on the night before the sanitation department is scheduled to pick up the trash. And try again to look at things with an artist's eye for the unconventional application. We've seen interesting pieces of furniture made out of such unlikely raw materials as automobile gas tanks, refrigerator coils, and cable spools. But *please, please, please* don't acquire a bed, sofa, or upholstered chair in this way. You may unwittingly carry an entire family of rats into your apartment.

Space: The Final Frontier

Space. For most apartment dwellers, the problem is not enough of it. Yet some people—believe it or not—have too much. Others must cope with odd-shaped spaces: slanting ceilings, for example, or rooms taller than they are wide. For some, the problem is dead space. For those who live in today's so-called luxury apartments, the problem is *dull* space. But no matter what particular puzzle you face, you can solve it by applying your brain to the task at hand, applying pen to paper, and applying a few simple principles of conserving, expanding, and organizing space.

LAYOUT

Even if your apartment is 97 percent empty, it's not too early to plan your furniture layout. In fact, now may be the *best* time, because a good layout will help you create and execute your five-year plan for buying furniture. Don't attempt to do this in your head; use a pencil and paper. If you really want to do it right, buy some graph paper and draw the layout to scale. To begin, draw the outline and floor plan of your apartment as precisely as you can. Be sure to indicate radiators, windows, and doors so you don't make the mistake of putting a piece of furniture in a place where it just can't go. Now start adding your furniture—the pieces you currently own and the ones you intend to buy soon. In doing so, follow these three principles:

USE ALL AVAILABLE SPACE Get rid of the notion that all your furniture must be shoved up against the wall. You're thinking like an amateur. Think like a pro, and use every bit of available space by bringing at least some of your furniture into the center of the room.

Let's look at some examples. Here are two layouts using the same pieces of furniture in the same size room. The layout in the drawing below, was designed by an amateur with the typical up-against-the-wall mentality. Look how dull it is! What is

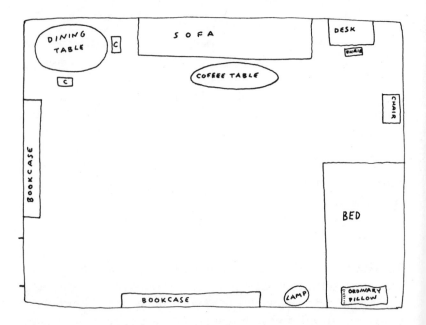

Dull.

she going to do with all that empty space in the center, hold a high school prom?

Now look at the same space designed by an expert. Notice how few pieces are placed with their backs to the wall. The sofa is placed perpendicular to the wall, thrusting dramatically into the center of the room. The easy chair is situated almost dead center. The coffee table is at the focal point of a cozy arrangement of the bed, sofa, and chair. The desk is angled into a corner. every square inch of available space is either covered by furniture or "defined" by it. There is, in short, nothing wasted. It is exciting, involving, and inviting.

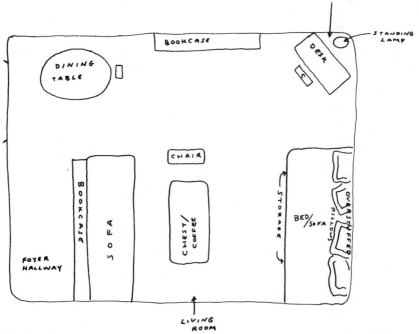

Exciting!

ORGANIZE SPACE BY FUNCTION Do you notice something else unusual about the layout in the second drawing? The furniture is placed in such a way as to define spatial areas by function—almost like a series of rooms without walls. The bookcase by the front door creates a little hallway or foyer. The table near the kitchen defines a tiny dining room. The arrangement of sofa, chair, coffee table, and bed establishes a cozy living room. Large pieces of furniture will double as psychological room dividers, and organizing your apartment in this way will ease the depressing sensation of living in a one-room cell.

How do you define your functional areas? Let your own lifestyle be your guide. As you pencil in your layout, keep a note on one side of the paper about how you like to spend your evenings and weekends. Do you like to entertain? Or do you cherish your privacy? Do you prefer to read, or watch TV? Run through a typical evening in your mind and picture your movements through the apartment. Let those movements, habits, and activities define your space.

USE DUAL-FUNCTIONAL PIECES WHENEVER POSSIBLE   One of the best ways to get the most out of your existing space is to use pieces of furniture that serve two or more functions. Notice the single bed in the lower right corner of the second layout. Throw a few overstuffed pillows along the right edge, and the bed becomes a sofa. See that coffee table in the center? It's actually a trunk stuffed with clothing and blankets. Until you can afford a desk, you can use your dining table for paperwork. Or you can use your desk for dining. Dual-functional furniture not only saves space, it saves money!

STORAGE

"I don't have enough closets!" is the plaintive cry of every apartment dweller. Now that you've had enough time to get settled in your new home and start stashing away your clothing and possessions, you may feel the same way. You can't just leave things lying around, or all your efforts to beautify your apartment will be wasted. So what do you do?

Let's approach the problem in four steps:

USE DEAD STORAGE   Ask your landlord if your building has an area for dead storage—a place for you to store items on a long-term basis. If, for example, you have a box of college memorabilia that you just can't part with but that you certainly won't be looking at more than once a year, consider stashing it here. These storage areas are usually in the basement, and they can be very damp and mildewy, so be careful about what you decide to keep there. Mark the boxes with a note of what's inside to spare yourself a huge hassle when you go looking for one particular item.

GET RID OF JUNK   If you live in a house with a large attic and basement, you can afford to get sentimental about an old candy wrapper and save it for twenty years. But apartment dwellers must be ruthless about junk. Junk is a fire hazard, an eyesore, a financial burden, and even a restraint on your personal freedom. Some people have so much junk in their homes, they literally can't move around. Instead of endlessly shifting the junk in your home from one place to another, why don't you throw some of it out? And in the future, don't save anything until you've made it pass a strict test of whether or not you'll ever use it again.

EXPLORE INNER SPACE   Astronauts explore outer space, but the canny apartment dweller must be a courageous explorer of inner space.

What is inner space?

It is the empty and usually wasted space inside or underneath furniture and other voluminous objects in your apartment. We've already talked about using an old trunk for a coffee table, for example. If you do, make sure the trunk is crammed with clothing, blankets, sheets, and whatever else you can stuff inside.

Mom used to yell at you about shoving stuff under your bed, but that was back in the days when you lived in a house and had closets. Now, the soft underbelly of your bed is a great place to stash boxes full of off-season clothing, shoes, or assorted goodies.

Is your suitcase sitting empty inside your closet? What a shameful waste of inner space!

Sometimes colonizing inner space requires a little ingenuity.

Go to the dime store and buy an item called a sink skirt. Wrap it around your kitchen or bathroom sink and no one will see all the stuff you have stored underneath. Visit the hardware store and buy do-it-yourself shelving, then go shelf crazy. Add shelves in the bathroom, in the kitchen, inside your closet, wherever you spot dead wall space.

Hanging things is another way to bring dead wall space to life. By hanging pots and pans on the kitchen walls, you can free your kitchen cabinets for additional storage and create a charming decorative effect in your kitchen. You can save space in the bathroom by putting your soap, shampoo, hair condi- tioner, and so forth in a shower caddy. By purchasing or build- ing a wooden rack, you can even hang drinking glasses from the ceiling, just like they do in your favorite bar. You can even "hang" your bed by installing a Murphy bed or a loft.

Once you've done everything to create additional space, start to create spaciousness—or the *illusion* of space. Strate- gically placed mirrors will almost double the apparent size of your apartment. Small rooms will be expanded by using com- paratively small pieces of furniture and light paint on the walls. Even a deep-perspective painting on the wall will help.

ORGANIZE YOUR CLOSETS Most closets are woefully under- utilized. Take a look inside your own closet and see if you don't

agree. You may think it's crammed to the gills, but wait. What about all the space *above* the top shelf; couldn't you add a few more shelves? Why just one pole? Couldn't you install a high pole and a low pole? Or a pole in the front and a pole in the back? If you have a hinged door (as opposed to a sliding or folding one), the back of the door can be covered with shelves. So can the side walls or even the back wall. And buy a shoe rack; it will help you clean up that snakepit on the floor (it'll prolong the life of your shoes, too).

TAKE THE EASY WAY OUT   What's the easy way out when you don't have enough closet space? Buy another closet. Freestanding closets are called armoires or wardrobes, and they can be very handsome pieces of furniture. They come in all price ranges, and best of all, you can take them with you when you move into your *next* apartment without enough closet space.

Decorating Your New Apartment

In case you're wondering, furnishing and decorating are not quite the same thing. Furnishing is an aspect of decoration, but while furnishing deals mostly with matters of function, decoration is largely a matter of style. Decorating your apartment is what makes it your own. It's the pictures and plants, the fabrics and colors that bring your apartment to life and make it a unique expression of your personality. It is—to borrow a trite but true phrase—what makes your house a home.

Here are a few fundamental guidelines people use when they're decorating a home:

• Unity with variety: A room in which each major piece of furniture matches all the others is neat but dull. Furnishings and decorative elements needn't match, but they should agree.

They should not—to use one of the interior decorator's favorite words—clash.

• Balance: Remember Richard's first apartment from the beginning of this chapter, where all the furniture was gathered on one side of the room? That's an extreme example of a lack of balance. Yet the same disaster can occur by having all the pieces on one side of the room in the same color.

• Focus: A well-decorated room has one major point of interest, not several different points vying for attention. This is a good principle to remember as you proceed with your five-year plan. Every time you get an exquisite new piece of furniture, you should rearrange the rest of the room to show it off.

• Proportion: Furnishings and decorative elements should be in proportion to the size of the room. This is a good principle for apartment dwellers to remember, because large pieces of furniture will have the effect of diminishing the size of a small apartment.

• Color: Color is probably the single most important element in any decorative scheme. The more you learn about color, the better a decorator you'll become. Here's a trick to identify the colors you'll be comfortable living with. Buy yourself a big, glossy magazine. The subject matter isn't important, just one with a lot of full-color ads and photos. Take exactly three minutes and leaf through the magazine, tearing out about twenty pages that appeal to you. See if there aren't two or three dominant colors or combinations of colors you instinctively like. Look for them when you buy furniture and decorations.

But there's only one principle of decoration that really counts:

Please yourself.

Never decorate to conform to some notion of what's correct or what's in style. (That is, unless you're a very correct or stylish person.) If the conventional principles of decoration are any help to you as a guideline, that's great. But don't follow them slavishly. And don't follow another person's idea of what's right for *your* apartment. You're the one who has to live in the joint.

Here are some specific tips on decorating your walls, ceilings and floors . . . plus some advice on decorating your apartment with pictures, plants, and lighting.

WALLS AND CEILINGS

When you move into a new apartment, your walls and ceilings are like the famous *tabula rasa* of modern psychology on which you are free to draw your own personality from scratch. Before you paint the walls of your apartment, check with your landlord and read the section in Chapter 9 on how to paint. By and large, it's a good idea to paint your walls white or in subtle colors, because dramatic color schemes are, ironically, easier to get tired of. Generally speaking, light colors will make a room look more spacious and airy; darker colors will make it look smaller and cozier.

Before you begin painting, you may want to consider one of the dozens of other wall-treatment options you have, including: wallpaper, paneling, fabrics, straw, cork, fake brick, or fake stone. We'll let you pursue those ideas on your own, but none of them is very hard to do.

WINDOWS

The windows in your apartment are your sole connection to the outside world: a source of light, pleasure, and even information. A good window is a thing of beauty and a joy forever, and you should treat it accordingly.

The most conventional way to decorate windows is to drape them. Measure the length and width of your windows carefully (including the distance between the windowsill and the floor) and go to a department store with moderate prices, like Sears or Penney's. You can choose from a wide variety of styles, colors, and lengths. You don't need fancy draw drapes; the kind that fit over a simple rod and that you draw by hand will do fine. The most important quality to look for in drapes is *washability*. Drapes get dirty in a hurry, especially in city apartments, so you'll want something you can throw in the washer from time to time.

But wait.

Are you daring enough to try something unconventional?

Why not consider vertical blinds, café curtains, roll-up shades, shutters, stained glass windows, or stencils? [*Richard:* I like shutters.] Or try "landscaping" your window with plants.

FLOORS

People tend to neglect their floors when decorating, but the floor can have a major impact on the overall look and feel of a room. Rugs and carpeting add a sense of coziness to your apartment, and if you've ever jumped out of bed on a winter morning and hit the cold floor with your bare feet, you know they add a measure of comfort, too. Think of your floor as a fifth wall, which must be decorated just as carefully as the other four.

You may not be able to afford wall-to-wall carpeting, but you could do just as well by going to a carpet-remnant store and buying a large piece of carpet left over from another job. You should be able to find a piece large enough to cover an entire room of your apartment. You can also buy area rugs to cover—as the name implies—specific areas. Don't leave the rug or carpet store without buying some padding to go under-

neath the carpet. It protects the carpet and prevents it from slipping.

If you're lucky enough to have genuine hardwood floors, you might prefer to go easy on rugs and let the natural beauty of the wood shine through. In that case, you may need only a few small throw rugs to add a cozy touch.

Your kitchen floor undoubtedly will be covered with a substance called linoleum. There's nothing wrong with this synthetic floor covering, but if you hate the design or it's in terrible shape, feel free to change it. Ask your landlord first, of course, and then look up "Linoleum" in the Yellow Pages. You should be able to find a shop where you can pick out a more pleasant design and have a new layer installed by professionals. It isn't very expensive, and it will make your whole kitchen look spanking new.

LAMPS AND LIGHTING

If you doubt the importance of lighting to your decorative scheme, imagine how your apartment would look without it. Lighting serves three purposes: 1) to illuminate the entire room and create an "atmosphere"; 2) to provide light for specific tasks, like reading or writing; 3) to focus the eye on a particular object and create an "accent."

As you plan your lighting, consider those three purposes of lighting in order. First, decide on what kind of lighting you need for general illumination. Extremely bright overhead lights will work well in the kitchen and bathroom. In the living room, however, it's better to use two or three large lamps with translucent (not opaque) shades. Good table lamps are expensive, by the way, so why don't you consider making a few of your own with an old wine bottle and a do-it-yourself lamp kit you can buy at the hardware store. If you can afford it, a standing lamp will serve well as the main source of light in your living room.

Next, decide upon your need for "task lighting." Make sure a bright, focused lamp is near the chair in which you like to read. You should also have a light for your dining table and one by your bed.

Finally, if you really want to be a clever decorator, consider using some "accent lighting." If you have a beautiful oil painting, a handsome vase, a valuable sculpture, or even an attractive "nest" of plants, you can achieve a fabulous effect by hitting it with a little spotlight. So-called track lighting attached to the ceiling is the most common way of doing this. But you needn't go to the expense of installing track lighting if you don't want to. You can achieve the same effect with a small reading lamp that can be clipped onto a piece of furniture. You'll love this look, but don't overdo it. Otherwise, your apartment will look like a museum.

PICTURES

Speaking of museums, we couldn't write a chapter on decoration without emphasizing the importance of pictures. There's nothing more dull than four empty walls staring glumly in your face every day. Don't live like a Buddhist monk when there are so many simple and inexpensive ways to bring art into your home.

Your local art museum is a great source of pictures. Don't steal one from the exhibition rooms, but go to the gift shop and buy several of the many inexpensive posters and postcards on sale there. Greeting-card shops and poster stores offer a variety of beautiful, amusing, or inspirational things to hang on your wall.

Framing shops are also a good place to go for artwork. They have a wide selection of art posters, both framed and unframed. Many of these shops will teach you how to matte and frame posters by yourself and earn a huge discount. Once you've acquired this skill, you can frame photographs, tear sheets from magazines, postcards, calendars, and any number of inexpensive things.

Don't think you have to be rich in order to afford original art, either. Go to student art shows at a nearby college or art school. You might be able to buy a painting from the world's *next* Picasso for fifty dollars or so. As long as a painting meets your own standards of beauty and craftsmanship, it doesn't matter where you bought it.

Now that you've acquired some beautiful pictures for your apartment, how do you hang them?

The most common mistake in hanging pictures is to hang them too high. Pictures should be hung with the center at eye level, or perhaps slightly lower (because you will usually be looking at them from a sitting position). But since your pictures will be of different sizes and shapes, it's a good idea to arrange them so the *bottoms* of the pictures line up at the same height. An exception to this is when you choose to hang a "nest" of pictures—a group of pictures hung together in the same section of the wall. We like nests, by the way, because it's a more involving look than just one picture per wall. To design a good-looking nest without turning your wall into swiss cheese, sketch it out on a piece of paper or arrange the pictures on the floor before you begin hammering.

Finally, consider the possibility of hanging more than just pictures on your walls. Do you have a collection of unusual items, like old musical instruments or woodworking tools or even theater programs? Try displaying your collection on the wall. You can also decorate your walls with rugs, quilts, bedspreads, towels, and any number of other fabrics.

PLANTS

We can't say enough good things about plants. Not only are they a beautiful form of decoration, but taking care of them will become a fascinating and relaxing hobby. What's more, plants are alive, and—for some people, anyway—they offer genuine companionship. You've probably read that talking to your plants is good for them, but we wouldn't be surprised to learn it's good for you, too!

Enter the wonderful world of plants gradually, though, because not everyone is cut out for it. Some people, for example, have a mental block about remembering to water their plants. Others just don't have the knack. If you buy a houseful of plants and later learn you are among this unfortunate group of people, you're not being fair to yourself . . . or to the plants. So take it one at a time.

Choose your plants primarily on the basis of the lighting in which you will be putting them. Only after you've found several plants that you're confident will survive in a given location should you make a decision about which plant is most attractive.

Don't forget plants can grow on *artificial* light, too. Make sure the plant is placed near the light source, but not near enough to burn it. Cool fluorescent lights are great for plants— especially in the bathroom, where the high humidity also helps.

Want a good plant to get you started? Try the philodendron. It survives in low light. It will forgive several missed appointments with the watering can. And it likes to climb and crawl and hang and do all sorts of amusing tricks. Also see the list of plants even Dorinne couldn't kill.

Of all the places to buy plants, the local nursery is the best. Nurseries rarely sell unhealthy plants. They will give you detailed instructions on how to take care of your plant, and they usually offer a guarantee. A good nursery will also act as a plant veterinarian, giving you advice over the phone and even emergency-room treatment of a sick plant. Florists are not quite as helpful as nurseries, but they will sell you a healthy plant and give you reliable advice on how to care for it.

If, however, you buy your plant at a dime store or supermarket, take a moment to make sure the plant is in good condition and that it comes with printed instructions. Look for mysterious holes or discoloration of the leaves. A healthy plant should have a robust, moist, lush overall appearance. Never buy a plant that doesn't *look* healthy . . . because it probably isn't.

Purists may hate us for saying this, but when you buy a plant, you are not marrying it "for better or worse, in sickness and in health." When it starts to look more worse than better, and it

PLANTS EVEN DORINNE COULDN'T KILL

Direct Sunlight	Water When the Soil Is . . .
Kalanchoe	almost completely dry
Baby tears	barely moist to the touch

Good Light	
Jade plant (Crassula)	almost completely dry
Gardenia	barely moist to the touch
Shefflera	dry down to 1–2″

Medium Light	
Prayer plant (Maranta)	dry down to 1–1 and 1/2″
Wandering jew (Tradescantia)	dry down to 1–1 and 1/2″
Dieffenbachia	dry down to 1–1 and 1/2″

Low Light	
Mother-in-law tongue (Sanseveria)	dry down to 1–1 and 1/2″
Philodendron	dry down to 1–1 and 1/2″
Chinese evergreen (Aglaonema)	dry down to 1–1 and 1/2″

[NOTE: The size of your pot affects how deep you must dig with your finger to check the dryness. For large pots, dig to the deepest level we suggest. For small pots, dig to the most shallow level.]

resists your best attempts to save it, give it the old heave-ho. Even under the best of care, plants don't live forever. After you've murdered five or six of them, however, it's time for you to come to grips with the fact that you don't have a green thumb.

Don't despair. The artificial plants they're making these days look wonderful.

[*Dorinne:* Not long ago, I bought an artificial plant for a dark corner of our bedroom, and I asked my husband how he thought it looked.

He said, "It looks great, but I don't think it's going to get enough light."

"It doesn't need much," I replied.]

**Real or artificial? Only her florist knows for
sure. Actually, it's artificial.**

ACCESSORIES

Accessories are those dumb little things that aren't quite appliances and definitely aren't furniture but are too nice to shove into the closet. Accessories are a vital part of your decorative scheme. Without them, even the most exquisitely decorated home would look like a museum piece or a tearsheet from a women's magazine. They give your apartment personality and life; they tell visitors a little about yourself and your interests. But like the pods in *Invasion of the Body Snatchers,* they easily can get out of hand.

Too many small accessories scattered casually about the apartment will make it appear cluttered and confused. Instead, choose your most attractive accessory and make it the focal point of a given area. It's better, for example, to decorate a coffee table with one nice vase than to clutter it with dozens of tiny figurines. If, however, your most prized accessories do consist of small pieces, group them together on a shelf or inside a curio cabinet.

The difference between accessories and plain old junk is largely a matter of how meaningful the piece is to you. Does it perform some useful function? Does it have personal or sentimental value? Does it reflect your cultural heritage or your intellectual interests? If so, display it with pride.

If, on the other hand, it was a birthday gift from someone forced to make a last-minute purchase at one of those gas station gift shops on the turnpike, the trashcan may be the most appropriate place for it.

CHAPTER FOUR

Cooking 101—
An Idiot's Guide to the Art of Cooking

If you don't know how to cook, you may be tempted to skip this chapter. But please don't. Because if you don't know how to cook, this chapter is going to change your life.

No, we're not going to preach to you about how much better you'll eat when you learn to cook at home or how much money you'll save. We assume you know all that. What's more, we assume you would in fact *like* to cook at home, but you just don't know how.

Have you tried using cookbooks to teach yourself how to cook?

Was it a total disaster?

We're not surprised. Giving a cookbook to someone who doesn't know how to cook is like giving a road map to someone who doesn't know how to drive. Even people who *can* cook tend to ignore their cookbooks. Oh sure, they *own* a lot of them, and every now and then on a Sunday afternoon they'll pull one off the shelf and struggle through a recipe for chocolate mousse. But when it comes to feeding themselves on a daily basis, most people depend on the two dozen or so meals they learned from Mom.

What if your mother never taught you how to cook?

Well, that's what this book is all about. And that's why this chapter promises to be different from any "cookbook" you've ever seen before.

Here's how:

• These recipes assume no prior knowledge: If you've ever tried to follow a recipe in an ordinary cookbook, you've probably had this experience. You're about halfway through the recipe and doing fine. In fact, you're just about ready to congratulate yourself on how clever you are . . . when suddenly, the directions say, "separate an egg."

"From what?" you shout.

What the heck does it mean to separate an egg? So you go running to another cookbook or, if you don't have another, you go to your Encyclopedia Britannica, and you try to find out how to separate an egg. But even if you succeed, by now your saucepans have boiled over, your butter has turned brown, and your adventurous spirit is defeated.

The problem? Most cookbooks *assume* you already know how to cook. They assume you know what it means to separate an egg, scald milk, or clarify butter.

The only thing we assume in the 21 recipes that follow is that your I.Q. is higher than room temperature. Each recipe has been painstakingly written step by step to take you by the hand and lead you through the process of cooking a meal. If you're smart enough to read, you're smart enough to make every meal in this book.

• Recipes for complete meals, not just main dishes: Strictly speaking, what follow are not recipes at all, but meal plans. A recipe tells you how to make a single dish. But these 21 meal plans tell you how to prepare 21 entire dinners. The step-by-step format is designed to let you cook an entire meal at once, so everything will be ready at the same time. If you don't want to eat a particular item on a meal plan (or if you don't have the necessary ingredients), you can just skip the steps that relate to it.

• These recipes use plain English: To people who don't know how to cook, cookbooks are written in a foreign language—a bizarre combination of French, Italian, pidgin English, and scientific notation:

> Saute ½ tsp. minced onion and add ⅓ dollop puree of prosciutto, pared and sifted gently before shucking.

Does that make any sense to you? Of course not. That's why the most complicated word you'll find in this chapter is *fry*.

• No surprises: Each recipe in this chapter begins with a complete list of all the things you need to cook the meal, including the main ingredients, the staples, *and* the utensils. You will never find yourself three-quarters of the way through a recipe and suddenly discover you need an electric blender to finish the rest of it. Nothing can go wrong!

• Small portions: Most cookbooks ignore the single cook. Dividing recipes designed for four to six people to make an amount suitable for one is a tricky business—especially for someone who doesn't know how to cook in the first place. That's why most of the recipes in this chapter are designed for just one serving.

• These recipes are based on reality: The people who write cookbooks don't always live in the real world. Recipes for a sandwich, for example, might begin with instructions on how to grind wheat and bake bread. But this chapter is different. It's written for people who live in the twentieth century, who use canned tomatoes, ready-made piecrusts, and (occasionally) frozen vegetables. We're not above telling you to buy a packaged hollandaise sauce mix or a box of frozen french fries. What's more, we've encouraged you to use leftovers whenever possible. Some of the 21 meal plans are based on leftovers from earlier meals, and some make use of ingredients that you've used earlier in the week. We've even given you three weekly shopping lists so you'll be sure to have everything you need.

• Recipes to suit your lifestyle: Most cookbooks are written under the mistaken notion that every day is just another long, lazy Sunday afternoon. Just what you need after coming home on a Tuesday night after a hard day at the office is a nice three-hour recipe for chicken cacciatore! That's why we've organized these recipes over three hypothetical weeks. We've tried, whenever possible, to put the big meals on Saturdays and Sundays and the lighter ones (especially those using leftovers) early in the week. Each recipe begins with a rating of the total cooking time:

> QUICKIE: 30 minutes or less
> AVERAGE: 30–60 minutes
> LONG: more than an hour

We'd rate the degree of difficulty, too, if it weren't for the fact that *all* these recipes are easy!

You don't have to do the recipes in order if you don't want, and you certainly don't have to eat things that don't appeal to you. But why not take three weeks out of your life and give it a try? By the time it's over, you'll be a darn good cook.

Are you ready to begin?

Good.

But do us a little favor. First, read (or at least skim) the rest of this introduction before you begin cooking: It covers some things you'll need to know. And second, *read each recipe all the way through before you start to make it.*

IT'S GOOD TO KNOW HOW TO COOK AN EGG

There will be days when you just don't feel like cooking. Maybe the boss didn't like the report you've been working on for the past two weeks, or maybe you're just tired. Well, that's why God invented the egg. So do yourself a favor. Master these simple instructions and you'll never starve.

How to make scrambled eggs [*Use one or two eggs per serving*]

1. Break the eggs by cracking the shell on the edge of a cup or small bowl. Let the eggs fall into the bowl and throw away the shell.

2. Add 1 teaspoon of milk (or water) for each egg and stir with a fork until the yellow part (the yolk) and the clear part (the white) are well mixed. Stir the eggs vigorously in a vertical circle so that your hand looks like it's reeling in a fishing line. This exposes the egg to the air and gives it a foamy, bubbly consistency. It's called beating the egg.

3. Heat 1 tablespoon of butter in a frying pan over medium-high heat until it coats the bottom of the pan. Try not to let it turn brown.

4. Pour the egg into the pan.

5. Wait a moment for the egg to get somewhat firm. Then, with a large spoon, gently stir or fold over the egg a few times until it's done the way you like it. Despite the name (scrambled), don't stir the eggs too vigorously. Two or three gentle stirring motions will do the trick. [Feel free to spark up your scrambled eggs by adding such things as chopped onion, chopped parsley, grated cheese, chopped peppers, mushrooms, or worcestershire sauce just after Step 4.]

How to make a fried egg

1. Melt 1 tablespoon of butter in a frying pan over medium-high heat until it coats the bottom of the pan. Try not to let it turn brown.

2. Break the egg against the edge of the pan and gently pour it into the pan, discarding the shell. If you are careful, the egg will remain whole. But don't worry if the yolk breaks and runs into the white. Some people prefer 'em that way.

3. Give the egg roughly one minute to become firm. Sprinkle about 1 teaspoon of water into *the frying pan cover* and place it over the frying pan.

4. Lower the heat to low and cook another minute, or until

the egg looks firm and there is a thin, transparent film over the yolk. Take it out of the pan with a spatula and serve. If you like your fried eggs "over easy," flip it over with a spatula and let it cook on the other side for about fifteen more seconds. Remove and serve.

HOW TO MAKE A SOFT-BOILED EGG

1. Put about 3 cups of water into a small saucepan and bring it to a boil over high heat.

2. When the water has come to a full boil, place the egg on a slotted spoon and lower it gingerly into the water. Raise and lower it a few times to ease the shock of the cold egg hitting the hot water. If in spite of this precaution the egg cracks, sprinkle the crack with some salt to help seal it. Submerge the egg and let it boil. Cover and lower heat to low.

3. If the egg has come directly from the refrigerator, let it boil 5 minutes. If the egg was at room temperature, let it boil for 4 minutes.

4. When time is up, gently remove the egg with your slotted spoon and hold it under cold running water until it is cool enough to handle.

5. Crack the egg by smacking it with a table knife and scoop out the inside with a spoon, letting it fall into a small bowl or, if you have one, an egg cup. Try not to let the broken shell get mixed in with the egg. Cut the egg into pieces and season with salt and pepper.

HOW TO MAKE A HARD-BOILED EGG

1. Fill a small saucepan with about 3 cups of cold water and add up to three eggs.

2. Bring the water to a boil over high heat.

3. When the water comes to a full boil, reduce the heat to low and let the water boil slowly for about fifteen minutes.

4. When time is up, drain the saucepan of hot water and run cold water over the eggs until they are easy to handle.

5. Gently crack the shells by hitting or rolling them on your countertop and peel off the shells entirely.

6. Put the eggs in the fridge until they're nice and cold.

[NOTE: To learn how to make *deviled eggs, see Friday, the 21st.* And to learn how to make something that looks and tastes like an *omelette* but requires none of the skill, see Frittata, on *Friday, the 14th.*]

IT'S GOOD TO KNOW
HOW TO MAKE A SALAD

Your opinion of salads may be based on either one of two stereotypes. If you tend to hate them, it's probably because you remember the pale hunks of iceberg lettuce, mushy tomatoes, and Elmer's Glue dressing popularized by school cafeterias and hospital food-service centers. If, on the other hand, you tend to love them, it may be because you're part of the "salad-bar generation" and you're really in love with mixed beans, sliced beets, artichoke hearts, bacon bits, chick peas, cottage cheese, and all the other goodies that comprise a salad that is, to say the least, hard to duplicate at home.

A good, everyday homemade salad lies somewhere in between these two extremes. To make one, you need only start with fresh salad greens and add a simple homemade dressing. Here's how:

SALAD GREENS
Most grocery stores stock a wide variety of salad greens, so resist the temptation to make all your salads with plain old iceberg. Experiment with different varieties, and try mixing them with each other, too.

• Bibb: Similar in shape to boston lettuce but slightly smaller, bibb has loosely packed tender, dark-green leaves. Marvelous by itself, its leaves also can be used as a "cup" to hold a main-course salad, like tuna or chicken salad.

• Boston: A good all-purpose lettuce with soft-green leaves and a delicate flavor. Good by itself or in combination with more bitter-tasting greens.

• Curly endive (chicory): The edges of these narrow leaves are irregular and crinkly, and they come from a stem that is almost pure white. Because of its strong and bitter flavor, it's best used in combination with other greens or as a garnish.

• Escarole: Similar to chicory, but the leaves are fuller, less curly, and it's not quite as bitter. A little of it goes a long way, though, so use it in combination with other greens.

• Iceberg: The most familiar variety of lettuce. Because of its crispness, it can't be beat for sandwiches. But salads made only with iceberg are boring. Spark it up with some chicory or escarole.

• Leaf: There are several different types of lettuce that the grocery store will lump together under the generic name leaf lettuce. Although the colors vary, they are all mild in taste, and each will serve as a good all-purpose lettuce.

• Romaine: With its long, broad leaves and dark green color, romaine adds a dramatic note to a salad. Chef salads, for example, are often served on a bed of romaine. Its flavor is very strong, though, so use it in combination with milder greens, like iceberg or Boston.

• Spinach: That's right, don't overlook spinach as a salad green. Use it by itself or in combination with others. Look for fresh loose spinach, not the kind that comes in packages. Remove the tough stems and wash the leaves very thoroughly.

PREPARING THE GREENS

Once you've chosen your salad greens, prepare them as follows:

1. Remove as many leaves from the stem as you want to eat in one serving. Tear the leaves into bite-size pieces (don't chop with a knife, but tear with your hands) and put them in a mixing bowl or salad spinner.

2. Rinse them with cold water.

3. If you have a salad spinner, spin the greens and repeat the process until there is no sand or grit in the water. If you don't have a spinner, simply pour off the water and repeat two or three times until you're confident the greens are clean.

4. Spin the leaves dry, or pat them dry with a paper towel. [Don't clean a whole week's worth of lettuce at once, because most of it will get soggy. Instead, simply wrap what remains of the head of lettuce in plastic wrap and store it in the fridge.]

TOSSING AND DRESSING THE SALAD

It takes three different men to make the ideal tossed salad: a generous man with the olive oil, a stingy man with the vinegar; and a crazy man to mix it up!

But if you can't find three such people, do it yourself by following these directions for a single serving:

1. Place the rinsed and dried greens in a mixing bowl.

2. Pour in a small amount of olive oil (start with about a tablespoon).

3. Lift and mix the greens with a fork and spoon until they are covered with a thin film of oil, adding more oil if necessary.

4. Sprinkle in about 1 teaspoon of vinegar. Continue to mix and toss the greens. [If making more than one serving, just remember the proportions are roughly three parts oil to one part vinegar.]

5. Add salt and freshly ground pepper.

Try eating your salad as a last course instead of the first. It's very Continental, and it makes sense—both from the standpoint of preserving your appetite and aiding your digestion.

IT'S GOOD TO KNOW
HOW TO CHOP A VEGETABLE

Chop is a deceptively simple word. Sure, it means to cut something into small bits. But how small should you chop them? And what's the best way to do it?

There are essentially three different levels of chopping: *mince*, which means to chop something into very tiny bits; *dice*, which means to chop something into small cubes about ¼" thick; and *chop coarsely*, which means to chop into bite-size pieces about ½" thick. Unless we specifically tell you to chop fine or coarse, you'll never go wrong by dicing vegetables into ¼" bits.

The key to good chopping is to use a carbon-steel chef's knife with a razor-sharp edge. Before you begin, peel the vegetable with your vegetable peeler or, if it's an onion or garlic clove, remove the outer layers of skin. Slice it thinly and arrange the slices into a pile. Then, with the knife pointing to your left, put your right hand on the handle and lay the palm of your left hand across the dull edge of the blade. Chop the sliced vegetables by making a series of guillotinelike motions with the knife, stopping every now and then to scoop everything back into a pile. Repeat the process until you've achieved the "grain" you want—minced, diced, or chopped coarse.

While we're on the subject, here's a quick way to chop an onion:

1. Peel the onion and slice it in half lengthwise from top to bottom.

2. Lay half the onion cut-side down on your cutting board and cut a series of thin *lengthwise* slices in it, taking care not to cut all the way through to the cutting board.

3. Turn the onion around and start cutting *crosswise* slices against the grain of the slices you just made. As you do, the onion will break into perfectly diced bits.

A FEW WORDS OF ADVICE ABOUT
THESE RECIPES . . .

A WORD ABOUT TEMPERATURES

To the novice cook, one of the most irritating things about cookbooks is their cavalier attitude about temperatures. "Simmer this," or "sauté that," they say, leaving the beginner screaming, "How hot? How hot?"

To make your life a little easier, we've divided stovetop temperatures into six different levels, which we've tried to use as consistently and accurately as possible. They are: very low; low; medium-low; medium; medium-high; and high. If you have an electric range, you'll probably be able to find a setting for each of these levels. If you have a gas range, you'll just have to estimate and experiment.

But there are a zillion variables in cooking, so there's no way to tell you exactly how high to set your heat. Just make sure the food is cooking in the way we've described. If, for example, we tell you to boil something slowly over low heat, *it should be boiling slowly*—even if you have to turn your heat up to medium or down to very low to make it do so. In short, use our heat levels as guidelines, not gospel.

When it comes to oven temperatures, we will always specify an exact figure. But keep in mind that oven temperatures vary. If you find your food is consistently undercooked or overcooked when you follow our directions exactly, go to the hardware store and buy a stove thermometer. Set your oven to a given temperature and give it a few minutes to get hot. Then check to see how it jives with the reading on the thermometer. If it's only a few degrees off, you can probably compensate by adding or subtracting to the temperatures we recommend. But if it's off by 25 degrees or more, call a repairman and have him adjust your stove.

A WORD ABOUT SAFETY

Most inexperienced cooks are afraid they'll poison themselves if they're left to their own devices in the kitchen. That's virtually impossible. But it is, unfortunately, very possible that you could burn, scald, lacerate, or otherwise maim yourself while learning to cook. We urge you to use extreme caution when you cook—especially when you're performing one of the following hazardous operations:

adding ingredients to a pot of boiling liquid

chopping vegetables with a sharp knife

adding ingredients to a frying pan filled with hot oil

draining hot liquid from a saucepan or pot

tasting something without letting it cool

working with electrical appliances

putting out an accidental pan fire (See Chapter 9)

A WORD ABOUT SERVING SIZES

Unless otherwise noted, all the recipes in this book are designed to feed one hungry person, but they can be expanded to feed two by simply doubling the proportions. The prepackaged meats you'll find in the supermarket nowadays often contain more than enough to feed one. If that's the case, you can either freeze the excess portion before you cook it or cook everything and repeat the meal in a few days. See Chapter 5 for some advice on freezing, refrigerating, and preparing leftovers.

A WORD ABOUT SEASONING

With a few minor exceptions, you won't find the word *salt* in these recipes. In recent years, salt has been linked to a variety of illnesses, especially high blood pressure. Without passing judgment on the merit of these findings or arbitrarily telling you how much salt to use, we've simply told you to add "seasoning" if you wish.

A WORD ABOUT MEASUREMENTS

From time to time, you will notice that we have a rather casual attitude about measurements. We may write, for example, "take a chunk of butter and mix it with a hunk of mayonnaise until it becomes a large gob of gunk." That's our way of saying the exact measurements aren't important. Don't worry. When they *are* important, we'll tell you exactly how much to use. But

---

CONVERSION TABLE: STANDARD LIQUID MEASURES

1 teaspoon = 60 drops	1 cup = 16 tablespoons
1 tablespoon = 3 teaspoons	2 cups = 1 pint
1 ounce = 2 tablespoons	16 fluid ounces = 1 pint
¼ cup = 4 tablespoons	2 pints = 1 quart
⅓ cup = 5 and ⅓ tablespoons	4 quarts = 1 gallon
½ cup = 8 tablespoons	

---

you'll never become a good cook if you remain a slave to the measuring spoons. A good chemist, maybe, but not a good cook.

Young single person's refrigerator.

Mom's refrigerator.

As long as we're on the subject of measurements, here's a handy tip you'll use often:

> To measure solid butter in tablespoons,
> use the hash-marks printed on the wrapper.

A WORD ABOUT LEFTOVERS

Is there anything more typical of a single person's apartment than an empty refrigerator?

We don't mean completely empty, of course. There is always exactly one can of beer on the top rack, still attached to the plastic six-pack holder, which now dangles off to the side. One individually wrapped slice of slightly green Kraft American cheese sits alone on the bottom shelf. The tray inside the door contains a small jar of mustard and a large bottle of ketchup, which has a crusty red growth near the cap.

Compare this barren wasteland to Mom's refrigerator! Here is a garden of delights and delicacies, a bountiful smorgasbord of delicious cold fried chicken, tasty leftover roast beef, crisp salad greens, and fresh vegetables. As you open the door, a huge bottle of milk beckons you inside, while Grade A eggs guard the door, standing rank and file in their neat little tray.

What makes the difference?

Several things:

Mom doesn't eat at McDonald's five days a week.

Mom does her grocery shopping as infrequently as possible.

And most important, Mom knows the three rules of leftovers.

When it comes to leftovers, the world can be divided into two groups: those who save every little scrap of food; and those who throw everything away. People who feel guilty about wasting food will fill the refrigerator with dozens of containers holding a half slice of meat loaf or two tablespoons of mashed potatoes, while others cast away full cartons of milk after a few days and throw out anything that isn't put to immediate use. Neither policy is strictly correct. Leftover rule #1 is simply this:

If there's enough left for a full helping, save it.
Otherwise, don't.

Of course, you also should save raw ingredients that you will use again in the course of a week or so: a half onion, a half lemon, a few sprigs of parsley, and so on.

Storing food in the refrigerator is easy. Just make sure you have an adequate supply of plastic wrap, aluminum foil, plastic storage bags (like Baggies), and—if possible—plastic containers.

Tupperware is the Rolls-Royce of plastic containers. Unfortunately, the only way to get it is to be invited to a horrid event called a Tupperware party, at which you will learn, among other things, how to "burp" your Tupperware. If the thought of going to one of these parties frightens you—and it should—you can buy perfectly acceptable plastic food containers at the dime store.

No matter what device you use to cover refrigerated foods, though, try to make it as airtight as possible. And don't delay. Refrigerate foods as soon as you get them home from the store or clear them from the dinner table. In the past, it was common to let food sit at room temperature before refrigerating it. *Wrong!* The key to storing food safely is to put it in the fridge while it's still fairly hot, bypassing the dangerous lukewarm temperatures in which bacteria thrive.

You'll never have to worry about food spoiling in your refrigerator if you'll follow leftover rule #2:

Don't save anything longer than one week.

There are some exceptions, of course. Condiments like mustard, ketchup, salad dressing, and pickles will last in your refrigerator for many moons. So will unopened soft drinks, beer, and tightly wrapped cheese.

But by "using or losing" your leftovers, fresh meats, vegetables, and dairy products within one week, you'll always be confident in their freshness. If a piece of food smells fresh and looks fresh, chances are it *is* fresh. Trust your senses, including your common sense. Spoiled meat and dairy products have an unmistakable odor. Spoiled fruits and vegetables look discolored and feel soft. Inspect anything that has been stored in your refrigerator before you use it, and follow leftover rule #3:

When in doubt, throw it out.

A WORD ABOUT WORDS

We promised you no hard words and we intend to keep that promise. But there are a few *easy* words we want to make sure you know and a few hard ones you'll need to know if you want to carry your cooking career any further than this book. So here is the shortest, most basic glossary of cooking terms in history:

BAKE: To put something in the oven and cook it in dry heat.

BASTE: To coat a piece of meat or poultry with its own pan juices, using a pastry brush or bulb baster.

BEAT: To stir something very vigorously in such a way that it is exposed to the air. [See "Scrambled Eggs."]

BROIL: To cook something in such a way that it is only a few inches beneath the source of the heat. How you broil varies from oven to oven. In most gas stoves, the broiling section is behind that little door below the main oven. In most electric ranges, you broil by raising one of the racks all the way to the spot nearest the heating element at the top of the oven.

BROWN: To bake, broil, or fry a piece of food until it turns slightly brown.

CLOVE: A single wedgelike section of a larger bulb (usually refers to garlic).

DICE: To chop something into small cubes, about ¼" square.

DOT: To apply small pats (of butter, usually) to the surface of a piece of meat or poultry.

DRAIN: To separate food from the liquid in which it was cooked by pouring it through a colander or a sieve, or by simply tipping the lid and pouring the liquid down the drain. Use caution when dealing with boiling-hot liquids.

DREDGE: To coat a piece of food in flour.

FILLET: A piece of meat or fish from which the bones have been removed.

GRATE: To rub food (usually cheese) against a grater until it is reduced to thin shreds.

MARINATE: To let a piece of food soak in a liquid solution until it becomes more tender or tasty than it would otherwise be.

MINCE: To chop into tiny bits.

OIL: An animal or vegetable fat in liquid form used for cooking. [Most of the recipes in this book call for olive oil because that's our favorite, but you can substitute any kind of oil or shortening you like.]

PINCH: The amount of a food (usually a spice) that you can hold between your thumb and forefinger, or an amount equal to less than ⅛ teaspoon.

PREHEAT THE OVEN: To set the oven to a given temperature, giving it sufficient time (usually about 10 minutes) to reach that temperature before adding food.

ROAST: Essentially the same as "bake," so don't let this word throw you.

SAUTÉ: We won't use this word in this book, but in case you see it elsewhere, don't worry. All it means is to fry something very slowly and gently over low heat.

SHORTENING: Animal or vegetable fat in *solid* form. (Crisco is one of the best-known brands.)

SIMMER: We use this word a few times, but not without explanation. It's an important word to know, though. It means to boil something very slowly over low heat. (The surface should be bubbling slightly.)

WHIP: To stir something so vigorously (with a whisk or electric mixer) that it acquires a fluffy consistency.

Weekly Shopping Lists

If you intend to follow these recipes in the order they are printed, you may find these shopping lists handy. Just take the list with you to the grocery store, and you'll have everything you need for the coming week. To make the plan work, do your shopping on Saturday, although you may want to make a second trip to the store around Wednesday to pick up fresh vegetables and meats for later in the week.

WEEK ONE:
SATURDAY, THE 1ST–FRIDAY, THE 7TH

beef chuck roast (2 lbs.)
5 baking potatoes
carrots (1 bunch or package, fresh)
celery (1 bunch or package, fresh)
5 medium-size onions
french bread (1 individual-size loaf)
parsley (1 bunch)
prepared horseradish (1 bottle)
red wine (1 bottle)

lettuce (1 head, your favorite kind)

chicken (1 package of your favorite parts)

spaghetti (1 8 oz. box)

broccoli (1 bunch)

2 tomatoes

cheddar cheese (1 small brick, or 1 small package shredded)

peach halves (1 can)

cream cheese (1 small package)

3 lemons

2 pork chops (roughly ½″ thick)

long-grain white rice (1 box)

applesauce (1 small jar)

ground beef (1 lb.)

stewed tomatoes (1 can)

spinach (buy it fresh and loose; as much as you want for 1 salad)

plain yogurt (1 small container)

1 fillet of fresh fish (buy this later in the week)

frozen asparagus (1 package)

cabbage (1 small head)

CHECK TO MAKE SURE YOU HAVE

flour

olive oil

red wine vinegar

butter

oregano

paprika

grated parmesan cheese

garlic (fresh)

bread (1 loaf, your favorite kind)

milk

mayonnaise

rosemary

eggs (½ dozen)

dijon mustard

WEEK TWO:
SATURDAY, THE 8TH–FRIDAY, THE 14TH

tomato sauce (1 small can)

carraway seeds (1 jar)

4 baking potatoes

5 medium-size onions

chicken (3 lbs. fryer)

3 apples

frozen peas (1 package)

seedless white grapes (1 bunch)

chopped walnuts (1 package)

lettuce (1 head, your favorite kind)

celery (1 bunch)

parsley (1 bunch)

potato sticks (1 can)

dried mint (1 jar)

1 lemon

liver (2 or 3 thin slices, preferably calf's)

bacon (1/2 lb.)

green beans (as many as you want for a single serving)

ham slice (precooked and prepackaged, 1/2–1" thick)

sweet potato

pineapple slices (1 can)

cottage cheese (1 small container)

1 acorn squash
bulk sausage (1 lb.)
watercress or endive or chicory (1 head)
brown sugar (1 box)
mushrooms (about 1/4 lb. fresh)
1 zucchini squash
french bread (1 individual loaf)
garlic salt

CHECK TO MAKE SURE YOU HAVE

butter
olive oil
paprika
mayonnaise
milk
flour
red or white wine
prepared horseradish
dijon mustard
eggs (1/2 dozen)
red wine vinegar
oregano
bread
cinnamon

WEEK THREE:
SATURDAY, THE 15TH–FRIDAY, THE 21ST

veal (1/4–1/2 lb., thin-sliced)
pasta (1 box mostaccioli, rigatoni, or penne)
2 16 oz. cans tomatoes (Italian plum style, if available)
dried crushed red peppers (1 jar)

dry white wine or dry vermouth

parsley (1 bunch)

3 medium-size onions

4 lemons

1 steak (New York strip, T-bone, porterhouse, or shell)

1 artichoke

lettuce (2 heads of iceberg)

1 apple

pickle relish (1 small jar)

chili sauce (1 small bottle)

cheddar cheese (1 small brick)

ground beef (1 lb.)

hamburger buns

ice cream

fudge sauce (1 small jar)

2 or 3 lamb chops

1 baking potato

brussels sprouts (1 small package, or enough for one serving)

water chestnuts (1 small can)

1 large green pepper

carrots (1 bunch or package, fresh)

scallions (1 bunch)

1 orange

1 mild red onion.

french salad dressing (1 bottle)

bread (1 loaf of firm white)

tomato sauce (1 small can)

mozarella cheese (1 package, sliced or shredded)

seedless white grapes (1 bunch)

tuna (1 6 oz. can)

celery (1 bunch or package, fresh)

potato chips (1 small bag)

1 cucumber

anchovies (optional)

mushrooms (optional)

pepperoni (optional)

sour cream (optional)

mint jelly (optional)

plain yogurt (optional)

CHECK TO MAKE SURE YOU HAVE

mushrooms (left over from previous week)

grated Parmesan cheese

olive oil

dijon mustard

butter

oregano

red wine vinegar

garlic (fresh)

mayonnaise

eggs (1/2 dozen)

paprika

sugar

RELAX

One last word before you start cooking:

Relax.

Take a nip or two out of the wine bottle from time to time—just like Julia Child does—so you won't start taking yourself or the job too seriously.

Just about the only thing that can go wrong is that you'll burn your food or leave it undercooked. There's very little chance you'll poison yourself and almost none that you'll cause an explosion and lose a limb.

Don't take our instructions too literally. If we suggest using a six-quart pot for a given recipe, for example, and you suddenly learn the biggest pot you have is four quarts, don't panic. Read the recipe carefully. You can probably do it just as easily with the smaller pot. The same goes for ingredients. While it may be hard to make Sunday, the 16th's steak dinner without steak, it's certainly possible to make Saturday, the 15th's spaghetti sauce without oregano. Use your common sense. Make substitutions. Be flexible. Be creative and innovative. That's what being a good cook is all about.

Don't be frightened by the large number of steps in some of these recipes. Lots of steps are a sign not of a recipe's complexity, but of its simplicity. We've broken our instructions into many small steps so you can easily follow them in a systematic way. We truly believe that a five-year-old child could understand and follow these recipes.

So, in the words of Groucho Marx, run out and find yourself a five-year-old child, and let's get started.

Saturday, the 1st

OLD-FASHIONED POT ROAST WITH
VEGETABLES, FRENCH BREAD, GREEN
SALAD (original meal)

It's Saturday. You've got some extra time, so this is the day to learn how to cook. We could have started you out with something simpler, but why not jump in head first? This recipe is somewhat lengthy, but it isn't difficult. When you're done, you will have gained three things: a feeling of real accomplishment; a delicious dinner; and some leftovers to save you time during the week.

COOKING TIME: long

THINGS YOU SHOULD BUY

beef chuck roast, approx. 2 lbs. (You can also use rump roast,
or any beef roast with a label marked "for pot roast.")

carrots (you'll use 4)

celery (you'll use 4 stalks)

2 medium-size onions

3 baking potatoes

french bread (1 small loaf)

parsley (a few sprigs)

prepared horseradish

dry red wine (optional)

lettuce (you choose what kind)

THINGS YOU SHOULD HAVE

flour

olive oil

red wine vinegar

butter

oregano

paprika

UTENSILS

6 qt. pot with cover

salad spinner (optional)

vegetable peeler

measuring cup and spoons

mixing bowl

cookie sheet or broiling pan

STEP-BY-STEP DIRECTIONS

   1. On a paper towel or plate, put about ½ cup of flour. Roll
the meat in the flour or pat it with your hands until the meat is

covered with a thin coating of flour. If the meat is too big or too oddly shaped to fit into your pot, you may want to cut it into two or three pieces and cover those with flour.

2. Put two or three tablespoons of oil in the pot to coat the bottom.

3. Over medium-high heat, fry the meat in the oil for about three minutes on each side until it turns brown.

4. When it is well browned, spoon about ¼ cup of horse-radish over the top of the meat.

5. Add one cup of water (or a 50-50 mixture of water and wine) to the pot and *put the cover on.*

6. When the water you just put in begins to boil, lower the heat to low until it boils very slowly ("simmers"), and cover. Let it cook like this for *three hours.* Check it from time to time to make sure the liquid hasn't boiled away completely. If so, just add a little more. Always remember to put the cover back on. Meanwhile, let's work on the vegetables.

7. Cut the ends off 2 onions. Run under cold water and peel off the outer layers until you have a smooth white onion. Cut in halves or, if they are big onions, in quarters. Set them aside in your mixing bowl.

8. Slice the ends off 4 carrots and scrape with a vegetable peeler. Slice lengthwise in halves or, if large, in quarters. Rinse in cold water. Put in mixing bowl.

9. Cut the leaves and the bottom ends off 4 single stalks of celery. Slice lengthwise in halves or quarters depending on the size. Rinse in cold water. Put in mixing bowl.

10. Peel 3 potatoes and cut in quarters. Put in mixing bowl.

11. Fill the mixing bowl with cold water until it covers all the vegetables. This will keep them fresh for the next hour or so, before you put them in the pot. Now relax for a while.

12. One hour before the meat is done (or two hours after you put it in), drain the water covering your vegetables down the sink and put the vegetables in the pot with the meat. Put the carrots and celery in first so they can get down into the simmering liquid. Season, and cover the pot. When you add all these goodies to the pot, it may stop simmering for a while. If so, just turn up the heat until you can hear the liquid boiling. Then turn the heat back down until the liquid boils very gently. Check occasionally to make sure there is enough liquid. If not, just toss in a shot of wine like Julia Child does.

13. Make your green salad (see section on salads).

14. About 10 minutes before the pot roast is due to be ready, slice your French bread lengthwise. If it's a long piece you may want to cut it in half, so you'll have four pieces of bread. Spread the cut sides with butter.

15. Rinse a few sprigs of parsley, cut off the stems, and chop the leaves very fine.

16. Sprinkle parsley, oregano, and paprika over the buttered bread.

17. Put the bread on a cookie sheet or broiling pan (buttered side up) and stick it under the broiler for just a few minutes until it's golden brown. Check it frequently, because it goes from golden brown to disgustingly black in a blink of an eye.

18. Is your pot roast ready yet? To make sure it's done, take a knife and pierce a few of the carrots. If the knife goes in smoothly, the pot roast is done. If it goes in making a crunchy sound, give it another 5 or 10 minutes and try again.

SERVING INSTRUCTIONS

Put the pot roast on a large plate or platter with the meat on one side and the vegetables piled up on the other. Slice as much meat as you want and spoon the vegetables onto your plate. The bread will look nice in a little basket lined with a napkin. Have a nice glass of milk, too; it's good for you.

LEFTOVER INSTRUCTIONS

Put the leftover meat and vegetables on a clean plate and wrap it up tight in plastic wrap or aluminum foil. Put it in the fridge. If possible, refrigerate the pot roast cooking liquid, too. Wash the leftover parsley and spin it dry. Pull the leaves off the stems and pat them dry with paper towels. Store them in a covered jar in the refrigerator, where they will stay fresh for two weeks. Cover your leftover lettuce with plastic wrap and put it in the refrigerator.

Sunday, the 2nd

OVEN-FRIED CHICKEN, PASTA BURRO,
BROCCOLI (original meal)

This is the easy way to fry chicken. No need to stand over the frying pan while you and the kitchen get splattered with grease. Just pop it in the oven, and the chicken will pop out crispy brown.

COOKING TIME: average

THINGS YOU SHOULD BUY

1 package of your favorite chicken parts

spaghetti (¼ to ½ of an 8 oz. box), or your favorite pasta

broccoli (2 or 3 stalks; we'll cook all of it and save some for leftovers)

THINGS YOU SHOULD HAVE

parsley (left over from yesterday)

grated parmesan cheese

butter (1 stick)

garlic (2 cloves)

paprika

flour

olive oil (optional)

UTENSILS

baking pan

6 qt. pot

3 qt. saucepan with cover

colander

1 qt. saucepan

plastic bag, or brown lunch bag

vegetable peeler

salad spinner (optional)

measuring cup and spoons

STEP-BY-STEP DIRECTIONS

1. Turn on the oven and set for 450°.

2. Put ½ stick of butter in the baking pan and put it in the oven. Take it out as soon as the butter has melted completely.

3. Meanwhile, put about ½ cup of flour into the brown paper bag, put in two or three chicken pieces at a time, and shake the bag until the pieces are covered with flour. (If you don't have a bag, just put flour on a plate and roll the chicken in it until it's covered with a thin layer.)

4. Put the floured pieces of chicken skin side down in the baking pan with the melted butter. Season and sprinkle with paprika. Put it in the oven for 30 minutes.

5. Now, while that's cooking, let's work on the rest of the meal. Rinse the broccoli in cold water. Take a sharp knife and trim the broccoli a little: cut off the tough ends, slice off the leaves, cut off the individual stalks so they will be a manageable size to eat. Use your vegetable peeler to scrape off the outer skin. Set the broccoli aside.

6. Rinse the parsley, cut off the stems (if there are any), and chop it fine. (Or use what you have in the refrigerator.)

7. Separate 2 cloves of garlic from the garlic bulb. Peel them and chop fine.

8. Combine about 4 tablespoons of the chopped parsley, the chopped garlic, and at least 3 tablespoons of butter in the small saucepan. Put it on the stove, but don't start heating it until we tell you.

9. Boil about 2 or 3 quarts of water for the spaghetti over high heat in the 6 qt. pot. Add 1 teaspoon of olive oil and give it a few shakes of the salt shaker.

10. Has time elapsed on the chicken? If so, remove the chicken from the oven and turn each piece over. Season and sprinkle with more paprika. Return it to the oven and time for

15 minutes. If time expires before you're done with the rest of the meal, don't worry. Just turn off the oven and let the chicken stay warm in there while you finish.

11. Boil about 2 quarts of water in a 3 qt. saucepan over high heat. Add the broccoli. You won't eat all of it tonight, but you can save what you don't eat for soup on Tuesday. When you drop the broccoli in the saucepan, the water will stop boiling. When it starts up again, time it for 8 minutes.

12. Has your spaghetti water come to a boil yet? If so, drop in the amount you want and cook for as long as the directions on the box specify (usually about 8–10 minutes).

13. With the heat as low as you can get it, slowly heat the butter/parsley/garlic mixture you made earlier. Don't let it boil or turn brown. When the butter has completely melted, turn off the heat.

14. Is your broccoli ready? Check and see if the tip of your knife pierces it easily. Drain out the water and bring it to the table.

15. Is your spaghetti ready? Remove it from the stove, hold it over the sink, and dump it into the colander. (Don't burn yourself.) See what a clever instrument the colander is? It separates the water from the spaghetti. Shake the colander up and down to get rid of all the excess water. Now put the spaghetti back into the pot it just came from (make sure there's no water left in it) and add your melted butter/parsley/garlic mixture. Add some grated parmesan cheese and mix it up well. Put the cover on to keep it hot.

16. Is your chicken ready? Just take it out of the oven and serve.

SERVING INSTRUCTIONS

Put your spaghetti in a bowl and bring a little extra parmesan cheese with you to the table. Put several pieces of chicken on a small plate, with your broccoli on the side. Or you can eat the spaghetti as a first course, keeping the rest of the meal warm in the oven.

LEFTOVER INSTRUCTIONS

Put the remaining chicken on a dinner plate, wrap it with foil or plastic wrap, and put it in the refrigerator. Put the leftover broccoli in a little bowl or container, wrap it up, and refrigerate.

Monday, the 3rd

POT ROAST ENCORE, HOME FRIES,
SCALLOPED TOMATOES, GREEN
SALAD (leftover-based meal*)

This is the present you gave yourself when you worked so hard on Saturday. Tonight's dinner is almost ready before you start.
COOKING TIME: quickie

THINGS YOU SHOULD BUY

2 tomatoes (fairly large)

cheddar cheese

1 medium-size onion

THINGS YOU SHOULD HAVE

*leftover pot roast (with potatoes and cooking liquid)
*leftover lettuce
bread (2 slices)
olive oil
butter
paprika (optional)
red wine vinegar

UTENSILS

casserole dish with cover (or baking pan with aluminum foil as cover)
10" frying pan

cookie sheet or pie tin

spatula

cheese grater (unless you bought grated cheese)

salad spinner (optional)

STEP-BY-STEP DIRECTIONS

1. Heat oven to 350°.

2. Place leftover pot roast with vegetables in the casserole dish. Take out the potatoes and set them aside.

3. Add 1 cup of liquid for the pot roast to heat in. This could be your leftover cooking liquid, water, or water and wine, or a combination of all three.

4. Cover the casserole and put it in the oven. Just let it stew there until everything else is ready.

5. Slice tomatoes crosswise in 4 or 5 slices about ¼" thick.

6. Peel and chop the onion. Set aside.

7. Crumble 2 slices of bread by rolling them around in your hands until they break into crumbs. Set aside.

8. Grate approximately ½ cup of cheese. Set aside.

9. Take the baking pan and grease it with oil or butter. (Pour 1 tablespoon of oil on the pan and rub it around with a paper towel.) Put half the tomato slices on the pan. Using about one-fourth of the chopped onions you set aside a moment ago and some of the bread crumbs, sprinkle the sliced tomatoes with bread crumbs and onions, put the remaining slices on top (like a sandwich), sprinkle again with onion and crumbs, and top with some grated cheese. Put it in the oven next to the pot roast (same temperature). It will cook about 20–30 minutes or until the cheese is melted and golden brown.

10. Cut the leftover potatoes into bite-size chunks.

11. Heat about 2 tablespoons of butter and 2 tablespoons of oil in a frying pan over medium heat.

12. When the butter is melted, toss in the remaining onions. Let the onions fry slowly by themselves for a minute or two and then put in the potatoes. Season and sprinkle with paprika. Turn the potatoes over from time to time with a

spoon, and taste them every now and then. When they're crispy and brown, they're ready.

13. Make your green salad (see section on green salads).

14. When the potatoes are done to your satisfaction and the cheese on the tomatoes is melted and slightly brown, dinner is ready. Remove the pot roast and serve.

SERVING INSTRUCTIONS

A serving of pot roast and the home fries will go nicely on your dinner plate. Put your salad in a little bowl and your scalloped tomatoes on a small plate.

LEFTOVER INSTRUCTIONS

If you have leftover meat, keep it in the fridge and use it for sandwiches. It probably has another two or three days of life in it.

Tuesday, the 4th

BROCCOLI SOUP, COLD FRIED
CHICKEN, PEACH AND CREAM-CHEESE
SALAD (leftover-based meal*)

Who me? I can't make soup! Sure you can. This kind is easy, and it can be made with a variety of leftover vegetables. Tonight, it's broccoli from Sunday's dinner.

COOKING TIME: quickie

THINGS YOU SHOULD BUY

peach halves (1 can)

cream cheese (a small package)

1 lemon (optional)

lettuce (optional)

1 medium-size onion

THINGS YOU SHOULD HAVE

* cold chicken left over from Sunday
* cooked broccoli left over from Sunday
milk (1 cup)
flour (1 tablespoon)
butter (1 tablespoon)
mayonnaise (optional)

UTENSILS

2 qt. saucepan
wire whisk
measuring cup and spoons

STEP-BY-STEP DIRECTIONS

1. Peel an onion, cut 2 slices about ½" thick, and chop them very fine.
2. Cut the leftover broccoli into bite-size pieces and set aside.
3. Melt 1 tablespoon of butter in a saucepan over low heat.
4. Slowly fry the chopped onion in the butter over low heat until it becomes soft, but not brown.
5. Stir in 1 tablespoon of flour. Lower the heat as far as you can and use your whisk to stir everything into a mixture of butter, onion, and flour, which is called a *roux*.
6. When the roux is smooth, add a cup of milk and continue stirring with the whisk (or a spoon) until the sauce begins to thicken slightly.
7. Add the broccoli. Season and let it stay over very low heat until it gets hot. Watch it to make sure it doesn't boil, however, because that's *too* hot.
8. Put a couple of clean lettuce leaves on a small plate and put a few peach halves on top. Put a spoonful of cream cheese in the center. Add some mayonnaise too, if you like.
9. Your soup is ready when it's hot to the taste.

SERVING INSTRUCTIONS

Put several pieces of leftover cold chicken on your dinner plate with a few slices of lemon. Mayonnaise is also good with cold chicken. Ladle the soup into a soup bowl. And keep your plate with peaches on the side.

LEFTOVER INSTRUCTIONS

Wrap the unused chicken in plastic wrap and refrigerate. It will be good for at least another two or three days, so eat it for lunch or a late-night snack.

Wednesday, the 5th

BRAISED PORK CHOPS, BUTTERED RICE, HOT APPLESAUCE (original meal)

If you've had "minute rice" all your life, you'll be shocked at how good regular rice tastes. It takes a little longer to cook than minute rice, but it's just as easy. Since the pork chops in this meal simmer for a half hour, you'll hardly notice the extra time on the rice.

COOKING TIME: average

THINGS YOU SHOULD BUY

pork chops (2 chops, roughly ½" thick)

long-grain white rice (you'll use ¼ cup)

applesauce (a small jar)

1 lemon

THINGS YOU SHOULD HAVE

butter (1 tablespoon)

flour

olive oil (2 tablespoons)

paprika

rosemary

Utensils

8″ frying pan with cover

2 qt. saucepan with cover

1 qt. saucepan (cover not necessary)

measuring cup and spoons

Step-by-step directions

1. Trim the excess fat off your pork chops and pat them dry with a paper towel.

2. Put about ½ cup of flour on a paper towel or plate. Season, and sprinkle with enough paprika to turn the flour slightly pink.

3. Coat the chops with the flour.

4. Heat 2 tablespoons of oil in the frying pan over medium-high heat. After the oil has had a moment to get hot, put in the chops. Brown on one side, turn, and brown on the other.

5. While you're watching the chops brown (which will take about 10 minutes altogether), take a lemon and cut it in half, remove the seeds with a fork, and throw them away. Squeeze all the lemon juice you can into a cup or small glass.

6. Are your chops golden brown on both sides? Remove the chops temporarily and carefully pour the grease into your grease jar (or anywhere but down the sink!). Turn the heat down to low. Return the chops to the frying pan. Sprinkle them with rosemary (a pinch or two on each chop is enough, more if you like) and the lemon juice you just squeezed. Add about ¼ cup of water—or however much it takes to barely cover the bottom of the frying pan. Put the cover on the pan and let the chops cook in there for another 30 minutes.

7. Pour slightly less than 1 cup of water into one of your small saucepans (the one with the cover). Add 1 tablespoon of butter and a dash of salt. Bring to a boil over high heat. When it's boiling hard, add ¼ cup of rice. It will stop boiling for a moment. When it starts boiling again, lower the heat to low and cover the saucepan. Let the rice boil gently ("simmer") in there for 20 minutes.

8. Has time elapsed on the rice? If so, turn off the heat and let it sit covered for another 5 minutes.

9. Pour as much applesauce as you feel like eating tonight into the other small saucepan, heat it over very low heat, stirring occasionally, until it's hot to the taste. It'll only take a few minutes. By the time the applesauce is done, everything else should be ready too.

SERVING INSTRUCTIONS
The pork chops and rice will go nicely together on one dinner plate. Put your applesauce in a little salad bowl off to the side.

Thursday, the 6th

MEAT LOAF, PARSLEY POTATOES,
STEWED TOMATOES, SPINACH SALAD
(original meal)

Have you ever heard the old saying "Don't order meat loaf in a restaurant; you don't know what might be in it"? Well, this is the world's best meat loaf: moist, tasty, and easy to make.
COOKING TIME: average to long

THINGS YOU SHOULD BUY

ground beef (1 lb.)

stewed tomatoes (1 can)

spinach (as much as you want for a serving of salad)

plain yogurt (1 small container)

celery (you'll use 2 stalks)

1 medium-size onion

1 baking potato

THINGS YOU SHOULD HAVE

1 egg

milk (¼ cup)

bread (2 slices)
butter (2 or 3 tablespoons)
parsley (1 or 2 sprigs)

Utensils

loaf pan
mixing bowl
1 qt. saucepan
2 qt. saucepan
salad spinner (optional)
vegetable peeler
measuring cup and spoons
wooden spoon (optional)

Step-by-step directions

1. Heat oven to 350°.
2. Break an egg into the mixing bowl and beat with a fork.
3. Break the hamburger into chunks and put it in with the egg.
4. Chop 2 celery stalks (*including* the leafy tops) into small pieces and add to the hamburger and egg mixture.
5. Peel and chop 1 small onion to yield about 2 tablespoons' worth. Add it to the mixing bowl.
6. Crumble 2 slices of bread and toss that in, too.
7. Add ¼ cup of milk.
8. With your clean hands, gently mix everything up in the bowl. The result should be a gob of meat that is moist but not wet. If it's too dry, add a little more milk. If it's too wet, add another slice of crumbled bread. Season.
9. Put the whole blob into your loaf pan. If it does not fill the entire width of the pan, don't flatten it out, but rather shape it with your hands until it comes almost to the top of the pan when shoved over to one end.
10. Put the loaf pan in the oven for 1 hour.

11. Using as much spinach as you want for your salad, tear off the tough stems and leathery outer leaves and discard.

12. Place the remaining tender leaves in your salad spinner (or rinse and pat dry with paper towels) and spin. Repeat at least three times until no grit shows in the water. (Fresh spinach tends to be dirty.) Set aside.

13. Peel 1 large potato and cut into quarters or large chunks.

14. Put the potatoes in your 2 qt. saucepan. To preserve the potatoes until you're ready to begin cooking them, add enough cold water to cover (by that we mean just enough to keep them completely submerged).

15. Chop a few sprigs of parsley.

16. About 20 minutes before meat loaf is due to be ready, drain the potatoes and add enough fresh water to cover. Cover the saucepan and bring to a boil over high heat.

17. After it boils, lower the heat to low and boil the potatoes gently for 15 or 20 minutes.

18. Open the can of stewed tomatoes and pour the contents into a 1 qt. saucepan. Break up the tomatoes with a fork (if necessary) and bring them to a boil over medium-high heat. Once boiling, lower the heat to low, and let them boil slowly ("simmer"), uncovered, until you're ready to eat.

19. When the potatoes are ready, drain the water and shake the pan over the burner for a moment until they are dry.

20. Remove the potatoes from the heat, add 2 or 3 tablespoons of butter and some chopped parsley, and mix gently with a wooden spoon. Cover the pan to keep them warm.

21. Place the spinach in a bowl, season, and toss with a few tablespoons of plain yogurt.

LEFTOVER INSTRUCTIONS
Cover the remaining meat loaf in plastic wrap and save it for Saturday's dinner. Put the remaining stewed tomatoes in a small bowl, cover with plastic wrap, and refrigerate for tomorrow night's dinner.

Friday, the 7th

BROILED FISH, COLD STEWED
TOMATOES, ASPARAGUS WITH
CHEESE, COLE SLAW (a partially
leftover-based meal*)

The most difficult part about preparing a fish dinner is buying
the fish. The taste of fish varies in direct proportion to how
fresh it is, so avoid the frozen kind if you possibly can. Truly
fresh fish has almost no "fishy" smell. Many large supermarkets now carry fresh fish, and most cities have seafood
stores. The latter are specialists who will help you choose the
right fish in the necessary amount and give you cooking tips,
too. For this recipe, you may use any piece of fish 1 to 1½"
thick.

COOKING TIME: quickie

THINGS YOU SHOULD BUY

fish (½ lb. fillet should be enough)

frozen asparagus (1 package)

cabbage (1 small head)

1 lemon

grated parmesan cheese

THINGS YOU SHOULD HAVE

olive oil

butter

paprika

rosemary

mayonnaise

red wine vinegar

dijon mustard

*leftover stewed tomatoes

Utensils

broiling pan

2 qt. saucepan with cover

mixing bowl

aluminum foil (enough to line the broiling pan)

Step-by-step directions

1. Pull the outer layer of leaves off the head of cabbage and discard them. Slice the remaining cabbage in half and cut out the tough inner core.

2. Lay half the cabbage cut side down on a cutting board and slice it into strips. Then chop the strips. (Save the other half of the cabbage for Saturday's meal.) Put chopped cabbage into a mixing bowl.

3. In a small glass or cup, mix ¼ cup mayonnaise, 1 tablespoon wine vinegar, ½ teaspoon dijon mustard. Add this mixture to the mixing bowl and mix it with the chopped cabbage. Cover the mixing bowl with plastic wrap and refrigerate until you're ready to eat.

4. Take yesterday's stewed tomatoes from the refrigerator and stir once or twice. Pour them into a small saucer, and allow them to sit at room temperature.

5. Wash the fish gently in cold running water and pat dry with a paper towel.

6. Cover the broiling rack with aluminum foil (to make it easier to clean later.) Lightly grease the foil with some oil. Place the fish on the foil, skin side down (if there is a skin). Season, dot with a few dabs of butter, and sprinkle with paprika and rosemary.

7. Begin cooking the frozen asparagus in your 2 qt. saucepan according to the directions on the package.

8. About 5 minutes before the asparagus is ready, place the fish in the broiling section of the oven with the temperature set to broil. Cook it for 5 minutes. Check doneness by gently inserting a fork into the fish: It should easily break into "flakes." If it does, the fish is done. (It does not need to be turned.)

9. When the asparagus is ready, drain the water, add a small chunk of butter, and sprinkle with paprika and grated parmesan cheese.

SERVING INSTRUCTIONS

Don't forget your cole slaw! The stewed tomatoes taste good cold, and the asparagus may be served on the same plate as the fish.

LEFTOVER INSTRUCTIONS

Save the uncooked half of cabbage by wrapping it in plastic wrap and putting it in the fridge. We'll use it again tomorrow.

Saturday, the 8th

COLD SLICED MEAT LOAF WITH HOT TOMATO SAUCE, QUICK FRIED POTATOES, BOILED CABBAGE
(a leftover-based meal*)

Here's a fast meal that uses leftover raw materials but changes the preparation.

COOKING TIME: quickie

THINGS YOU SHOULD BUY

tomato sauce (1 small can)

carraway seed

1 baking potato

1 medium-size onion (you'll use only half)

THINGS YOU SHOULD HAVE

*meat loaf from Thursday

*cabbage (the half-head you saved on Friday)

butter

olive oil

paprika

UTENSILS

8" frying pan with cover

2 qt. saucepan with cover

1 qt. saucepan

measuring cup and spoons

STEP-BY-STEP DIRECTIONS

1. Thoroughly scrub the potato under cold running water and dry with a paper towel. You're using the skin, so you'll want it clean.

2. Cut the potato into bite-size chunks.

3. Peel, slice, and chop half an onion.

4. Heat about 2 tablespoons each of olive oil and butter in a frying pan over medium-high heat. When the oil is hot, add the chopped onion and fry until it turns soft but not brown.

5. Add the potatoes to the onion. Season, and sprinkle with paprika. Turn them frequently so they'll brown on all sides. If they absorb all the oil, add a little more (be careful not to pour oil into the flame). When potatoes are brown, cover the pan and lower the heat to low.

6. Take the leftover half-head of cabbage and cut it into 2 or 3 wedges.

7. Pour about ½ cup of water into your 2 qt. saucepan and bring to a boil over high heat. Add the cabbage. It will stop boiling for a moment. When it returns to a boil, lower the heat to low, cover the saucepan, and let it boil gently ("simmer") for about 10 minutes.

8. Open the can of tomato sauce and pour it into your 1 qt. saucepan over low heat. Then forget about it until Step 12.

9. Slice the meat loaf into slices about ¾" thick.

10. Pierce the potatoes with a fork. If they are tender, they're done. Uncover the pan and lower the heat to very low (or warm).

11. The cabbage is done when the leaves are slightly transparent and feel tender (not crunchy) when pierced by a fork.

Pour off the remaining water. Season. Add a tablespoon of butter and sprinkle with carraway seeds.

12. Spoon the hot tomato sauce over the meat loaf and serve.

Sunday, the 9th

ROAST CHICKEN, MASHED POTATOES, PEAS, WALDORF SALAD (original meal)

It's been said the test of a good kitchen is how well the cook prepares a simple roast chicken. Now, here you are just beginning your second week of cooking and you're ready for the test. Don't worry, you'll pass.

COOKING TIME: long

THINGS YOU SHOULD BUY

1 whole chicken, about 3 lbs. (sometimes called a fryer)

1 apple

seedless white grapes (1 bunch)

frozen peas (1 package)

chopped walnuts or pecans (1 package)

lettuce (you'll use only a few leaves)

celery (you'll use only one stalk)

3 baking potatoes (or 2, if they're large)

1 onion

parsley (3 or 4 sprigs)

THINGS YOU SHOULD HAVE

mayonnaise

butter

milk (you'll use only ¼ cup)

olive oil

paprika

UTENSILS

roasting pan

mixing bowl

3 qt. saucepan

2 qt. saucepan

vegetable peeler

colander

pastry brush (optional)

apple corer (optional)

measuring cup and spoons

STEP-BY-STEP DIRECTIONS

1. Heat oven to 350°.

2. Remove the package of giblets you'll find inside the cavity of the chicken and discard.

3. Rinse the inside of the chicken with cold water and pat dry with a paper towel.

4. Cut a lemon in half and rub the cut side around inside the cavity.

5. Peel and cut an onion into quarters and put them inside the cavity. Throw a small handful of parsley in there too.

6. Pour some olive oil into the palm of your hand and rub it all over the outside of the chicken.

7. Put the chicken in the roasting pan, breast side up, and put a half dozen or so small "dots" of butter on the skin. Season, and sprinkle with paprika.

8. Put the chicken in the oven and let it cook for about 18 minutes per pound. A 3-pound chicken, for example, will cook just about 1 hour.

9. Peel the potatoes with your vegetable peeler and cut them into quarters or, if the potatoes are large, eighths. (We're

making a heckuva lot of mashed potatoes, but you're going to save some for Tuesday.)

10. Put the potatoes in a 3 qt. saucepan. Add just enough cold water to keep them completely submerged.

11. Remove grapes from the stem and put them in a colander. Rinse with cold water and let them drip dry for a few minutes. Then slice them in halves.

12. Cut the tough bottom and leafy end off one stalk of celery. Rinse with cold water, pat dry with a paper towel, and chop into small bits.

13. Rinse and dry 1 apple, but don't peel it. Remove the core and seeds, and cut it into bite-size pieces.

14. Combine apple, celery, and as many grapes as you wish in a mixing bowl. (Save a handful of grapes for tomorrow night's meal.)

15. Add 2 tablespoons of mayonnaise (which you might mix with a teaspoon of lemon juice, if you have it) to the mixing bowl and toss the salad well until everything is covered with a coating of mayonnaise. Sprinkle with some chopped nuts. Cover the mixing bowl with plastic wrap, and put it into the refrigerator until you're ready to serve.

16. Sneak a peek at that chicken. If there are some juices in the roasting pan, take your pastry brush, your bulb baster, or just a large spoon, and pour the juices over the chicken. This is called basting, and you should repeat the process every 10–15 minutes.

17. About 25 minutes before the chicken is due to be ready, drain the potatoes and add just enough fresh cold water to get them completely submerged. Cover the saucepan and bring to a boil over high heat. When it starts to boil, lower the heat to low and let it boil gently ("simmer") for 15–20 minutes.

18. About 10 minutes before the chicken is due to be ready, cook the frozen peas in your 2 qt. saucepan according to the directions on the package. If they are done before the rest of the meal, keep them warm over very low heat before draining.

19. When the potatoes are ready, drain off the water and shake the pan over the heat for a moment to evaporate the remaining moisture in the saucepan. Then mash the potatoes with your potato masher or electric hand mixer.

If using a masher: When the lumps are gone, add a hunk of butter (about 2–3 tablespoons), and just enough milk to moisten (a few tablespoons for starters). Beat vigorously with a fork, a wooden spoon, or a wire whisk. Add more milk to soften the potatoes to the consistency you prefer.

If using a mixer: Add a chunk of butter and a few tablespoons of milk as you continue mixing. Add more milk, if necessary, to attain the consistency you prefer.

SERVING INSTRUCTIONS

Carve the chicken with a very sharp knife, and put as much meat as you plan to eat tonight on a plate with your peas and mashed potatoes. Since you have no gravy for the mashed potatoes tonight, season with a dab of butter and some freshly ground pepper. Use a small plate to serve your waldorf salad on top of a few lettuce leaves.

LEFTOVER INSTRUCTIONS

Just about everything is saved from this meal. Put the chicken on a clean plate, cover it with aluminum foil, and refrigerate. Put the remaining peas in a small salad bowl, cover with plastic wrap, and refrigerate. Stick the remaining grapes in the fridge. Save the remaining chopped nuts in your cupboard. Take whatever is left of the mashed potatoes and shape them into little patties about the size of a McDonald's hamburger. Put them on a small plate, wrap them in plastic wrap, and refrigerate.

Monday, the 10th

CHICKEN SALAD, POTATO STICKS,
MINTED PEAS (a leftover-based meal*)

There are as many recipes for chicken salad as there are church cookbooks, and you'll eventually experiment and create your own. This one uses the leftovers from last night's roast chicken and borrows some of the raw ingredients from yesterday's waldorf salad.

COOKING TIME: quickie

THINGS YOU SHOULD BUY

potato sticks (1 can)

dried mint (you'll find it in the spice section)

1 lemon (or a teaspoon of lemon juice)

THINGS YOU SHOULD HAVE

*roast chicken left over from Sunday

*grapes left over from Sunday

celery (1 stalk)

*chopped nuts left over from Sunday

mayonnaise

UTENSILS

mixing bowl

1 qt. saucepan

cookie sheet (or just a piece of aluminum foil)

STEP-BY-STEP DIRECTIONS

1. Heat oven to 350°.
2. Remove the skin from the leftover chicken and discard. Tear as much chicken as you can from the carcass and cut it into bite-size pieces. Put them in a mixing bowl. (You'll probably get a yield of about 1½ to 2 cups of chicken.)

3. Remove the tough bottom and the leafy top from 1 stalk of celery and discard. Rinse the remaining celery stalk in cold water, pat dry with a paper towel, and chop into tiny bits. Add it to the chicken.

4. Slice about ½ cup of seedless grapes in half and add them to the chicken.

5. Add ¼ cup of chopped nuts.

6. Starting with about ¼ cup, judge for yourself how much mayonnaise to add to the mixing bowl to get a consistency and moistness of chicken salad that suits your taste, mixing with a large spoon. (Everything should be covered with mayonnaise, but not drenched with it.) Add 1 teaspoon of lemon juice as you mix.

7. Open a can of potato sticks and put them on a cookie sheet, a small baking pan, or just a piece of aluminum foil. Put them in the oven for about 10 minutes.

8. Put your leftover peas in a small saucepan with a dab of butter and 2 or 3 tablespoons of water. Heat over low heat until they are hot to the taste. Then season and add a pinch or two of dried mint leaves.

SERVING INSTRUCTIONS

You may want to serve your chicken salad over a few lettuce leaves. It's great for sandwiches, too. Put a pile of potato sticks off to the side of the same plate, and put the peas in a salad bowl.

Tuesday, the 11th

LIVER AND BACON, GREEN BEANS,
POTATO CAKE (a partially leftover-based
meal*)

Almost everybody hates liver! The truth is, "almost everybody" has never tried it (or at least not since they were young and, like the little boy in the cereal commercial, hated everything).

So before you decide to skip this menu entirely and eat out tonight, take a chance. The real trick is finding a good piece of liver. If possible, buy it in a butcher shop or specialty grocery, where you can request a slice of calf's or young beef liver, about ½" thick.

COOKING TIME: average

THINGS YOU SHOULD BUY

liver (1 or 2 slices, or about ¼ lb.)

bacon (you'll need 2 slices tonight)

green beans (if you're unsure of how much to buy, just pick up a handful and see if it looks like the amount you'll eat)

1 onion

THINGS YOU SHOULD HAVE

butter

flour

red or white wine (optional)

*mashed potato patties left over from Sunday

olive oil

paprika

UTENSILS

8" frying pan

10" frying pan

3 qt. saucepan with cover

colander

slotted spoon (optional)

measuring cup and spoons

STEP-BY-STEP DIRECTIONS

1. Snap the ends off the green beans, and if they're long ones, snap them in half. Place in the colander. Rinse with cold water and drain.

2. Peel 1 onion and chop half of it. Set aside.

3. Fill the 3 qt. saucepan about three-quarters full of water and bring to a boil over high heat.

4. As you're waiting for the water to boil, put about ½ cup of flour on a paper towel and coat the potato patties you made on Sunday in it. Season both sides and sprinkle with paprika.

5. Heat about 1 tablespoon of butter and 1 tablespoon of oil in a small frying pan and fry the potato patties over medium-high heat, watching that they don't get too dark. When they're golden brown on the bottom, flip them over and brown the other side. When they're brown on both sides, turn the heat down to very low (or warm, if you have that setting) and forget about them.

6. Meanwhile, wash the liver slice in cold water and pat it dry with a paper towel. Set aside.

7. Lay 2 slices of bacon in a frying pan and heat on high heat until you hear it spattering and frying, then turn the heat down to medium-low. When the bacon starts to shrink and turn slightly brown, turn it over and cook on the other side. When it looks crispy, like the bacon Mom used to make, it's done. Remove both slices from the pan with a fork and put it on a double thickness of paper towel, which will absorb the excess grease.

8. Turn off the heat under the bacon grease, but let it stay in the pan because we're going to cook the liver in it.

9. The water for the beans is boiling by now, so put them in. When you do, the water will stop boiling for a moment. Put the cover on until it starts to boil again. When it does, remove the cover and time for 8 minutes.

10. Coat the liver slice in what remains of the flour you used to coat the potato cake, adding more if necessary.

11. Turn the heat on low underneath the pan with the bacon fat and add your chopped onion. Fry it slowly until the onions get soft but not brown. Take the pan off the burner and remove the onions with a slotted spoon. Put them aside in a cup or saucer.

12. When the beans are ready, drain the pot into a colander and return the beans to the empty pot from which they came. Add a dab of butter, season, and put the cover on to keep them warm.

13. Now, you're ready to fry the liver, which only takes a minute. Put the frying pan with the bacon grease back on the burner and turn the heat to medium-high. Gently, put in the liver slice and cook it 1–3 minutes on each side.

14. Remove the liver and put it on your dinner plate. Drain the fat into your grease jar (not down the sink, of course) and pour about ¼ cup of wine into the frying pan. Add the chopped onion and swish it around in there for a minute over low heat. Then pour the mixture over the liver. If you're not using wine, simply cover the liver with plain fried onions. Lay the bacon slices on top, too.

SERVING INSTRUCTIONS
The liver and onions, potato cake, and bacon should all fit on one large dinner plate. Put the green beans in a salad bowl to the side.

Wednesday, the 12th

BROILED HAM SLICE, BAKED SWEET
POTATO, PINEAPPLE AND COTTAGE
CHEESE SALAD (original meal)

A ham slice is a convenient way to enjoy the flavor of smoked ham when it wouldn't make sense for a single cook to bake a whole one. We've suggested horseradish sauce and mustard as a topping, but if you have a sweet tooth, you might prefer to spread the ham with a few spoonfuls of orange marmalade when you turn it.

COOKING TIME: average

THINGS YOU SHOULD BUY

1 ham slice, about ½–1″ thick (precooked and packaged)

1 sweet potato

pineapple slices (1 can)

cottage cheese (a small container)

chopped walnuts

THINGS YOU SHOULD HAVE

mustard

prepared horseradish

butter

lettuce (you'll need only a few leaves)

UTENSILS

broiling pan

STEP-BY-STEP DIRECTIONS

1. Heat oven to 400°.

2. Rinse the sweet potato in cold water and pat dry with a paper towel. Put a dab of soft butter on your fingers and coat the potato with it. Prick the potato skin a few times with a fork and put it in the oven. It will take 45 to 50 minutes to cook.

3. Rinse a few leaves of lettuce, pat dry, and put them on a small plate.

4. Open the can of pineapple and arrange two slices on top of the lettuce leaves. Top with a scoop of cottage cheese and sprinkle with nuts. Set this in the refrigerator until you're ready to eat.

5. Wipe the ham slice with a paper towel. With a sharp knife, cut small slices, about ¼″ long, all around the perimeter of the ham. This will prevent it from curling when it broils.

6. When the potato is done, wrap it in aluminum foil to keep it warm while you cook the ham. (But if you have a separate broiler, you can cook them both at the same time.)

7. Put the ham slice on your broiling pan and stick three or four small dots of butter on the ham. Turn the oven temperature to broil, and put the ham in the broiling compartment of your oven. Cook 5 minutes. Turn. Add a few more dots of butter to the other side, and cook another 5 minutes.

SERVING INSTRUCTIONS
Serve the sweet potato just as you would an ordinary baked potato—split open, with a dab of butter inside.

LEFTOVER INSTRUCTIONS
If this is too much ham for one serving, you can cut off a piece before broiling and fry it for tomorrow's breakfast. Or cook it all tonight and use the leftovers in a sandwich.

Thursday, the 13th

BAKED SQUASH WITH SAUSAGE,
FRIED APPLE SLICES, WATERCRESS
AND MUSHROOM SALAD (an original
meal)

Besides tasting good, this meal looks attractive on the plate. The visual aspects of a meal should be considered as your cooking skills improve. Just think of creamed chicken, mashed potatoes, and braised celery staring up at you. That's enough to take your appetite away for a week!

COOKING TIME: average

THINGS YOU SHOULD BUY

1 acorn squash (it's a round, dark green squash shaped like an acorn)

bulk sausage (1 lb.) [Note: By "bulk," we mean not patties or links]

2 tart apples

watercress or endive or chicory (enough for a single salad)

brown sugar

1 onion

mushrooms (¼ lb.)

THINGS YOU SHOULD HAVE

2 slices of white bread

olive oil

red wine vinegar

dijon mustard

butter

cinnamon

UTENSILS

baking pan

10″ frying pan

1 qt. saucepan

mixing bowl

apple corer (optional)

measuring cup and spoons

slotted spoon (optional)

aluminum foil

STEP-BY-STEP DIRECTIONS

1. Heat oven to 400°.

2. Boil a couple of cups of water in a small saucepan or tea kettle.

3. Rinse off the squash in cold water. With a sharp knife, cut in half, lengthwise. Be careful not to cut yourself.

4. With a spoon, scoop out the seeds and stringy goop and discard.

5. Place the two halves in a baking pan, cut side down. Pour the boiling water around the squash so that it comes up

¼–½″ on the sides of the squash. Cover with a piece of aluminum foil. Place in the oven for 30 minutes.

6. Take about 6 medium-size mushrooms. Authorities vary as to the best way to clean mushrooms, but considering how they are grown, it's wise to clean them well. An easy way is to dampen a paper towel and gently wipe off the dirt. Cut off the stems, discard, and slice lengthwise. Set aside. (Save the mushrooms you don't use for Saturday's meal.)

7. Remove the long stems from the watercress, leaving just the short stems and leaves. Wash them in your salad bowl by filling it with cold water for a minute or two. Drain. Pat it dry with paper towels.

8. Mix your salad dressing, using roughly 3 tablespoons olive oil, 1 tablespoon vinegar, and 1 teaspoon dijon mustard.

9. Peel and chop 2 slices of onion and fry them over low heat with a dab of butter in the frying pan.

10. Add ½ pound (probably half the package) of sausage to the onions and butter, turning the heat up to medium. Break it up into small pieces, using a fork. Crumble two slices of bread and add that, too. Season as you wish. And cook until the sausage is brown.

11. If time has elapsed on the squash, remove it from the oven and carefully remove the foil cover; don't burn yourself with the steam. Pierce the skin side of the squash with a fork. If it goes in easily, you're ready to proceed. If not, cover it and return it to the oven for 5 or 10 more minutes. When the squash is tender, turn it cut side up and fill the cavity with your sausage, onion, and bread mixture. Drain the pan of whatever water remains. Return the pan (uncovered, this time) to the oven and bake another 15 minutes.

12. Wash the apples. Don't peel them, but with an apple corer or a small knife, remove the core and seeds.

13. Slice the apples crosswise in ¼″ slices.

14. Rinse out the frying pan in which you cooked the sausage and heat 2 tablespoons of butter over medium-high heat. Lay the apple slices in the pan, sprinkle with brown sugar, and add 1 tablespoon of water. Cover, and lower the heat to low.

Cook for about 5 minutes. Then remove the cover and continue frying over medium-high heat, turning occasionally so the apple will brown slightly without burning. This will take around 5 more minutes. Sprinkle with cinnamon.

15. Toss the watercress and mushrooms with the salad dressing.

SERVING INSTRUCTIONS
Put your baked squash and fried apples on a large dinner plate. The salad should go into a bowl on the side.

LEFTOVER INSTRUCTIONS
Store the remaining brown sugar in a covered glass jar, if you have one. This will keep it from turning into a brown rock. Be sure to save unused mushrooms for Saturday's meal.

Friday, the 14th

FRITTATA, GREEN SALAD, FRENCH
BREAD (original meal)

Here's a supper, as opposed to a dinner, menu for a night when you're not terribly hungry. It's just right for a late supper and can be used for a brunch as well. Believe it or not, the frittata tastes good cold the next day.

COOKING TIME: quickie

THINGS YOU SHOULD BUY

1 zucchini squash

lettuce (your choice)

french bread (1 small loaf)

garlic salt

1 medium-size onion

THINGS YOU SHOULD HAVE

4 eggs

butter

olive oil

red wine vinegar

dijon mustard

parsley

paprika

oregano

UTENSILS

10″ frying pan with cover

dinner plate about the same size as the frying pan

salad spinner (optional)

wire whisk (optional)

cookie sheet (or aluminum foil)

STEP-BY-STEP DIRECTIONS

1. Heat oven to 450°.
2. Make your green salad (see section on salads).
3. Thoroughly rinse the zucchini, pat dry with a paper towel, cut a slice off each end, and discard the endpieces. Then slice the remaining zucchini crosswise into thin slices.
4. Peel and slice the onion into thin slices.
5. Break 4 eggs into a small salad or soup bowl. Add 2 tablespoons of milk and beat with a fork or whisk.
6. Slice the loaf of French bread in half lengthwise. Spread the cut sides with butter and sprinkle with garlic salt, oregano, paprika, and a little chopped parsley. Put the two half loaves on a cookie sheet or a piece of aluminum foil and set them in the oven. (One of these half loaves may be all you need; you be the judge.)
7. Heat about 2 tablespoons of butter in the frying pan over

medium heat. Don't let it brown. Add the onion slices and fry slowly until they become soft. Add the zucchini slices and fry slowly until they are tender, or about 5 minutes. Season as they cook.

8. Beat the eggs again briefly and pour them gently over the zucchini and onion.

9. Cover the pan and lower the heat to low. Let it cook like that for 6 minutes.

10. After 6 minutes, sneak a peek at the eggs. If they are not quite firm, allow a few more minutes.

11. When the eggs are firm (not too wet), the fun is about to begin. Remove the cover from the frying pan and place your dinner plate upside down on top of the frying pan as if to cover it. Holding the frying pan handle in one hand, put the other hand on the dinner plate and flip the pan over so that it is now on top of the plate. The frittata should now be on the plate, not the floor! Put the frying pan back on the stove and carefully slide the frittata back into the pan to brown the other side.

12. In the minute required to finish the frittata, you have time to pop the bread under the broiler for a moment to turn it golden brown. Don't let it burn.

13. Slide the frittata onto your dinner plate and remove the bread from the broiler.

LEFTOVER INSTRUCTIONS

Four eggs is a lot for one person, so unless you're sharing this meal, eat what you want tonight and enjoy the rest cold tomorrow.

Saturday, the 15th

VEAL PICATA, PASTA FULVIA (a partially leftover-based meal*)

An Italian friend named Fulvia taught us this light sauce for use when the pasta is not the main course. Veal picata is a classic

Italian dish found on many restaurant menus. Why not invite a friend for dinner tonight?

COOKING TIME: long

THINGS YOU SHOULD BUY

thinly sliced veal (¼ to ½ lb. is plenty)

1 package of mostaccioli (or any small-noodle type of pasta, like rigatoni or penne)

1 can of tomatoes (16 oz. size or thereabouts; Italian plum style, if you can find them)

crushed dried red peppers (look for them in the spice section)

grated parmesan cheese

dry white wine (or dry vermouth)

parsley

1 medium-size onion

1 lemon

THINGS YOU SHOULD HAVE

*mushrooms left over from Wednesday night

olive oil

dijon mustard

butter

oregano

garlic (1 or 2 cloves)

UTENSILS

6 qt. pot

2 qt. saucepan

10″ frying pan with cover

8″ frying pan (no cover needed)

colander

measuring spoons and cup

meat hammer (optional)

STEP-BY-STEP DIRECTIONS

1. Fill a pot half full of water. Put it over high heat until it begins to boil. (If it starts to boil before you're ready to put in the pasta, just turn the heat down until you're ready.)

2. Peel and chop 1 onion.

3. Separate 1 large or 2 small cloves of garlic from the bulb. Peel and chop into tiny bits.

4. Place the veal slices on a cutting board or some other sturdy surface. If you have a meat hammer, use it to pound the meat, flattening it as thin as you can get it. (If you don't have a meat hammer, use the bottom of a coffee mug.) Set the veal aside.

5. Chop enough parsley to make roughly 4 tablespoons when chopped. Set aside.

6. Slice 4 thin slices of lemon. Set aside.

7. Take about 6 medium-size mushrooms and remove the stems. Wipe them clean with a damp paper towel. Put them down on the cutting board so they look like the dome of the U.S. Capitol. Cut them into thin slices. Set aside.

8. Now it's time to start the spaghetti sauce. Heat 4 tablespoons of olive oil in a frying pan (use the one without the cover for this) over low heat. Drop in the chopped onion and chopped garlic, and fry them slowly until they are soft but not brown.

9. Add the can of tomatoes, half the parsley, a dash of oregano, and a dash of crushed red pepper. If the tomatoes look larger than bite size, you may want to cut them in half or quarters or simply mash them down. Keep the heat low and let this boil very gently ("simmer") until you're ready to put it on the pasta.

10. If the water is boiling, put in as much pasta as you feel you can eat tonight. (Don't let your eyes be bigger than your stomach; remember you have the veal, too.) Cook it for as long as the directions specify, probably about 14 minutes.

11. Put about 2 tablespoons of butter in the frying pan and melt over medium-high heat. When the butter has melted (but not browned), put in the veal slices and fry about 3 minutes on each side. Season.

12. Put the lemon slices on top of the veal, and sprinkle on the remaining parsley and mushroom slices. Turn the heat down to very low.

13. Pour ¼ cup of dry white wine or dry vermouth into the frying pan with the veal. (Be careful not to expose the alcohol to the flame because it can ignite.) Cover the frying pan. Now forget about it until after you're finished with your first course (Pasta Fulvia). As long as the heat is on very low, it can simmer for 15 minutes or so without burning.

14. When the pasta is done, drain it through a colander and return it to the pot you cooked it in (without the water, of course). Pour the Sauce Fulvia on top of it and toss gently.

SERVING INSTRUCTIONS
Serve the pasta with grated cheese as a first course. When you've finished eating that, the veal picata will be ready. Serve it on a small plate.

Sunday, the 16th

STEAK, ARTICHOKE, LETTUCE WEDGE
WITH THOUSAND ISLAND DRESSING,
APPLE AND CHEDDAR CHEESE (original
meal)

Steak seems to be everyone's favorite meal, and because it's relatively easy to cook a steak, we'll add an artichoke to the menu so you won't get too lazy!

COOKING TIME: average

THINGS YOU SHOULD BUY

1 steak (New York strip, T-bone, porterhouse, shell steak, etc.)

1 artichoke

1 head of iceberg lettuce

1 apple

1 lemon

pickle relish

chili sauce

cheddar cheese (just a small chunk to enjoy with your apple)

THINGS YOU SHOULD HAVE

butter (½ stick is enough)

mayonnaise

dijon mustard

UTENSILS

broiling pan

saucepan with cover (use the smallest one in which the artichoke will fit with the cover on)

1 qt. saucepan

scissors

measuring spoons

STEP-BY-STEP DIRECTIONS

1. Cut off the stem and the pointed top of the artichoke with a sharp knife and then pull off the bottom two rows of leaves. Holding the artichoke in one hand, snip off the prickly tops of the remaining leaves with your scissors.

2. Place the artichoke upright in the saucepan, add 2 or 3 inches of water and 1 slice of lemon (save the rest of lemon for later). Cover the pan and bring the water to a boil over high heat.

3. After it comes to a boil, lower the heat to low and boil gently for 40 to 45 minutes.

4. Remove the dark green outer leaves from your head of lettuce. Cut the head in half and then cut the half into a couple of large chunks or wedges. Put several of these chunks (as much as you want to eat) in a single-serving salad bowl.

5. Cut away excess fat from the steak. Place on a broiler pan and sprinkle with pepper, but salt only the remaining fat at the edge.

6. Put about half a stick of butter in a small saucepan and squeeze the juice from the rest of lemon you used earlier onto the butter. Set aside.

7. Now make your thousand-island salad dressing by mixing 1 tablespoon of chili sauce, 2 or 3 tablespoons of mayonnaise, 1 teaspoon of pickle relish, and a dab of dijon mustard in a small salad bowl. Pour it over the lettuce.

8. About 15 minutes before the artichoke will be ready, set the oven to broil.

9. Put the steak in the broiling compartment of your oven. A 1 inch-thick steak will cook 5 minutes each side for rare, 6 minutes each side for medium.

10. As the steak is cooking, slowly melt your lemon butter in a small saucepan over very low heat. Don't let it bubble or brown, just melt.

11. Is your artichoke ready? Remove it with tongs or two large spoons and hold it over the sink to let the excess water drip out.

12. When you've cooked both sides of the steak, it's time to eat!

13. For dessert, enjoy the apple with a slice of cheddar cheese on the side.

SERVING INSTRUCTIONS

If artichokes are new to you, here's how to handle them. Pull the leaves from the artichoke one at a time and dip them into the lemon butter. Then scrape the lower part with your upper front teeth as you pull each leaf away from your mouth. Discard the leaf on the side of your plate and move onto the next one. You'll eventually come to a fuzzy section. Pull this out with your fork and discard. Continue eating until you reach the meaty chunk at the very bottom, called the heart, which many people consider the reward for all this effort.

Monday, the 17th

HAMBURGER WITH FRIED ONIONS ON
A TOASTED BUN, "SALAD-BAR" SALAD,
ICE CREAM SUNDAE (original meal)

We know you could go out and get this meal at any number of
restaurants, but try it at home. There will come a night when
the rain is falling and the wind is blowing and you'll just want to
stay inside. You'll be glad you learned how to cook fast food at
home.

COOKING TIME: quickie

THINGS YOU SHOULD BUY

ground beef (1 lb.) [Note: Save what you don't use tonight by
shaping it into patties, wrapping them in foil, and freezing. See
Chapter 5 for advice.]

hamburger buns (you can freeze the unused buns, too)

lettuce (your choice)

ice cream

fudge sauce

1 medium-size onion

THINGS YOU SHOULD HAVE

some or all of the following leftover vegetables: carrots, celery,
tomato, cheddar cheese, cabbage

butter

olive oil

red wine vinegar

UTENSILS

8″ frying pan with cover

salad spinner (optional)

cookie sheet (or just a piece of aluminum foil)

STEP-BY-STEP DIRECTIONS

1. Tear the desired amount of lettuce for your salad and wash in your salad spinner or by hand.

2. Check the fridge for available salad fixings. Do you have some or all of the following: carrots, celery, tomato, uncooked cabbage, cheddar cheese? If so, chop or slice the ingredients you choose and put them in a salad bowl. Don't ignore any raw vegetables you wrapped in plastic wrap and forgot about. If they're still crisp, they make a great addition to a salad. If your refrigerator is bare, make a piece of toast. Melt some butter on top and sprinkle it with garlic salt. Then chop it into small chunks for homemade croutons!

3. In a small salad bowl, mix 3 parts oil to 1 part vinegar for homemade salad dressing (see section on salads).

4. Peel 1 onion and cut it in half. Save half and slice the other half into thin slices.

5. Shape a hamburger patty, using about ¼ lb. of ground beef. If you're hungry, make two.

6. Add a small dab of butter to the pan. Place the hamburger(s) in your frying pan. Brown the meat well over medium heat on one side. Turn. When the meat is browned on both sides, add the onion slices to the pan, cover, and lower the heat to low. Cook for 5 minutes, and then slice into it with a knife or fork to see if it is done enough for you. Continue cooking until it is.

7. A few minutes before the hamburger is due to be ready, spread both halves of a hamburger bun with butter.

8. Add the dressing to the salad and toss.

9. Moments before the hamburger is ready, put the hamburger bun (buttered side up) under the broiler on a cookie sheet or aluminum foil for just a minute. Watch it carefully because it will go from golden brown to charred black in a wink.

10. For dessert, give yourself a big scoop of ice cream topped with chocolate fudge sauce. There may be some chopped walnuts in your cupboard as well, so sprinkle them on and pig out.

Tuesday, the 18th

LAMB CHOPS, MINT JELLY, BAKED POTATO, BRUSSELS SPROUTS WITH WATER CHESTNUTS (original meal)

Some folks just don't like brussels sprouts. You may be one of them, but there are whole nations on earth for whom this vegetable is a staple. They're usually available in the winter, when other fresh vegetables are either not in the stores or too expensive.

COOKING TIME: average

THINGS YOU SHOULD BUY

2 or 3 lamb chops (loin or rib)

1 baking potato

brussels sprouts (if not packaged, buy ¼ lb.)

water chestnuts (a small can)

sour cream or plain yogurt (optional)

mint jelly or pepper jelly (optional)

THINGS YOU SHOULD HAVE

butter

UTENSILS

broiling pan

3 qt. saucepan with cover

colander

aluminum foil

STEP-BY-STEP DIRECTIONS

1. Heat oven to 400°.

2. Rinse the potato in cold water and pat dry with a paper towel. Prick with a fork once or twice, and put it in the oven. (It will cook 50–60 minutes.)

3. Put the brussels sprouts in a colander and run cold water over them to rinse. If some are larger than bite-size, cut them in half. Cut off the stems and discard. Then cut small gashes in the shape of a cross on the ends where the stems were.

4. About 10 minutes before the potato is ready, fill your 3 qt. saucepan about two-thirds full of water and bring it to a boil over high heat.

5. Wipe the lamb chops with a paper towel and trim off excess fat. Then put them on your broiling pan and sprinkle them with pepper, salting only the fat that remains.

6. If you have only one oven and you must wait until the potato is done before you begin broiling your lamb chops, remove the potato after 50 minutes and wrap it in aluminum foil, shiny side in.

7. Set the oven temperature to broil.

8. Put the lamb chops under the broiler for 6 minutes. Turn, and broil the other side for 6 more minutes. Meanwhile, if the water in the saucepan has started to boil, throw in the sprouts. The water will stop boiling for a moment. When it starts again, continue cooking the sprouts for 10 minutes. They are done when the bottoms can be pierced easily with the tip of a knife.

9. Open the can of water chestnuts and drain.

10. When the sprouts are done, drain the saucepan of water, add a dab of butter and some water chestnuts to the sprouts. Keep the saucepan covered (to stay warm) until the lamb chops are ready.

SERVING INSTRUCTIONS

Mint jelly is a traditional accompaniment for lamb, but pepper jelly is a new flavor that you might like better. Slit open the potato, pinch the sides to soften it, and add a dab of butter. Season and top the potato with sour cream or yogurt if you wish. A good baked potato, however, is delicious with nothing on it . . . and a lot less fattening.

Wednesday, the 19th

STUFFED PEPPERS, CAROL'S
CARROTS, ORANGE AND ONION
SALAD (original meal)

Here's a different way to use that old standby, hamburger. Similar to meat loaf, the green pepper "container" makes the difference. Note that the meat is cooked *before* it is put in the pepper. Other recipes for this dish often call for an uncooked meat mixture and the added baking time tends to congeal the stuffing.

COOKING TIME: average

THINGS YOU SHOULD BUY

1 large green pepper

hamburger (You'll use only about ¼ pound for this recipe. Check your freezer to see if you have some left over from an earlier meal.)

4 carrots

green spring onions or scallions (1 bunch)

1 large orange

1 mild red onion

french dressing (a few tablespoons is enough)

lettuce (just a small amount, to serve as a bed for the salad)

1 lemon

THINGS YOU SHOULD HAVE

garlic (1 clove)

bread (1 slice)

butter (½ stick will be plenty)

parsley (a few tablespoons, chopped)

Utensils

baking pan (or pie tin)

8″ frying pan

1 qt. saucepan with cover

2 qt. saucepan with cover

measuring cup and spoons

Step-by-step directions

1. Heat oven to 350°.

2. Wash, and cut the top off the green pepper. Remove the membrane and seeds from the inside with your hand. Rinse it in cold water and put it in the small saucepan with about 1 cup of water. Cover.

3. Turn the heat on under the green pepper. Bring it to a boil over high heat, then reduce heat to medium and boil gently for 5 minutes. When time is up, carefully remove the pepper from the pan, and if there's moisture inside, turn it upside down to drain. (Don't burn yourself.) Set the pepper in a baking pan.

4. Meanwhile, rinse and scrape the carrots with your vegetable peeler. Then slice lengthwise into narrow strips, about 4 strips per carrot. Put them into a medium-size saucepan with enough water to just cover them. Cover the saucepan and bring the water to a boil over high heat. When it boils, lower the heat to low and boil gently for about 20 minutes.

5. Peel a clove of garlic and chop it into tiny bits.

6. Peel the outer layer skin off 4 or 5 scallions and slice them crosswise until you've sliced about halfway up the green stem.

7. Heat 2 tablespoons of butter in the frying pan and fry the scallions slowly over medium heat. Don't let them burn. Add the hamburger and garlic. Use a fork to crumble the meat and spread it around until it's brown all over. Hold a slice of bread under cold running water, and wring it out. Crumble it and let the crumbs drop into the meat mixture. Break an egg into a saucer and stir it with a fork until it turns completely yellow.

Add the egg to the hamburger. Season. Let everything cook another 5 minutes.

8. When the meat mixture is done, stuff it into the green pepper, and place it in the oven for 10 minutes.

9. Chop 1 or 2 tablespoons of parsley, and cut 1 lemon in half. Set them both aside.

10. Wash a few lettuce leaves and dry with a paper towel. Remove the skin from an orange and break it into wedges. Slice 3 or 4 thin slices of onion and break the slices into rings. Combine the onions and orange wedges and put them on a bed of lettuce. Now pour a little french dressing over the top.

11. Are your carrots done? Remove from the heat and drain. Add 1 tablespoon of butter and hold the pan over the heat until the butter melts. Squeeze the juice from half a lemon onto the carrots (remove the seeds first). Add the chopped parsley and season.

SERVING INSTRUCTIONS

We disagree about how to eat a stuffed pepper. Dorinne eats both the pepper and the hamburger at once (not in one gulp, though). Richard uses the pepper as a little bowl from which he spoons out the hamburger, and when the hamburger is gone, he eats the pepper. We each think the other's method is stupid.

Thursday, the 20th

CROSTINI ALLA NAPOLITANA, GREEN
SALAD, WHITE GRAPES (original meal)

Thursday is a good night to have something simple, so try Crostini alla Napolitana, a fancy name for pizza you don't have to send out for.

COOKING TIME: quickie

THINGS YOU SHOULD BUY

1 loaf of firm white bread (Pepperidge Farm's Toasting White Bread is perfect.)

Tomato sauce* (1 small can)

Tomatoes* (1 small can of Italian plum style, if available)

mozzarella cheese, sliced or grated (a slice or a handful)

anchovies (optional)

mushrooms (optional)

pepperoni (optional)

lettuce (your choice)

seedless white grapes (a small bunch)

*[If it's available in your grocery store, Ragout's Pizza Quick Sauce may be substituted for these two ingredients.]

THINGS YOU SHOULD HAVE

olive oil

red wine vinegar

oregano

UTENSILS

baking pan or cookie sheet

1 qt. saucepan

salad spinner (optional)

colander

STEP-BY-STEP DIRECTIONS

1. Heat oven to 375°.

2. Drain the tomatoes and mix them with the tomato sauce in your small saucepan. Heat over medium heat until it is hot to the taste.

3. As that simmers, make your green salad (see section on salads).

4. Put a few drops of oil on the baking pan and rub it around with a paper towel.

5. Place 2 slices of bread on the pan.

6. Remove the tomatoes and tomato sauce mixture from the burner and pour it on the bread, enough to cover but not

drown them. Place a slice of mozzarella or a small handful of
grated mozzarella on each piece of bread. Add small bits of
anchovy, mushroom, pepperoni, onion, or whatever you happen to like on pizza. Sprinkle with oregano. Pour roughly ½
teaspoon of olive oil on top.

   7. Place the "pizzas" in the oven for about 20 minutes.

   8. Rinse the grapes under cold water in the colander and
allow to drain. Enjoy them as a light dessert.

LEFTOVER INSTRUCTIONS

You probably made more tomato/tomato sauce mixture than
you needed for tonight's recipe. Pour it in a salad bowl, cover
with plastic wrap, and refrigerate. Believe it or not, it tastes
great over scrambled eggs.

Friday, the 21st

TUNA FISH SALAD, DEVILED EGGS,
CUCUMBER AND ONION, POTATO
CHIPS (original meal)

Here's a basic salad that makes a quick and tasty supper, and
you can use the leftovers for sandwiches.
COOKING TIME: quickie

THINGS YOU SHOULD BUY

Tuna (a 6 oz. can, either oil- or water-packed)
celery (you'll use 1 stalk)
potato chips
1 lemon
1 medium-size onion
1 cucumber
lettuce (a few leaves)

Things you should have

pickle relish

2 eggs*

mayonnaise

dijon mustard

red wine vinegar

paprika

sugar

Utensils

mixing bowl

1 qt. saucepan with cover

soup bowl (or any shallow dish)

measuring cup and spoons

vegetable peeler

Step-by-step directions

1. Half fill a small saucepan with water and place the eggs in it. Bring the water to boil over high heat. Then lower the heat to low and continue boiling gently for 15 minutes.

2. Rinse a stalk of celery in cold water and pat dry with a paper towel. Cut off the leafy top and the tough bottom sections. Chop the rest into roughly ¼" cubes.

3. Peel and cut 4 thin slices of onion. Chop one slice and set aside the others.

4. Cut 1 lemon in half.

5. Using your vegetable peeler, peel the cucumber and slice it crosswise into very thin slices. Put the slices in a shallow bowl and add the (unchopped) onion slices, separated into rings. Add ¼ cup of red wine vinegar and a tablespoon of sugar. Season. Mix it up until all the onions and cukes are well coated and let them sit, stirring from time to time.

6. If the eggs are ready, drain off the water and refill the saucepan with cold water. Let the eggs sit in the cold water until

they are cool enough to handle. Then gently crack the shells by hitting or rolling the eggs on your cutting board. Peel the shells off and stick the eggs in the fridge.

7. Open the can of tuna and drain off the liquid. Put the tuna in a mixing bowl. Add the chopped celery. Add the chopped onion. Add 1 tablespoon of lemon juice and 1 tablespoon of pickle relish. Starting with about ¼ cup, add enough mayonnaise to moisten—but not drench—the tuna salad. Mix it all up with a large spoon. Cover the mixing bowl with plastic wrap and put it in the refrigerator.

8. Slice the hard-boiled eggs once lengthwise. Scoop out the yolks and put them in a small salad bowl. Add ½ teaspoon of dijon mustard and ½ teaspoon of mayonnaise, and use a fork to mix it up to a smooth consistency. Spoon out this yellow goop and stuff it back into the eggs from whence it came. Sprinkle paprika on top.

9. Rinse and pat dry a few lettuce leaves. Mound as much tuna salad as you want to eat tonight on top of the lettuce.

SERVING INSTRUCTIONS

Put the tuna fish salad, deviled eggs, and potato chips on one large dinner plate. The cucumber and onions should be drained and put in a small salad bowl.

LEFTOVER INSTRUCTIONS

Cover the tuna fish salad with plastic wrap and refrigerate. It makes wonderful sandwiches.

*[Note: When you know a recipe calls for hard-boiled eggs, it's smart to prepare them ahead of time so they will be well chilled.]

CHAPTER FIVE

Spit and Polish . . . Mostly Spit—

How to Clean Your Home Quickly and Easily

Grandma said, "You have to eat a peck of dirt before you die."

By that she meant, no matter how much you clean, a certain amount of dirt, grease, grunge, and bacteria—a peck, to be precise—is going to find its way into your stomach. So there's no sense worrying about it.

Grandma, however, did not say you should eat a *bushel* of dirt or a *ton* of dirt before you die . . . unless you want to die a lot sooner than you expected. It's a good thing Grandma can't see your apartment now, isn't it?

Oh, it's not entirely your fault. A life full of dirt is part of the price you pay for living in an American city today. Except in Los Angeles, where they can actually see their air pollution and, as a result, keep pretty good tabs on it, most urban Americans never realize how dirty their air is until they let their apartments go a few weeks without cleaning. Then a thick layer of dust, grime, and soot forms on furniture, countertops, and windows. Walls mysteriously start to turn brown. Mildew forms in the bathroom. The dirt trudged in from outside grinds deeply into the kitchen floor until the linoleum loses any trace of its original color or design.

Does that sound familiar?

Don't worry. With the right strategy, the right weapons, and some plain old courage and determination, you *can* win the war against dirt. And that's exactly what we plan to give you in this chapter.

Most books and articles on cleaning are written for people who already know a lot about it. You know the kind we mean, don't you? "One Thousand Ways to Remove Stains, Using Vanilla Extract," "Vacuum Cleaners You Can Build at Home from Potatoes."

But this chapter isn't like that. This chapter is for people who know *nothing* about cleaning. It's for people who do their dishes by piling them in the middle of the living room and spraying them with a garden hose; who dry their towels in the oven; who are constantly being hounded by archaeologists for a peek under their couch.

If you're that kind of person, you may have thought a sparkling clean apartment was an impossible dream. But in this chapter we'll give you a simple strategy for cleaning house. We'll tell you what tools and detergents to buy and how to use them. We'll take you by the hand and walk with you from room to room, showing you how to clean everything in sight. And at the end, we'll introduce you to your mortal enemies: the mouse, the rat, the ant, and the roach.

Your Strategy: Planning, Prevention, and Procrastination

As in any war, it helps to begin with a clearly defined strategy. Our strategy in the fight against dirt is three-pronged: plan, prevent, and (don't) procrastinate.

PLANNING

A regular cleaning schedule is helpful both to the person who hates to clean and to the one who cleans too much. (Yes, there are such people.) By writing down and following a definite housekeeping schedule, you'll always know what needs to be done, yet you'll stop yourself from getting carried away—cleaning the toilet twice in one week, for example. Working people will probably find it most convenient to do all of their "deep cleaning" on the weekend. But no matter how you plan your schedule, the important thing is to stick to it. Here's an easy-to-follow schedule that will keep your home clean at all times.

DAILY
Tidy up the entire apartment.
Make the bed.
Do the dishes.
Wipe down the kitchen counters and stovetop.
Sweep the kitchen floor.
Take out the garbage.

ONCE A WEEK
Deep clean the bathroom (toilet, tub, sink, and shower).
Deep clean the kitchen (counters, stovetop, refrigerator surface).
Mop the floor in the kitchen and bathroom.
Dust all living areas.
Dry-mop floors, ceilings, and baseboards.
Vacuum carpets.
Change the bathroom and bed linen.
Do the laundry.

ONCE A MONTH
Clean the oven (if necessary).
Spray-wax wood furniture.
Quickie clean windows (inside only).
Remove food and sweep out kitchen cupboards.
Quickie-wax the kitchen floor.
Wash kitchen accessories and knick-knacks.

SEVERAL TIMES A YEAR
Clean the bathroom tile.
Polish wood furniture.
Squeegee-clean windows (inside and out).
Real-wax the kitchen floor.

ONCE A YEAR
Wash or dry clean drapes.
Shampoo the rugs.

When cleaning day arrives, remember these two additional planning tips: 1) always clean from the dirtiest room to the cleanest (it will keep the dust from spreading and give you a sense of accomplishment); 2) clean from high to low.

PREVENTION

The easiest apartment to clean is the one that never gets dirty. If you stick to your daily schedule of tidying and simple maintenance chores, your weekly cleaning will be a breeze. Start by establishing some good housekeeping habits: do the dishes every night; wash every glass and snack plate immediately after using it; throw away newspapers and magazines as soon as they're out of date.

In the kitchen, learn how to cook and clean up at the same time. If your vegetables need to simmer for another 10 minutes and there's nothing else to do for the meal, use that time to get a head start on cleaning. If you leave the kitchen fairly tidy before dinner, you won't be so reluctant to return to it afterward.

PROCRASTINATION

Next to term papers, cleaning is probably the world's easiest task to postpone.

[**Richard:** I had a professor once who said the only reason he assigned term papers was to give his students a chance to do their laundry.]

The analogy doesn't stop there, however. A dirty apartment is like a term paper that hasn't been started until late in the semester: It's always in the back of your mind, making you feel depressed and lazy. A clean house, by contrast, is like a term paper completed early and returned with an A. It makes you feel carefree and confident.

One way to overcome your procrastination is to take a goal-oriented, as opposed to a task-oriented, approach to the job. Don't say, "Today, I've got to scrub the toilet, mop the floor, and clean the oven." Instead, say, "Today, I'm going to turn this drab apartment into a gleaming palace."

Borrow a tip from the experts on behavior modification and promise yourself a treat after you finish: a high-calorie sundae or a mindless evening in front of the TV. Turn some music on while you work, take frequent breaks, and have a beer if you feel like it. (Not too many, though, or you'll forget what you were doing.)

The best way to overcome your procrastination, however, is simply to begin! Take what efficiency experts call a leading task—a small part of the job, which doesn't look as intimidating as the whole thing. Rather than tackling the entire kitchen, for example, promise yourself you'll only wipe down the refrigerator. Once you get started, you'll probably wind up cleaning everything.

And if you don't?

Well, at least you'll have a clean refrigerator.

Your Weapons

You'd need more than a knife and a fork to fix yourself a gourmet meal, wouldn't you? The same is true of keeping house. A broom and dustpan alone won't do the whole job. So use this list to outfit your home with a basic battery of cleaning tools. You don't have to spend a lot of money, but please don't skimp on quality. Good equipment lasts longer and does a better job than the cheaper stuff. In many cases, it also helps you clean *faster,* and—as the saying goes—time is money, too.

Most of the things we've mentioned here can be found at the grocery store, the dime store, the hardware store, or one of those huge new drug stores that sell everything except drugs. If you live in a house, not an apartment, you might also consider going to a janitorial supply store for some really heavy-duty equipment. In a big home, industrial strength equipment is worth the extra investment.

• Broom: We like the old-fashioned kind best, the kind with long, thin natural bristles. The newfangled brooms with nylon or plastic bristles have a tendency to skim the dirt across the floor, making it harder to round up into the dustpan.
• Dustpan: Buy one with some heft, so it won't go slip-sliding away when you try to sweep dirt into it.
• Whisk broom: This is a short-handled broom that is good for cleaning in tight spots or upholstery. If you have a canister vacuum cleaner or a Dustbuster,™ you may not need a whisk broom.

• Sponge mop: Used for cleaning floors, the sponge mop looks like a broom with a sponge on the end of it. Sponge mops come in two basic styles that are distinguished by the type of wringer they use. The older model has a wringer at the end of the handle that you pull over and press against the sponge. The newer kind has the wringer in the middle of the handle. You push down and the sponge wrings out "automatically." The new kind is easier to work with, but the older model wrings out the sponge more thoroughly, so take your pick. Don't forget you can replace the sponge without buying a whole new mop.

• Mop pail: Your sponge mop is useless without a bucket to keep the hot water and detergent in. You can get the plastic kind, but make sure it's sturdy enough to hold a few gallons of water without buckling.

• Dust mop: An underrated tool, the dust mop looks like a broom handle with a giant centipede on the end of it. Dust-mops are great for cleaning floors, baseboards, and even ceilings. A daily dustmopping of your kitchen floor, for example, will make your weekly wet-mopping a breeze.

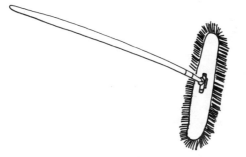

• Dustrags: You can buy a commercially treated dustrag, but it's just as good to use an old pair of cotton underwear. Whatever you do, don't buy a feather duster. They look charming, but the only effect they have on dust is to spread it around.

• Sponges: Buy several of these and segregate them by use: one for the dishes and one for the rest of the kitchen, one for the toilet and one for the rest of the bathroom, etc.

• Toilet bowl brush: Buy the kind that comes in its own little stand-up holder. That way, you can keep it near the toilet at all times.

• Scrub pad/doodlebug: Some jobs require something a little tougher than a sponge but not abrasive enough to scratch the surface you're trying to clean. Look for a little nylon scrub pad with a handle on it. The 3M company makes a good one. If you take the same pad and put a broom handle on it, you have a doodlebug. 3M makes one of these, too.

• Measuring cup: Buy one specifically for cleaning, because you don't want to measure your Mr. Clean in the same cup you measure your milk.

• Garbage can/wastebaskets: Buy a big strong garbage can with a tight-fitting lid for your kitchen. You'll want to keep it lined with plastic trash bags, so you can just lift out the trash when it's full and keep the sides of your garbage can clean. A tight lid keeps roaches and mice away.

• Rubber gloves: Cleaning house is rough on the hands. You're constantly sticking them in boiling hot water or in chemicals even your neighborhood toxic waste dump wouldn't permit. So buy some rubber gloves. Don't worry about how silly they look; nobody's going to see you.

• Paper towels: Carry a roll of paper towels around with you as you clean, and plan to use a lot of them. They're an indispensable tool for all the wiping, dabbing, rubbing, and blotting that housekeeping entails.

• Window squeegee: The gas station attendant uses one of these to wipe your windshield. They work just as well on the windows in your apartment, but few people know it. You can get one at the hardware store.

• Dishwashing aids: The well-prepared *escuelier,* or dish-washer, owns a soft sponge, an abrasive sponge, a soap pad (like Brillo or S.O.S.), a steel wool pad (sometimes called a choregirl or choreboy), and a *non-metal* choreboy for non-stick pans. You should also have a dish drainer with a rubber tray underneath it. A sink strainer—a little rubber container that fits into the corner of your sink—comes in handy when you're scraping food off dirty dishes or peeling potatoes and carrots.

• Vacuum cleaner: Ideally, you should own three vacuum cleaners: an upright for carpets and rugs; a canister for hard-wood floors and upholstery; and a hand-held electric for quick spills and touch-ups. But as an apartment dweller, you can probably get by nicely with just one vacuum cleaner. If that's what you want to do, buy the canister style, because it's the most versatile. Most canister vacuum cleaners come with a wide variety of attachments designed to tackle a range of clean-ing tasks. If you live in a very small apartment, you have an-other, even less expensive option: the electric broom. An electric broom is a very lightweight, inexpensive upright vac-uum cleaner that is perfect for small jobs. You can find vacuum cleaners at a department store or (surprise!) a vacuum cleaner dealership. Check the Yellow Pages.

• Cleaning tool caddy: One of the biggest frustrations and time wasters in cleaning your house is not having the right tools or detergents nearby when you need them. That's why we sug-gest you put together a little box or tray full of cleansers, rags, and scrub pads that you can carry around with you wherever you go. Look for one with a handle on it.

Your Ammunition: Detergents and Cleansers

You have your cleaning weapons. Now, let's stock up on am-munition. Don't be frightened by the rows and rows of cleansers and detergents glaring at you when you visit the grocery store. The world of cleaning fluids is not as complex as it looks. The most important thing to know about cleansers, in fact, is that they're pretty much alike. In recommending them to you, we've used brand names not necessarily because we think they are the best product on the market, but simply so you'll know what *we* use and so you'll have a name to look for in the store. Don't be afraid to experiment. You never know when you'll find something "new and improved!"

One important warning. The ingredients of household cleaning products include some very strong chemicals. Always read the label and follow the directions when you use them. Never *mix* chemicals—especially ammonia products and bleach products, which will combine to create poisonous gas. Wear rubber gloves, and don't expose yourself to the fumes for long periods of time or in poorly ventilated areas. Always wear old clothes when you're cleaning, because some of the products we've mentioned (Soft Scrub, in particular) will bleach fabrics. Finally, keep your pets in a different room when you clean.

Here are some of the basic cleansers you should have around the house:

• Dish soap: Try a few until you find one that works for you. We like Dawn, because it cuts grease well. If you have an automatic dishwasher, try Cascade.

• Floor cleaner: For weekly cleanings, we like Top Job. But if you find evidence of past civilizations trapped in the layers of wax on your linoleum, you might try Spic and Span (it's stronger).

• Floor wax: For quickie wax jobs, Mop & Glo puts a nice shine on both wax floors and no-wax floors. When it's time for a real wax job, we use Future, an acrylic-based floor wax.

• All-purpose bathroom cleaner: Soft Scrub is a good all-around bathroom cleaner for the toilet, tub, and tile. Don't be tricked into buying one product for the sink, one for the toilet, and one for the tub when there are many cleansers that do all three. We don't care for the *powdered* bathroom detergents on modern tubs, toilets, and sinks. Powdered cleansers leave a rough and scratchy residue behind them and will damage new porcelain. An exception to this is the older toilet or tub with deep brown stains on it. If you are unlucky enough to have a bathroom like that, try a powdered cleanser called Zud.

• All-purpose kitchen cleaner: For countertops, stovetops, Formica cabinets, refrigerators, and many other shiny surfaces, Fantastik is *fantastic*. It works on stuff in the bathroom, too. Be careful with varnished wood, however, because it may streak.

• All-purpose glass and chrome cleaner: What would we buy if we could only have one commercial household cleaner? Windex, definitely. Use this ammonia-based product on anything made of glass, chrome, or metal. Ammonia is a versatile and effective cleanser, and when you buy Windex, you get a safe strength of ammonia in a handy spray bottle.

• Furniture dusting and polishing: For the weekly dusting, spray your dustrag with Endust; it picks up dust but doesn't leave any waxy residue. Once a month, or when you're expecting company, dust with Pledge. It dusts and waxes at the same time. When the day comes for a genuine wax job on your fine wood furniture, we suggest you make your own polish by mixing a homemade brew (see instructions under *Dusting and Polishing*).

• Laundry products: For the sake of simplicity, buy an all-temperature detergent. We like Fresh Start, but there's scarcely any difference among brands. Clorox makes America's favorite liquid bleach, and Spray 'n Wash is an effective pre-wash treatment for minor food stains.

• Oven cleaners: You can wipe up small spills on the surface with Fantastik, but when the *inside* of the oven gets dirty, use Easy Off and follow the directions carefully.

A Room-by-Room Battle Plan

Now that you've stocked up on tools and chemicals, you're ready to begin.

What follows is a room-by-room description of what we would call a good weekly cleaning. If you're a relatively tidy person, you may need to clean this deeply only once every two weeks, maybe even once a month. You certainly wouldn't do this much cleaning every day, although some of the things we've discussed (the dishes, for example) are daily jobs.

We're not saying this is the only way to clean house. We're not even saying it's the best way. It's *our* way, that's all. And if you're the kind of person who just doesn't know where to begin when it comes to cleaning house, it can be your way, too.

Before we begin, get a plastic trash bag to carry with you wherever we go. Spend a minute *tidying* each room before you start to clean it. Throw away newspapers, magazines, tissues, and assorted junk. Put books and clothes back where they belong. Pick up pencils and pocket change and whatever happens to be lying around.

Things look better already, don't they? But don't stop there. Now, let's begin cleaning room by room . . . in this order.

KITCHEN

Dishes   A sinkful of dirty dishes makes a kitchen look dirtier than it really is, so that's usually the best place to start. If you already have a method of washing dishes that works for you, stick with it. If not, try ours.

First, walk through the apartment and look for any glasses or saucers you've left by the bed or TV set. Nothing's more frustrating than to spend forty-five minutes washing dishes and suddenly find a bunch you forgot.

Scrape the food off the plates into your garbage can or sink strainer. Unless you have a garbage disposal, try not to let too much solid food go down the drain.

Quickly rinse off each dish in hot water and stack them up on the side. Put the stopper in the drain and fill the sink with soapy water, as hot as you can stand it. (Rubber gloves help.) Drop in your utensils and let them sink to the bottom. Then start washing dishes in this order: drinking glasses first, dinner plates second, utensils third, pots and pans last.

To wash, just rub and scrape each dish with a soapy sponge. If you encounter baked-on grease or stains, try a steel wool soap pad or a choreboy. (Don't use these on non-stick pans, however. On those pans, use your non-metal pad.)

As you finish each piece, dip it once in the water and stack it in the dish drainer to your side. Make sure the dish drainer is resting on its rubber tray and that it's placed so the excess water will run back into the sink. When all the dishes, pots, and pans are stacked up in the drainer, fill a saucepan with hot water (boiling, if you want to be a perfectionist), and pour it over the dishes. If you have a modern sink, spray them with that little black gun. This will rinse away the remaining soap and dry the dishes in a much easier and more sanitary way than if you dried them with a towel. Finally, rinse your drinking glasses individually under the faucet or with the gun.

[*Dorinne: Before you turn on the water, check that little black gun. Make sure no one has tied it up with a rubber band so it sprays in your face.*]

[*Richard: What kind of person would do something like that?*]

When the dishes are dry, *put them away*! Don't let clean dishes sit in the drainer, making the kitchen look messy when it really isn't.

THE OVEN   Check inside the oven after every meal for spills or stains that can be wiped off easily with a soap pad. If your oven starts to smoke when you turn it on (even though you haven't put any food in it), if you notice many stains and dark spots when you look inside, or if it's just been a while since your oven was cleaned, buy a commercial oven cleaner (we like Easy Off) and follow the directions explicitly. Most oven cleaners include directions for both a quickie job (using a warm oven) and an overnight job (using a cold oven).

Use a sponge treated with Fantastik to clean the outside of your stove. Just apply it to the surface, let it sit for a moment, and wipe it off with a paper towel. Windex sprayed directly on the stove and wiped off with a clean paper towel works well, too.

From time to time, you should clean in and around the heating elements of your stove. This area of the stovetop usually can be broken down into pieces and brought to the sink, where you'll scrub the elements with a steel wool soap pad. The little saucerlike metal fixtures beneath the heating element in particular can be washed and dried just like dishes. You can also use a soap pad to scour out stains underneath or around the heating elements if you're careful not to scratch the pretty surface of your stove.

REFRIGERATOR   Check it once a week or so (right before you go grocery shopping is the best time) to make sure nothing has died in there. For reasons scientists are still debating, an open box of Arm & Hammer baking soda in your refrigerator and freezer miraculously absorbs the food odors inside. Wipe down the shelves inside with a wet sponge from time to time. Spray Windex or Fantastik on the outside of your refrigerator and wipe it off with a sponge. Take your whisk broom and gently brush the coils on the back of your refrigerator to remove dust and dirt. Keeping these clean will help your refrigerator work more efficiently.

COUNTERS, CUPBOARDS, AND SO ON   Kitchen counters are a snap. Just spray them with Fantastik and wipe it up with a damp sponge. Once a month or so, you may want to treat your Formica countertops with a wax polish to protect the surface from stains and scratches. We recommend Jubilee.

How you clean your cupboards depends on what they're made of. If they are Formica, plastic, or metal, spray with Fantastik and wipe dry. If they are wood, follow our directions for treating wood furniture under *Dusting and Polishing.* No matter what your cupboards are made of, check inside from time to time for evidence of spilled food or crumbs and wipe them clean with a damp sponge.

Like most people, you probably have an assortment of knick-knacks in your kitchen: decorative bowls and plates, figurines, samplers with homey messages on them like "God Bless the Cook" and so on. In no time at all these items can acquire a thick layer of grease from the smoke of frying foods in your kitchen. Promise yourself you'll clean these accessories once a month by adding them to a pile of dirty dishes. The exteriors of tea kettles and toasters shine up beautifully with Windex. And don't forget your toaster has a little trap door underneath it which you can open up to remove all the bread crumbs.

KITCHEN FLOOR   Ah, the kitchen floor. Think how many great commercials it has inspired over the years. Remember "Johnny's black heel marks," "the white tornado," "Mr. Clean?" Isn't it funny you could watch those commercials hundreds of times, whistle their jingles, mimic their slogans, even memorize the lines, and yet have absolutely no idea what they were talking about?

Well, you're about to find out.

It's not so bad, really—especially if you sweep often. Make a habit of sweeping the kitchen floor every night after you do the dishes (dust-mopping too, if you feel like it), and mopping the floor will never become the horrid task it is thought to be on Madison Avenue.

Always sweep the floor before you mop, otherwise you will simply be rearranging the dirt. After you've swept, go over it once with a dust mop (sprayed with Endust) to pick up whatever dirt and dust remains. [If you have hardwood floors, stop here, because you should never wet-mop a wood floor. But if you have a linoleum kitchen floor (as 99 percent of us do), you may proceed to wet-mop it.]

Fill your mop pail with about a gallon of hot water and add the recommended amount of Top Job, or whatever floor cleaner you prefer. Dip the sponge mop in the pail, wring it out once, and start mopping the floor. Stop every few minutes to wring out the dirty water, dip the mop back in the pail, wring it once, and continue. Don't paint yourself into a corner! Just keep mopping until you've mopped yourself right out of the kitchen, and then give it five or ten minutes to dry.

You can stop here if you like, but for extra protection and a beautiful shine, let's apply some wax.

For a quickie wax job, we like Mop & Glo. Fill the mop pail with clear hot water. Now pour a line of Mop & Glo directly onto a small section of your kitchen floor. Spread it around evenly and gently with your mop. Rinse the mop in the pail, and move on to the next section, where you'll repeat the process.

Mop & Glo is good for touch-ups, but once every six months or so, you'll want to give your floors a real wax treatment. For this job, we like Future. [But wait. Before you apply real wax, make sure yours is not a no-wax floor. Not that any harm will come to the floor, but it just isn't necessary.]

First, remove all the old wax by scrubbing the floor with a pad of #2 steel wool and a strong solution of detergent (like Spic and Span). Once your floor is as clean as you can possibly get it, rinse out your mop thoroughly and apply Future (or your favorite wax) directly to the floor. Follow the directions on the can, but go easy on the areas that don't get much traffic. There's no point in building up a thick coat of wax where it isn't needed.

What do you do if you have a no-wax floor? Well, the Mop & Glo treatment described above works well. There are also— believe it or not—a wide range of specially formulated waxes for no-wax floors. (Yes, you heard us right . . . only in America.) Perk and Brite are two of the most popular. Try them and decide for yourself if waxing your no-wax floor is worth the effort.

Throughout this section we've assumed you've started out with a fairly clean floor, but that's a big assumption, isn't it? If you're facing a dull, stained, greasy kitchen floor, you need to work a little harder. Fill a bucket with hot water and the recommended amount of Spic and Span. Fill a second bucket with clear hot water. Using a scrub pad or #2 steel wool, get on your hands and knees and scrub one small section of the floor vigorously with the Spic and Span solution. Once you've loosened up the old wax and dirt, dip your sponge mop in the clear water bucket, and mop the area you just scrubbed. Repeat until the whole floor is clean. When the floor is dry, coat it with Mop & Glo or Future as explained above.

BATHROOM

Bathroom cleaning goes faster if you keep a few cleansers and cleaning tools stored in the bathroom at all times. A cabinet under the sink is the ideal place to store your weapons, but if you have no cabinet, you can use a sink skirt.

BATHTUB Start by applying Soft Scrub to your sponge or scrub pad and wipe down the entire bathtub, including the tile, the soap tray, and everywhere you see signs of dirt or soap scum. You don't have to scour and scrape (unless you're going after a particular stain), but just make sure the entire surface is covered with cleanser. Let it sit for a moment, then turn on the hot water in the tub, rinse out your sponge, and splash the clear water around in the tub until all the cleanser has rinsed away. If there's any excess soap that hasn't rinsed away, wipe it up with a paper towel. For a little extra sparkle, spray the chrome fixtures with Windex and wipe them off with a dry paper towel.

[If you've just moved into one of those ancient urban apartments with deep brown ghastly stains in the bathtub and toilet, the light cleaning described above probably won't even make a dent in your tub. Don't despair. Try a powdered cleanser called Zud. Follow the directions on the can and be prepared to scrub hard. Once you've got it white and shiny, you can keep it that way by following the much simpler procedure outlined above.]

SHOWER If you have a separate shower stall, clean that in the same way you did the tub. Wipe everything down with a sponge treated with Soft Scrub, then rinse. If you prefer, you can spray Fantastik around your shower stall and rinse it off with a sponge. Pay particular attention to the corners and soap tray, where soap scum and mildew tend to accumulate.

Once every few months, your shower stall could use a more astringent cleanser. We recommend Tilex, by Clorox. Wear your rubber gloves, read the label carefully, and spray Tilex over the tile on one wall of your shower stall. Leave the room to avoid the fumes and let it work by itself for two or three minutes. Fill a saucepan with water and pour it down the wall of the shower from the top so it "sheets" down and rinses away the Tilex. (Don't splash it on the wall, though, or the chemical might bounce back into your face.) No need to scrub. Then repeat the process on the next wall of tile. If you have a combination shower and bathtub, do this job *before* you clean the tub.

Toilet Squirt your Soft Scrub or Fantastik full strength on the inside of the toilet bowl and underneath the rim. Scrub it vigorously with your toilet brush. When it comes to cleaning the outside of the toilet, use the nonabrasive sponge or scrub pad that you set aside specifically for the toilet. Spray the entire surface of the toilet with Fantastik, let it sit a moment, and wipe it off with the sponge.

Sink Moving to the bathroom sink, work from top to bottom by spraying the mirror and chrome fixtures with Windex and wiping them dry with a clean paper towel. Next, clean your sink just like you did the bathtub. You can spray Fantastik or wipe a sponge treated with Soft Scrub around the outside of the sink and over the countertop. Rinse out the sponge, wipe again, and dry up any soapy spots with a paper towel.

The final step in cleaning the bathroom is to mop the floor just like you did in the kitchen.

LIVING ROOM/DINING ROOM/BEDROOM

We can lump these three areas together because the same principles apply, and if you live in an efficiency, they're all the same room anyway.

Tidy up first. Make the bed, pick up old newspapers, put everything back where it belongs. When the room is reasonably neat, do the following tasks in order.

DUST-MOPPING   Spray your dust mop with Endust and run it quickly over the baseboards, radiators, ceiling beams, hardwood floors, corners, and wherever else dust might accumulate (except on furniture). Work from high to low, and keep an eye out for any cobwebs that may be starting to form. When you're done with the dust mop, you can remove the mop part and throw it in the wash.

UPHOLSTERY   Take the cushions off your upholstered furniture and clean underneath with a whisk broom or canister vacuum cleaner. The little food crumbs that fall down here attract mice, who, upon seeing the cozy upholstery, say to themselves, "Hey, this looks like a nice place to live." If you see a little hole about one or two inches in diameter underneath your upholstery, you are looking at the mouse equivalent of a co-op conversion. Don't worry if you're just sweeping everything right out onto the floor; we'll scoop it all up with the vacuum cleaner in a moment.

DUSTING AND POLISHING   You should dust your furniture once a week, spray-wax it about once a month (or when you're expecting company), and—if you have fine wood furniture—apply real polish five or six times a year. To dust, spray your dustrag with Endust and wipe the wood once over lightly. Don't limit yourself to furniture, though. Do the windowsills, picture frames, lamps, vases, television sets, stereos, accessories, and in short, everything that doesn't bite back.

Spray-waxing is just like dusting, but you do it only on wood furniture. Spray some Pledge directly on the surface you want to polish. Wipe it around with a clean dustrag until the Pledge disappears and the wood shines. This both polishes *and* dusts the wood, so you don't need to go over the same furniture with Endust. Don't spray-wax your furniture every week, though, or you'll get what Madison Avenue calls waxy build-up.

If you've invested money in fine wood furniture, you owe it to yourself to protect it and keep it looking good by giving it a genuine wax job from time to time. Go to the hardware store and buy some boiled linseed oil and turpentine, then stop by the grocery store and get a bottle of white vinegar. In an old jar, mix 1/3 cup of each of those ingredients and shake well. Apply it sparingly to the wood with a clean cloth. Then take a second clean cloth and wipe it. When you're done, throw those cloths away, because they are a fire hazard.

VACUUMING   By now, all the dirt in your living room should have cascaded down to the floor, where you can suck it up with the vacuum cleaner. Before you start to vacuum, take your broom and sweep out areas where your vacuum cleaner can't reach: under sofas, in corners, around radiators, and so on. You don't have to sweep the dirt into a dustpan, just get it out where the vacuum can reach it.

WINDOWS   Washing windows is not as hard as it's cracked up to be, especially if you use the professional method. Fill a clean pail with a gallon of hot water and add two or three tablespoons of dishwashing liquid or ammonia (no more). Dip a clean sponge into the solution and lightly wipe the window with it. Take a moist paper towel and wipe the rubber blade on your window squeegee once to clean and lubricate it. Then wipe the squeegee vertically down the length of the window until you've removed all the liquid. Wipe off the blade after every pass and make sure each pass overlaps slightly into the previous one.

If you don't own a squeegee, you can clean windows adequately by spraying them with Windex and wiping them off with a clean paper towel.

WALLS Don't clean the walls unless you notice a particular stain on them, in which case you can spray it with Fantastik and wipe with a moist rag (not a sponge). When your walls get really dirty, paint.

Laundry

If kitchen-floor detergents have given us a lot of great commercials over the years, laundry products deserve to be enshrined in some kind of advertising hall of fame. Think of all the great thirty-second dramas that have been played out in the laundry rooms on television over the past thirty-five years: ambitious wives of hard-driving junior executives agonizing over the embarrassment of "ring around the collar"; young mothers fretting about Billy's grass stains; newlywed brides horrified to learn their husbands think the pile of laundry done with Final Touch is softer and whiter than their own.

WASHING AND DRYING

Now, somewhere in all these commercials, you probably heard the word *sorting*. Did you wonder what they meant by that? Did you ever wonder, for example, why your mother always spent five or ten minutes separating the laundry into different piles before she began to wash it? Why didn't she just throw it all in at once like everybody used to do at college?

Well, the reason is that your mother took pride in her housework and she wanted to get her family's clothing as clean as possible. Now that you're out in the cold cruel world—and people are judging you by (among other things) how well you dress—maybe you should consider sorting your laundry, too. It isn't hard.

Separate your laundry into three piles:

durables: blue jeans, socks, towels, sweatshirts, and so on.

delicates: brightly colored shirts and blouses, colored slacks, "permanent press," and anything made of synthetic fabrics like nylon and polyester.

whites: underwear, T-shirts, sheets and pillowcases, dress shirts, and handkerchiefs—but nothing delicate (even if it happens to be white).

If you're in doubt about whether an item is durable or delicate, look at the label inside. If it says "machine wash—cold water" or "machine wash—warm water" or "tumble dry—low heat," it's delicate. If not, and it feels pretty sturdy—as a pair of jeans obviously does, for example—it's a durable. Don't put anything marked "dry clean only" in the washing machine, and don't wash wool sweaters either. Sweaters and fine clothing (like business suits, for instance) should be taken to your dry cleaner.

For the sake of convenience, buy an all-temperature laundry detergent so you can use the same soap in all three loads. And buy a liquid bleach. (We would be downright un-American if we didn't recommend Clorox.) Now put your three piles into three different machines. Or, if you own your own washer and dryer, plan to do three separate loads. Bring a measuring cup with you to the laundromat, too.

• Wash your durable load in *hot* water with the recommended amount of detergent.

• Wash your delicate load in *warm or cold* water with the recommended amount of detergent.

• Wash your white load in *hot* water with the recommended amount of detergent *and* the recommended amount of liquid bleach.

[Can't get three machines and you want to know if there's a way to cheat? Okay. Throw your whites in with your durables and skip the bleach.]

When it's time to dry, remember this simple rule: *What washes together dries together.*

• Dry your durable load and your white load under the setting marked "hot" or "regular."

• Dry your delicate load under the setting marked "low" or "permanent press."

REMOVING STAINS

If you occasionally have food stains on your clothing—and who doesn't?—buy a can of Spray 'n Wash. As you sort your laundry, find the stains and spray them directly with a healthy squirt of this effective product. Sometimes it helps to tie the sleeves of a stained shirt together as soon as you take it off at night. On laundry day, the tied sleeves will remind you the shirt is stained.

For more difficult stains (in both clothing and carpets), remember this key principle: *blot, don't rub.* Try to catch the stain as soon as possible after it occurs. Blot it with a dry cloth to get up the excess moisture. Then blot it with cold water. If that doesn't work, buy a commercial stain remover like K2r, by Texize, and follow the directions carefully.

IRONING

The sooner you fold your clothes or hang them up after taking them out of the dryer, the less wrinkled they will get. Nevertheless, some items of clothing—men's dress shirts and women's dresses, in particular—will need to be ironed.

Ironing requires considerably less technique and skill than it would appear. Basically, a hot slab of metal is applied to a damp fabric until the wrinkles in that fabric disappear, and one man's method for doing so is as good as the next man's. But there are a few points to remember:

• Buy a steam iron, and fill it with water before you begin. If you don't have a steam iron, buy a sprinkle bottle, fill it with water, and lightly sprinkle each garment until it's *damp* but not *wet.* Roll it up, let it sit a few minutes, and then iron.

• Move the iron quickly: Don't let the iron sit on one area of the fabric too long or it will burn clear through.

• Do all your ironing at one time: Ironing is a pesky job—not difficult, but time-consuming and easy to postpone. As a result, you may be sorely tempted to iron your shirts one at a time as you need them. When you consider how long it takes to heat the iron, fill it with water, and set up your ironing board, ironing shirts in that way is a time waster. Instead, pick one of your favorite television shows and set aside that hour to do the whole week's ironing while you watch TV.

DORINNE'S SIX-STEP DIRECTIONS FOR IRONING A SHIRT

1. Start with the shirt inside-down on the ironing board with the collar unfolded and turned up. Iron the back of the collar. If you like your cuffs and collars stiff, squirt it with a spray starch, like Niagara.

2. Turn the shirt over and iron the inside of the collar.

3. Put the shirt at the end of the ironing board so the sleeve and shoulder fit over the rounded end of the board (just as if the ironing board were *wearing* the shirt). Iron the shoulder section. Iron across the back between the two shoulders. Put the other shoulder over the end of the ironing board as before, and iron the other shoulder.

4. Put one cuff at the center of the board. Iron the inside of the cuff. Then the outside of the cuff. Lay the sleeve lengthwise along the board. Iron one side of the sleeve, then the other side.

5. Repeat Step Four with the other cuff and sleeve.

6. Put the shirt on the board inside down so the sleeves hang off on either side like a dead man. Moving the shirt as necessary, iron the entire outside of the shirt (except for the shoulder area, which is already done), from the button area on one side all the way over to the buttonhole area on the other.

Know Your Enemy: The Mouse, the Rat, the Ant, and the Roach

Roaches, rats, ants, and mice are imperialists. They want to take over your apartment. They want to sleep on your furniture, eat your food, drink your water, and watch your TV. They will settle for nothing less than total domination over your home.

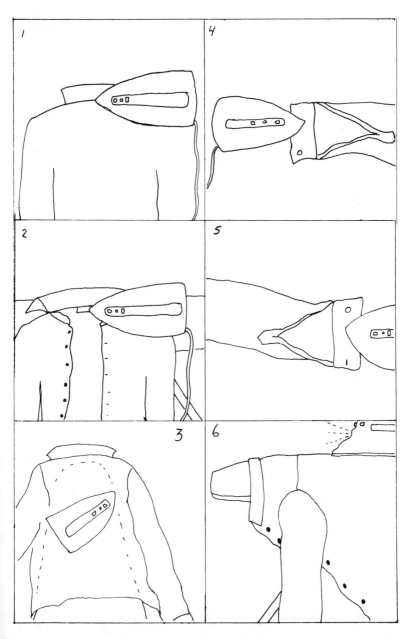

You must fight them with every ounce of your strength and wit and will. Sure, they will talk out of one side of their mouths about peaceful coexistence and détente. But with the other side of their mouths they are chewing on your Twinkies.

Occasionally, they will try to gain your sympathy by sending out a poisoned, dying soldier in broad daylight to stagger around your living room in plain view. But like the Rudolf Hess flight to England, it's a meaningless gesture.

Like the Viet Cong, they are guerrilla fighters. For example, they almost always attack at night. As soon as you turn off your light and go to sleep, you hear mice scratching away at your garbage can. You walk into your bathroom in the middle of the night, turn on the lights, and thousands of black roaches run for cover. Heaven knows when a hulking, ugly rat is prowling around your living room waiting to strike.

In planning your strategy, it's wise to remember that you can never hope to win an unconditional surrender against these enemies. No matter how many you kill, there are always more where they came from. The best you can do is to force a tactical retreat.

How?

Follow one of the most basic rules of military strategy: Cut off the enemy's supply lines. Or in civilian terms: Take away their food and water.

Simply putting a tight-fitting lid on your kitchen garbage can may reduce the insect and rodent population in your apartment by 75 percent or more. If, in addition, you make a special effort to wipe up kitchen counters, wash the dishes immediately after dinner, sweep the floor daily, clean the bathroom regularly, remove the crumbs from kitchen cupboards frequently, you can make visiting your apartment as unappealing to a mouse as attending a cat show. The roaches won't be too happy either, although they can survive on things most of us wouldn't even consider food.

Once you've done everything humanly possible to take away their source of food, follow these specific strategies for causing enemy casualties and forcing a retreat.

THE MOUSE

Mouse poisons are effective, but they have some serious drawbacks. After eating the poison, the mouse starts to feel a little ill. He decides to leave work early and go back to his home to spend the rest of the day watching soap operas and drinking hot tea. No sooner does he get home, however, than he immediately drops dead. Since mice like to build their houses in very remote areas (like inside walls or behind the refrigerator), there is often no way to find and remove the corpse, which, after a day or two, begins to smell like certain neighborhoods in New Jersey. The odor will go away eventually, thank God, but until it does, your apartment will be a very unpleasant place to live.

Using poison on mice is also not a good idea for people who have curious and hungry pets—especially if you own one of those dogs who cruise around with their mouth open, like sharks, sucking in everything that's in their way.

For those reasons, we prefer using mousetraps. There are two basic kinds: the old-fashioned spring bar trap and the new "sticky doormat" type. They are both effective, so it's a matter of which one you like best. Try using peanut butter instead of cheese in your spring bar traps, and put them where you've actually seen mice (or their droppings) in the past. (Mouse droppings, just in case you're wondering, look like carraway seeds.)

By contrast, you should put the newer kind of mousetrap on the floor flush against an open area of wall, because this is where mice like to run. These mousetraps are not for the squeamish or the animal lover, however, because the mouse is caught alive and, quite literally, tortured to death. The mouse runs along your baseboard minding his own business when suddenly he steps into quicksand. The harder he tries to free his little feet, the more he gets stuck. Chances are, he'll still be alive when you find him, although in a state of shock. You'll throw him down the garbage chute, where eventually he will die a slow, painful death of starvation or exhaustion.

Serves him right.

THE ANT

Compared to the invincible roach, getting rid of ants is child's play. The ant responds nicely (and by that we mean he dies) when confronted with commercial sprays, especially Crack 'n Crevice. (Follow the directions carefully, of course.) In areas where you'd rather not spray (in your cupboard, for example), use the sticky-paper ant traps. Unlike the roach, who will eat anything up to and including the kitchen sink, the ant has a more sensitive palate and must be tempted with something truly delectable, like an open sugar bowl or a three-day-old peanut butter and jelly sandwich. So keep your garbage cans closed, your food containers tightly sealed, and your cupboards free of crumbs.

THE ROACH

Scientists believe roaches may be the only creatures alive today capable of surviving a full-scale thermonuclear war. Why? Because they are indestructible: They can eat anything, and while they carry scores of diseases, they themselves are susceptible to none of them. Of course, using thermonuclear weapons on your roaches may be out of the question for most people anyway. But what's left? Not much, unfortunately. They laugh at commercially formulated insect sprays, and they never stick around long enough to be battered or swatted to death.

When dealing with roaches, it's important to remember they don't need *food*—in the conventional sense of the word—to survive. They can eat the glue behind your contact paper, envelopes, and postage stamps, the starch in your shirts, and God knows what in the bathroom. So it's vital to keep your home clean and picked-up at all times.

Roach "hotels" work well to control the roach population in areas where food is present. We especially like the brand called Combat. Some people swear by boric acid, which you can buy at the hardware store and spoon out full-strength along the baseboards and in the corners of your kitchen and bathroom.

But the best way to kill roaches is to have your apartment sprayed by a professional exterminator. Before you hire one yourself, ask your landlord to do it for you.

THE RAT

Speaking of landlords and exterminators, you should call both of them immediately if you ever have the misfortune of seeing a rat. The presence of rats in your apartment makes it legally uninhabitable for humans, and your landlord had better fix the situation or he is (in most states) criminally liable. Don't bother with rat traps (which are only larger versions of the same things that catch mice). Instead, call a professional exterminator and—we're serious—consider moving.

[*Dorinne:* I just couldn't let this chapter end without telling you about my neighbor and her Have-a-Heart mousetrap.

My neighbor is the biggest animal lover who ever lived; she even picks up ants gently in a tissue and moves them outdoors rather than kill them.

When she found a mouse in her basement, she bought a Have-a-Heart mousetrap—designed to trap mice alive so that you can free them outside.

But one day, she went on vacation and forgot all about her mice. When she came back, guess what she found?

An emaciated, gnarled, decomposed mouse starved to a slow and painful death by the Have-a-Heart mousetrap.

War is hell.]

CHAPTER SIX

The Trickle-Out Theory—

Managing Your Money

Like most people, you've probably gone through high school, college, and maybe a few years in the "real world" without knowing much about money. Of course you knew what it was, and you knew you liked it. But when it came to spending it, investing it, saving it, insuring it, and paying taxes on it, you probably scraped by on very little expertise.

Surprisingly, the amount of money you earn is often less important than how well you handle it. If you make $15,000 a year and manage it well, you might find yourself in better shape than the guy making $50,000 and blowing it.

That's what this chapter is all about: how not to blow your dough. We'll talk about budgeting, taxes, investments, insurance, and banks. Although our discussion of these complex topics will be brief, we hope it will be enough to make you want to learn more, because managing your money is nothing less than managing your life. It is a way to plan for the future, to set personal goals, to achieve life-long dreams, and to meet present needs while guarding against unforeseen dangers.

"When I was young," wrote Oscar Wilde, "I thought money was the most important thing in life. But now that I'm old, I know it is."

How to Create a Budget

Does the word *budget* scare you?

It shouldn't. Because a budget is a *good* thing. Think of your budget as a dam that controls the flow of money through your life. Build it right, and you'll enjoy a billion kilowatts of added financial power. Build it wrong (or fail to build one at all), and you may have trouble keeping your head above water.

The first step in creating a budget is to find a good place to put it. If you're the neat and orderly type, buy one of those handsome budget books at the dime store. If you're a slob, a regular notebook will do fine.

Now, open up to page one and draw a horizontal line across the top of the page and a vertical one down the left margin, just as we've done. On the horizontal line, write the month (or months) of the year, leaving enough room underneath for three vertical columns. Mark those columns: A) Planned; B) Actual; and C) Balance. Now, divide the vertical line into three main sections: 1) Income; 2) Fixed Expenses; and 3) Variable Expenses.

First, write down all the income you anticipate during the first month of your new budget. Second, enter your *fixed* expenses, including such things as your rent or mortgage payment and the monthly payment on your car. Third, estimate your *variable* expenses for the coming month, including food, household items, clothing, transportation, and health care. By adjusting your variables until your income and expenses are in balance, you gain the financial control that enables you to achieve your goals—whether those goals are as sensible as saving for a house or as frivolous as buying a VCR.

Once your budget is balanced, all you have to do is live up

	JANUARY		
---	Planned	Actual	Balance
INCOME			
Salary			
Other			
Total Income			
EXPENSES			
F Savings			
I			
X Rent or mortgage			
E			
D Insurance:			
E Hospitalization			
X			
P Major Medical			
E			
N Disability			
S			
E Tenants'			
S			
Auto			
Debts:			
Car			
Credit cards			
TOTAL FIXED EXPENSES			
V Utilities			
A			
R Telephone			
I			
A Food			
B			
L Household expenses			
E			
Clothing			
E			
X Public Transpo			
P and/or			
E Auto Expenses			
N			
S Medical			
E			
S Personal Care			
Pocket Money			
Fun			
Gifts/Contributions			
Misc.			
TOTAL VARIABLE EXPENSES			
TOTAL ALL EXPENSES			

to it! And the best way to do that is to keep a record of your spending. Every time you make a significant purchase, bring home the receipt (or make a note) and drop it in a shoebox or file folder. Don't try to watch every penny, but do try to get a general picture of where your money is going. Then set aside an hour at the end of each month to work with your budget and keep it on track.

If the amounts in your Actual columns come reasonably close to those in the Planned columns, you're doing fine. If not, ask yourself why. Were your original estimates unrealistic or too rigid? Perhaps you had an unexpected expense. Or maybe you just overindulged. Whatever the cause, don't be too discouraged if your first attempt isn't perfect. Keeping a budget is an ongoing process requiring constant reappraisal and revision. Eventually, you'll get it right. And when you do, you'll enjoy the enormous freedom and power of having your money under control.

LYDIA'S BUDGET

All that sounds good in theory, you say, but does it really work?

To find out, let's look at Lydia's budget.

Is Lydia a real person?

Yes, she is Dorinne's daughter and Richard's sister.

Is this Lydia's real budget?

Don't be silly. This is the budget we *wish* Lydia had—based on her actual income and expenses. Lydia's real budget looks more like the Rosetta Stone, and it's about as balanced as a drunken sailor.

Lydia is twenty-five years old, and she works in the insurance department of a large bank in New York City. She earns $18,400 a year and lives in a rent-controlled efficiency apartment in Manhattan. She commutes to and from work by subway. Let's look at her numbers.

On the income line, you'll notice what a big bite taxes take out of Lydia's paycheck. Of that $18,400 a year, she pays $2,815 in federal income tax, $945 in state tax, $355 in local

		JANUARY	
	Planned	Actual	Balance
INCOME			
Salary	1088	1088	—
Other			
Total Income	1088	1088	—
EXPENSES			
F I X E D E X P E N S E S Savings	25	25	—
Rent or mortgage	350	350	—
Insurance:			
Hospitalization	9	9	—
Major Medical	3	·3	—
Disability	1	1	—
Tenants'	10	10	—
Auto			
Debts:			
Car			
Credit cards	50	50	—
TOTAL FIXED EXPENSES	448	448	—
V A R I A B L E E X P E N S E S Utilities	25	25	—
Telephone	25	61	-36
Food	180	201	-21
Household expenses	25	60	-35
Clothing	25	0	+25
Public Transpo and/or Auto Expenses	27	27	—
Medical	16	16	—
Personal Care	25	25	—
Pocket Money	100	100	—
Fun	100	121	-21
Gifts/Contributions			
Misc.			
TOTAL VARIABLE EXPENSES	548	636	-88
TOTAL ALL EXPENSES	996	1084	-88

tax, and $1,232 in Social Security. After doing the necessary arithmetic, we see her take-home pay comes to just $1088 a month.

Lydia's biggest fixed expense is the rent on her apartment, which is $350. Like every true American, she has a hefty balance on several credit cards, and her minimum monthly payment on these comes to $50. Although her employer pays most of her insurance, she adds $9 a month in hospitalization, $3 on major medical, and $1 in disability out of her own pocket. She also has tenant's insurance, for which she pays $120 a year, or $10 per month. No matter what, Lydia stashes $25 per month in her passbook savings account.

Now, let's look at those variable expenses. Gas and electricity usually come to about $25 a month, and her phone bill hovers around $25. She averages about $45 a week at the grocery store, or $180 per month on the food line. Household expenses come to $25, and clothing to $25. At 90 cents for every trip, she spends about $18 a month getting to and from work and another $9 bouncing around town on weekends—a total of $27. Just to be careful, she puts away $16 per month to pay for her two annual visits to the dentist, and that leaves enough to cover the $100 deductible on her health insurance. Hairspray, nylons, makeup, aspirin, and so forth come to $25 per month. And look at this: She budgets a big $100 for pocket money and another $100 just for fun.

Her total expenses come to $996, or $92 less than her total income.

Sounds great, doesn't it?

Of course it does, the planned column always sounds great. Now, let's look at the actual.

As it turns out, Lydia spent the entire month making long-distance calls. "Who do I know in Anchorage?" she wondered when she saw the bill. She had planned $25 for the telephone bill. Actual: $61. Balance: −$36.

"I couldn't help it; I got hungry." Food line, planned: $180. Actual: $201. Balance: −$21.

Lydia didn't count on her television breaking down. It cost her $35 to get it fixed. Household expenses, planned: $25. Actual: $60. Balance: −$35.

Some good news. She bought no new clothing this month. Clothes, planned: $25. Actual: $0. Balance: $25.

"Well, a couple of the girls asked me if I wanted to go out for drinks after work, and I said fine. I thought it would only cost $5 or so, but we had a few, and a few more, and then we ordered some food. The next thing you know, it was eleven o'clock, and when the bill came, my share was $21." Fun money, planned: $100. Actual: $121. Balance: −$21.

Lydia went $88 over budget this month, or about $4 less than her margin of error. While not perfect, her budget is, as the saying goes, "good enough for government work." As it happens, she did a number of things right:

• *She put aside a small amount each month for large annual and semi-annual expenses like dentist's bills and insurance:* Each month, she carried over the amount saved and added it to the next month's balance column. So when the huge $120 bill for tenant's insurance arrived in December, the money was sitting in her budget waiting for it.

• *She recognized her own human frailties and budgeted a large amount for fun:* "Let's face it," she said. "I'm going to spend a certain amount on discos and movies anyway, so I might as well plan for it. If I don't, I'll probably just chuck the whole budget out the window." Good thinking.

• *She made her savings a fixed expense, not a variable:* By putting $25 in her passbook savings account before doing anything else, she did what financial planners call "paying yourself first."

There are, however, several things Lydia could do to make her budget work better:

• *She could fine-tune her variables:* It's possible she's allocated too much for clothing, for example, and too little for food.

• *She could increase her income* by getting a part-time job or simply by changing her tax withholding status. Since she gets a big tax refund every year, her employer is probably with-holding too much money from her paycheck. (See *The Facts of Life: Taxes and Death*)

• *Finally, she could get a grip on her overspending*, especially her long-distance calls. By keeping a record of her spending, Lydia knows exactly where she's overindulging and does not have that where-did-it-all-go? feeling most of us suffer at the end of the month.

Abandon Hope Ye Who Enter Here: Banks

Why do you need a bank?

Three reasons:

You need a place to keep you humble if you start to think your time is valuable;

You need a place where you can stand in line for several hours to get your weekly daydreaming done; and

In a world where mere acquaintances call you by your first name and everyone is always urging you to "have a nice day," you need a place where you can still be treated like a perfect stranger.

In addition to these services, banks can also provide you with a checking account and a savings account—both of which, unfortunately, you must have.

Does it matter which bank you choose?

Not much. But don't just walk into the first one you see. Look for a bank . . .

• with branch offices convenient to both your apartment and your job;

• with lots of automatic teller machines throughout the city;

• with an inexpensive or free basic-checking account;

• with a policy of clearing out-of-town checks and checks drawn on other banks in three days or less.

YOUR CHECKING ACCOUNT

There are only two types of checking accounts you need to worry about: *regular* and *special*.

How do you tell the difference?

Easy. Regular checking is called a "special account" and special checking is called a "regular account."

Typical.

In a regular account, you get free checking, but you may have to keep a minimum balance—usually $500 or more. If you find a bank that will give you free checking with no minimum balance (or a minimum balance of less than $200), you've found the banking equivalent of a four-leaf clover, so open an account before they change their minds.

In a special account, there is no minimum balance, but you have to pay a small fee per check and a monthly service charge, too. The check charge usually runs about 20 cents per check and the service charge about $5 a month. Anything lower than that is probably a bargain.

Which one is for you? It depends. If you don't have very much money and don't plan to write many checks (more than 10 a month, let's say), you'll do fine with a special account. If, however, you can afford to keep a large minimum balance and you plan to write a lot of checks, consider opening a regular account.

HOW TO BALANCE YOUR CHECKBOOK

It happens to everyone at least once in their lives. [*Dorinne:* It happened to Richard at least once a week.] You'll walk into the bank ready to make a big withdrawal, and—when you least expect it—the teller will utter his favorite line:

"I'm sorry, sir, but we can't do that for you."

"Why?" you ask.

"Because you have overdrawn your account," he replies.

So you ask him for your balance. He writes the figure on a tiny slip of paper and hands it to you like a warrant for your arrest. You look at it and nearly faint. It says − $328.53.

Did you mess up?

Maybe. Maybe not. Take a look at that teller again. Does he look like Albert Einstein? Isn't it possible the *bank* made a mistake? You bet it is, but there's only one way to find out. You must perform an arcane task known as balancing your checkbook. Here's how.

Every month, you'll receive a friendly little note from your bank crammed with cancelled checks and a long computer printout of all your transactions. This is called your statement. Take your statement, your pile of cancelled checks, and your checkbook register and follow these six easy steps:

1. Put your cancelled checks in a big pile . . . in numerical order.

2. Go through the pile, one by one, and match each check with the corresponding record in your register. Put an *x* in the register for every check in the pile. (Many checkbook registers have a handy box for you to do just this.)

3. Do you have any records of checks in your register that do *not* have an *x* by them? If so, these are your *outstanding* checks—the ones that have not yet cleared the bank. Make a list of these and add up the total amount.

4. Now make a list of all the *deposits* that are listed in your register but not in the statement. These are deposits you made *after* the bank's closing date for the statement. Add up the total.

5. Look at your statement for the check charge and the service charge, if any. Subtract them from the balance in your register. Write down your new balance.

6. Now just fill in the blanks and do the arithmetic:

A. The balance in your checkbook register: _____

B. Closing balance on your statement: _____

C. Total of deposits after closing (See Step 4) _____

D. Total of B and C _____

E. Total of outstanding checks (See Step 3) _____

F. Subtract Line E from Line D, and enter here: _____

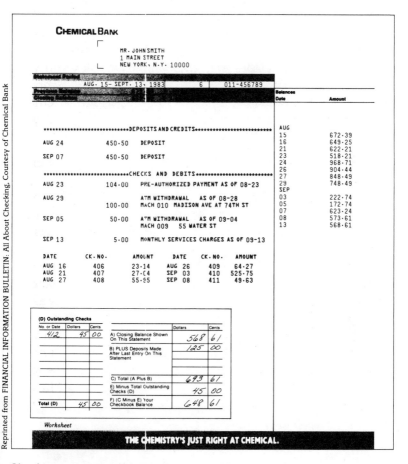

Checking account statement.

Does Line F equal Line A? If so, congratulations! Your checkbook is balanced!

If not, kill yourself.

No, wait, don't do that yet. Try this first. Double-check your arithmetic—both in the balancing operation and in the check register itself. Make sure you've counted all the outstandings, even ones from past months. (Some people hold on to your checks forever just to drive you crazy.) Double-check those maintenance charges, service charges, check charges, automatic teller machine withdrawals, automatic deductions, and all those other sneaky devils. And make sure the amount you entered in your register corresponds with the amount you wrote on the check. It's very easy to transpose numbers and write, for example, $38.95 on the check and $39.85 in the register.

ITEM NO OR TRANSACTION CODE	DATE	DESCRIPTION OF TRANSACTION	AMOUNT OF PAYMENT OR WITHDRAWAL	✓	OTHER DEDUCT	AMOUNT OF DEPOSIT OR INTEREST	BALANCE FORWARD
		PLEASE BE SURE TO **DEDUCT** CHARGES THAT AFFECT YOUR ACCOUNT					649 25
407	8/18	TO ACME HARDWARE FOR (VACUUM REPAIR)	27 04	✓			27 04 / 622 21
	8/23	TO CAR PAYMENT FOR PRE-AUTHORIZED TRANSFER	104 00	✓			104 00 / 518 21
408	8/23	TO NEW YORK FOR TELEPHONE	55 95	✓			55 95 / 462 26
	8/23	TO DEPOSIT FOR (PAYDAY)		✓		450 50	450 50 / 912 76
409	8/25	TO SHOE DESIGN FOR (RUNNING SHOES)	64 27	✓			64 27 / 848 49
	8/28	TO ATM WITHDRAWAL FOR (MADISON at 74th)	100 00	✓			100 00 / 748 49
410	9/2	TO FIRST CITY MGMT FOR (RENT)	525 75	✓			525 75 / 222 74
411	9/4	TO CON EDISON FOR	49 63	✓			49 63 / 173 11
	9/4	TO ATM WITHDRAWAL FOR (55 WATER ST.)	50 00	✓			50 00 / 123 11
	9/7	TO DEPOSIT FOR (PAYDAY)		✓		450 50	450 50 / 573 61
412	9/10	TO CHEMICAL BANK FOR (MASTERCARD)	45 00				45 00 / 528 61
	9/14	TO DEPOSIT FOR (AUNT SUE)				125 00	125 00 / 653 61
	9/13	TO MONTHLY SERVICE CHARGES FOR	5 00	✓			5 00 / 648 61

Checkbook register.

Still doesn't balance? Okay, now kill yourself.

NO, WAIT. There's one more thing to try. Go to the bank and tell them it must be their fault. Tell them they had better correct it right away or you're going to take action. Tell them you demand to be treated like a human being.

On second thought . . . might as well go ahead and kill yourself.

YOUR SAVINGS ACCOUNT

There are two basic kinds of savings accounts: passbook savings and statement savings. The difference is only a matter of how the records are kept; the interest you'll earn on both kinds of accounts is exactly the same—low.

If you open a passbook savings account, the bank will give you a little booklet to carry around as a record of your balance. When you want to make a deposit or a withdrawal, you must bring it to the bank and the teller will stamp it with a record of the transaction, plus your latest interest payment. A statement savings account is more like a checking account. Every month the bank will send you a statement of your balance, and you can make deposits by mail. Some people find statement savings more convenient; others like keeping their money in a passbook they can clutch in their hand. You decide which is best for you.

How much should you save?

That depends on your household budget, but the size of your monthly savings isn't as important as the *regularity* of it. In other words, the $5 you actually deposit every month is better than the $500 you hoped to deposit but couldn't. In general, you should keep saving at a comfortable pace until you have about three months' worth of monthly take-home income in your savings account. If your take-home pay is $1,000 a month, for example, a savings account of $3,000 is plenty. Once you've reached that level of security, it's time to think about channeling your extra dollars into areas that will pay a higher return.

THE DO'S AND DON'TS OF BANKING

• *Don't* ever write a check hoping to cover it later: You're breaking the law for one thing, but legal matters aside, it's just a dumb thing to do. A million things can prevent you from covering the check. After it bounces, you'll not only have to pay the bank a heavy fine, but you'll have a black mark on your record.

• *Don't* overuse checks: If you have a special checking account, each check costs money, so don't get in the habit of writing checks for shoeshines, newspapers, and telephone calls.

• *Do* make a note in your register *immediately* after writing a check: With an angry crowd behind you in the grocery line, you may be tempted to shove your checkbook in your pocket and fill out the register when you get home. Don't. Delaying the process of recording checks is the single biggest cause of messing up your account. Get in the habit of recording checks immediately after you write them, no matter how rushed the circumstances.

• *Do* keep a check file: You can buy a little check file at the dime store. It's a good investment. Just drop your cancelled checks and bank statements in there every month and save them for 3–5 years. That way, you'll always be armed with evidence if the bank questions your account. It's handy for taxes and budgeting, too.

The Facts of Life: Taxes and Death

With the possible exception of the Department of Defense, the IRS is the only branch of the federal government you'll ever need to take seriously. But unless you have the misfortune of being audited by them, the only interaction you'll probably ever have is filling out their silly forms. So here are a few of the most common ones, with some tips on how to use them:

The W-4

Even if the IRS trusted you to save an appropriate amount from your paycheck to pay your taxes at the end of the year, they probably wouldn't let you hold the money when they could be spending it themselves. That's why your first confrontation with the IRS will be a little form called the W-4, which determines how much money your employer will *withhold* from your paycheck as a down payment on your annual tax bill.

All the IRS wants to know on the W-4 is how many "allowances" you claim. In other words, how many people (including yourself) does your meager paycheck have to support? If you have a wife and six kids, for example, you would write 8 and the IRS would generously let you keep most of your paycheck because you obviously need it. As a single person, however, you only have a choice of writing 1 or 0.

If you write 0, you will get *less* money in your regular paycheck and (probably) *more* money on your tax refund at the end of the year. If you write 1, you will get *more* money in your paycheck and *less* money in your refund. Unless you anticipate any special tax liabilities (if, for example, you have more than one job), you're better off taking the money now by choosing 1.

The W-2

Late in January, your boss will hand you a little form called the W-2. This is your receipt for all the money you've sent to the IRS throughout the year. The W-2 will show your total salary, the amount of federal taxes withheld, the state and local taxes withheld, and the amount of Social Security you paid. It comes in triplicate: one for the IRS, one for your state tax agency, and one for you. If your boss hasn't coughed up your W-2 by the first week in February, complain about it because he's not doing you a favor: You can't complete your tax returns without it.

FILING YOUR TAX RETURN

Let's pretend it's a Friday afternoon late in January when the boss walks in and drops your long-awaited W-2 on your desk.

You didn't have anything planned for this weekend, did you? Why not do your taxes?

If you've played this game before, the IRS remembers you and has thoughtfully sent you the same forms you used last year. If, however, this is your first time, stop by the nearest bank or post office and pick up every state and federal tax return form they have. Don't forget to grab the instruction booklets, too.

Now sit down at your dining room table (your desk won't be big enough) and spread all the junk in front of you: tax return forms, W-2's, and all your records of taxable income. Gather your records of potential tax *deductions* too, including: doctor's bills, state and local tax payments, contributions to charities and political candidates, interest payments, and expenses you had in connection with your job. If you have enough of these expenses, you may be able to list them individually (itemize) and deduct them from your taxable income.

But first, you must decide what form to use: 1040EZ, 1040A, or 1040.

THE 1040EZ

Did you catch that name? 1040EZ? That is what passes for a sense of humor at the IRS. In fact, that's the funniest thing you'll see for the next seven hours.

Everything about the 1040EZ is easy. It looks like a coloring book, doesn't it? Glance at the upper right corner and you'll find a section that shows you how to write the numerals from 1 to 9—something most of us mastered in kindergarten. Yes, a fool could use the 1040EZ, and that's only fitting, because in most cases you're a fool if you do. In the war between you and the IRS, the 1040EZ is the moral equivalent of surrender. That's why the IRS loves this form so much. They're always trying to get you to use it. They sponsor TV ads about it. They put their agents on talk shows to promote it. They even write little notes all over the 1040 and the 1040A saying, in effect, "Tired of all this work? Wouldn't you rather use the 1040EZ?" . . . or, "If you used the 1040EZ, you'd be in bed by now."

Don't fall for it.

Unless you're in a big hurry, use one of the other returns. They're longer, sure. But the reason they're longer is that they give you more ways to save money.

THE 1040A

Not much better than the EZ, the 1040A at least lets you take a few deductions: payments to an individual retirement account (IRA); partial credit for political contributions; and credit for child- and dependent-care expenses. If you have other legitimate deductions, however, you could be paying money for the privilege of filling out a simple form, so turn to the 1040.

THE 1040

Did you move because of a change in your job? Do you ever spend money on business for which your employer doesn't pay you back? Did you have a lot of doctor's bills last year? If

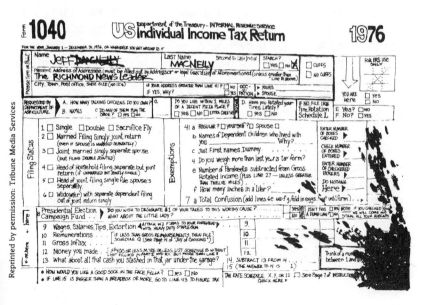

An improperly completed 1040.

you can claim these or any other legitimate tax deductions, you'll probably save money by using Form 1040. The 1040 is nowhere near as complicated as the IRS wants you to believe. Just follow the directions, and you'll do fine.

STATE TAX FORMS

Don't forget your friends in the state capital; they want to dip their beaks into your paycheck, too. Your state may or may not have its own equivalent of the federal "EZ" forms. If it does, the same principle applies. Use the longer form, and you'll save money. Always do your federal taxes before the state. Most state returns are designed to let you copy many lines directly from your federal return.

THE DO'S AND DON'TS OF TAXES

• *Do* save your tax forms for *at least* three years: The IRS can audit you up to three years after you file your return, and once they've got you, they may ask to see returns from up to seven years ago. So find a nice safe spot for old tax returns and let them sit there for a decade or so.

• *Do* hire professional help: If your tax return is complicated, you'll save money by hiring a tax accountant. A good one will often cost less money than he saves you, and his fee is deductible, so you can hardly lose. Ask your boss to recommend a good local accountant who handles personal tax returns, and don't wait until April 14 to call him.

• *Do* file early: Especially if you're expecting a refund, it makes sense to file before the April deadline. File in January, for example, and you could be enjoying your refund by February. Wait until the crunch around April, and your check might be delayed for months.

The Protection Racket: Insurance

So far in this chapter we've talked about expenses you expected and spending that you planned for. But what about those expenses you didn't expect and that nobody can plan for? What about the accident that totals your car and lands you in the hospital? How about the night you come home to find your apartment ransacked and all your valuables gone? Or the day you go to the dentist for a $50 check-up, and he says you need a $500 root canal? For these unexpected pleasures in life, you need something called insurance.

Insurance is, without a doubt, the most complex and boring subject in the financial world. Unfortunately, it also happens to be one of the most important. Although we can't tell you everything you need to know about insurance in the confines of this short chapter, we'll alert you to the major varieties and give you a few tips on how to buy it.

HEALTH INSURANCE

There's no getting around it, you *need* health insurance. Before you buy it at high individual rates, though, find out if you're covered at work in a group insurance plan. Fortunately, most companies give their employees some kind of health insurance, but it's up to you to know if your policy is enough.

There are three basic kinds of health insurance policies: *hospitalization, major medical,* and *disability.*

HOSPITALIZATION   As its name implies, this policy pays the bill if you go into the hospital. It should also include benefits for medical and surgical charges during your hospital stay and immediately afterward. To make sure it does, ask your boss for a copy of your company's insurance policy. Look for a section that lists all sorts of gruesome medical procedures and tells how much will be paid for each of them: "Flywheel removed—$500; Neckbone connected to headbone—$1,000"; and so on. Can you find something like this? If not, you may need to shop around on your own for a supplemental medical-surgical policy.

MAJOR MEDICAL   This policy covers bills that aren't necessarily related to a stay in the hospital. If you visit the doctor for a stomachache, for example, you can get some or all of the bill paid by your major medical. More important, if you develop a long-term illness requiring many visits to the doctor, a major-medical plan will save you from bankruptcy. Unfortunately, your boss isn't as likely to have a good major medical plan as he is to have hospitalization.

Do you need it?

Maybe not, but if you have any doubts about your health— or if you just want to play it safe—you should shop around for some major medical. As you do, pay attention to three words that are bound to appear in any major medical plan:

1. *Deductible:* You pay the first few dollars of your bill; the insurance company pays the rest. If you have a $1,000 doctor bill, for example, and a *$200 deductible* on your major medical, you'll pay $200, and the insurance company will pay $800.

2. *Co-insurance:* A co-insurance provision means you and the insurance company will *share* the cost of your medical bills. Isn't that sweet? Most plans call for you to pay 20 percent of the bill and for them to pay 80 percent.

3. *Stop-loss.* Trying to figure out what 20 percent of a zillion is? Don't worry. Your co-insurance provision should also have a "stop-loss" clause, which limits your expenses to a set amount, usually around $2,000.

Instead of a major medical policy, your employer may offer you one of several new kinds of health coverage. Many companies nowadays are switching to Health Maintenance Organizations, or HMOs. Your company pays the HMO a lump sum every month so you can go to the HMO clinic for *all* your medical needs and pay almost nothing. Or you may have a Preferred Provider plan. If so, you'll get a list of dozens of local doctors. When you go to one of the doctors on the list, you'll pay only a tiny charge for each visit.

DISABILITY The third major type of health insurance is disability, a policy that pays all or part of your salary if you're too sick to work. At this stage in your life, the most valuable thing you own is your ability to earn money, so this is an important type of insurance to have. A good disability policy pays you up to 80 percent of your net income for as long as you're unable to work, even if that happens to be for the rest of your life.

Since your employer is less likely to offer disability than he is other kinds of health insurance, you may have to shop for it on your own. If so, keep your costs down by getting a policy that: 1) does not start paying benefits until 30, 60, or 90 days after you become disabled; or 2) stops paying benefits after you reach age 65 (when Social Security takes over).

In most cases, your employer's health insurance plan will be just fine, but don't *assume* so. Read all the booklets the personnel department gave you on your first day of work. If you find any gaps in your coverage, you may need to shop for some supplemental policies. Ask your colleagues if they ever made a claim and if they were satisfied with the results. Become an expert on your own health insurance, and you can't go wrong.

DENTAL INSURANCE

If your employer has a dental insurance plan, consider yourself lucky. If not, don't worry about it. Dental insurance costs a lot, and it's usually not worth it to take out an individual policy at your own expense. If, however, your company has a plan that asks you to pay part of the cost, you must judge for yourself if it's worth the expense. Do your teeth look like Stonehenge? Then by all means take the dental plan. But if you never get any cavities, don't worry about dental insurance, because you don't need it.

LIFE INSURANCE

As a young single person with no dependents, you may wonder if you need life insurance at all, and perhaps you don't. But consider this: If you die, someone—probably your father—is going to have to bury you and pay off all your bills. This is not the kindest legacy you can leave your parents.

There are two basic kinds of life insurance: term and whole life. Term insurance is less expensive (especially while you're young), but it only pays off when you kick the bucket. Whole life insurance, on the other hand, gives you other benefits while you're waiting to die, including a way to: a) save money; b) borrow money at low interest rates; and c) protect yourself against the high cost of buying life insurance when you're old. To get the best deal, see an *independent* certified life underwriter, one who can write policies with more than one insurance company.

TENANT'S INSURANCE

You never really find out how many valuable things you own until they're stolen from you. When you return to your apartment after a burglary, you'll be amazed to learn how rich you used to be. You may even wonder why you never bought any tenant's insurance.

Unfortunately, theft isn't the only thing that can turn you into a pauper. There's fire. Or smoke damage from someone else's fire. A main water pipe might break and submerge everything you own in six feet of water. Even little Rattles, your pet snake, could get you in trouble if he bites the mailman and causes a lawsuit.

A good tenant's insurance policy should cover all these mishaps at a modest price. Plan to pay about $100 a year for $10,000 of comprehensive protection.

THE DO'S AND DON'TS OF INSURANCE

• *Do* join group plans whenever possible: Group insurance plans always cost less than individual policies. If your employer does not have a group plan, don't run out and buy an individual policy until you've explored your other options. Do you belong to a labor union or a professional association? If so, you might be able to buy group insurance from them.

• *Do* take the higher deductible: This is the "golden rule" for saving money on all kinds of insurance policies, from automobile to major medical. Can you afford to pay the first $500 worth of damage to your car, for example? If so, you'll save a bundle on premiums.

• *Don't* overlap insurance: Be careful your various insurance policies do not overlap each other. You don't want medical coverage on your car insurance, for example, if you already have a health insurance policy that covers car accidents.

• *Do* cover yourself between jobs: One of the most important things to look for in your employer's health insurance policy is a *conversion clause*. This means that if your boss ever calls you into his office and "converts" you into an unemployed person, you can have your health coverage extended (at your own expense, of course) while you look for another job. Expect your benefits to drop a little and your premiums to go up, but it's a lot better than buying an expensive individual policy on your own.

Investing your Money

Until now, we've spent all our time telling you how to keep up with the money game. Now it's time to tell you how to get ahead of it—investments. Are you too young to be worrying about investments, pensions, and retirement? Look around you. The world is full of old people wandering the streets who always thought they were too young to worry about such things.

INVESTING OR SAVING?

Knowing the difference between investments and savings is the first step to a sound financial strategy. The money you put aside for savings is money you want to keep; the money you invest is money you can afford to lose. Not that you *want* to lose it, of course. You want it to grow. But the more potential for growth in an investment, the more likely you'll blow the whole wad. Until you've established a financial security blanket with your savings account, you can't afford the risk.

EVALUATING AN INVESTMENT

Here's a handy formula for evaluating any investment. Just ask yourself these five questions, and don't invest unless you're happy with the answers:

1. *How much does it cost?* Most investments require a minimum commitment. Can you afford it?

2. *How much can it earn?* Professionals call this the yield. Quite simply, what do you stand to gain?

3. *How safe is it?*

4. *How liquid is it?* Can you get your money back if you need it (without penalties), and how quickly?

5. *How will this investment affect your taxes?* Some investments help your tax picture; some don't.

YOUR INVESTMENT OPTIONS

Now, let's take those five measures and apply them to the three most likely investment options for a person of your age and income.

STOCKS

MINIMUM INVESTMENT: $100 or less
YIELD: can be very high
SAFETY: varies from highly risky to moderately safe
LIQUIDITY: very liquid, but you may suffer a loss when you sell

TAXES: income on dividends is taxable; increased value of stock is not taxable until sold

When you buy a share of stock, you're buying a small part of the company which issued it. You become a "part owner" of the company, and you can even vote at its annual meetings. By purchasing a share of stock, you're betting the company will do well in coming years, because you will share in its profits through *dividends*. If the company thrives, the price of the stock will also go up—earning you an additional return on your investment when you sell. To get your feet wet in the stock market on a small investment, see someone called a "discount broker," a broker who will buy the stock you want without charging extra for advice. Look him up in the Yellow Pages.

MUTUAL FUNDS

MINIMUM INVESTMENT: $100 and up

YIELD: very good, but not a way to get rich overnight

SAFETY: generally safe, but aggressive funds sometimes suffer losses

LIQUIDITY: extremely liquid

TAXES: all income is taxable (although some funds are designed to be tax-exempt)

A mutual fund is a way to pool your dollars with many other investors and have the total sum managed by professionals. Mutual funds can be invested in a variety of "instruments," including stocks, bonds, money-markets, or some combination of all of them. When you invest $100 in a mutual fund, you are in effect buying a share of the fund. That share can earn money for you in two ways: 1) through dividends; and 2) through an increase in the value of your share when you decide to sell it back. There are many different kinds of mutual funds, and you can pick the one that suits you best. Some offer big dividends. Some concentrate on growth. Some are safe, some speculative. Every year, *Forbes* magazine rates the major mutual funds for their performance in the past year, so be sure to read that issue at the library before you buy. When shopping for a mutual, look for the word *no-load*, which means you won't have to pay commissions. You'll find the major mutual funds listed in the business section of your newspaper, and you can call them directly.

CERTIFICATES OF DEPOSIT (CDs)

MINIMUM INVESTMENT: $500 to $1,000 and up
YIELD: modest, but better than a savings account
SAFETY: nothing safer
LIQUIDITY: very poor (loss of interest and substantial penalties for early withdrawal)
TAXES: income is taxable

When you buy a CD, you are simply depositing money in the bank and promising you won't withdraw it for a certain period of time. In short, you're loaning the bank money, and they're paying you interest on it. As long as you're dealing with a federally insured bank, CDs are probably the safest investment around, but their liquidity is poor and their yield is nothing to brag about. In a diverse group of investments, use your CD as an anchor for a more speculative foray into stocks and mutuals. How do you get one? Just go to the nearest bank.

THE ALL-POWERFUL INDIVIDUAL RETIREMENT ACCOUNT (IRA)

The IRA is the single best idea our government has had since the invasion of Normandy, and like all good ideas, it's a simple one. The government says you can deduct up to $2,000 every year from your taxable income if you put the money in a retirement account. The interest and growth on your investment is also tax free. All you have to do is promise you won't touch it until you're 59½ years old.

Everyone should put at least some of his income into an IRA. You don't need to invest the maximum $2,000; you can start an IRA with as little as $100. Kiss the money goodbye, though, because you can't get it out without paying taxes and a 10 percent penalty. For now, the real benefit of your IRA is how it helps on taxes. If you use Form 1040 (or 1040A), you can subtract your IRA payments off the top of your taxable income. You can put your IRA in stocks, bonds, mutuals, CDs—just about anything. All you have to do to open an individual retirement account these days is to go out into the street at high noon and whisper, "I want to open an IRA." Thousands of stock brokers, bankers, insurance agents, and financial planners will descend on you like something out of an Alfred Hitchcock movie.

THE DO'S AND DON'TS OF INVESTING

• *Do* be daring while you're young, cautious when you're older: Now is the time of life to be bold in your investments— especially if you've followed our advice about savings. You can afford to accept a high risk in the hope of a long-term gain. Later, as you approach retirement, you should put your money in more sensible stuff—like companies that make nuclear weapons and carcinogens.

• *Do* enroll in dividend reinvestment plans: One of the best ways for a young person to "play the market" is to buy a single share of stock and enroll in the company's *dividend reinvestment plan*. There are two advantages: 1) the dividends you earn will be used to buy additional shares of the same company; and 2) you can buy more shares directly from the company itself, without paying commissions to a broker. If the stock does well, your shares will multiply like bunnies.

• *Do* "diversify" your investments: This is financial jargon for "Don't put all your eggs in one basket." One of the best ways to diversify is to follow the investment criteria we mentioned earlier. Buy some investments with high liquidity, some with high yield, some with a high degree of safety, and some with tax advantages.

Savings Strategies

Perhaps the best way to manage your money is to spend it wisely. After all, money was made to be *spent*—not saved, invested, or insured. So let's conclude this chapter with a list of ten tips on how to spend your money well.

• Don't shop for food on an empty stomach: This is the golden rule of grocery shopping. Follow it, and you could save $20 or more a week.

• Shop for food once a week, not once a day: This will cut your grocery bill in half. Just make a list of all your meals for the week before you go to the grocery store.

• Look before you leap on major purchases: Set a certain amount—let's say $100—above which you will never buy anything without researching it first. Read the consumer magazines, visit several stores, talk to your friends, and be sure you're making the right decision.

• Buy generic and house-brand goods: Generics and house brands are usually made by the same companies that make the better known brands. They're cheaper because less money is spent on packaging, advertising, and marketing. Generics may not suit your taste on everything, but with stuff like paper towels, floor mops, and hamburger buns, how can you miss?

• Watch for annual sales, and buy off-season: Become familiar with seasonal pricing and plan your purchases accordingly. You can get an air conditioner in the dead of winter, for example, at a fraction of what it costs you in July.

• Be creative about entertainment: Remember when you were a kid? Remember how much more fun it was to make up your own games with your pals than it was to play with expensive toys and participate in organized activities? The same is true as an adult. You don't need to spend money to have fun. Use your imagination.

• Buy from garage sales and thrift shops: These are especially good for furniture, casual clothes, books, and records.

• Shop by mail: Mail-order shopping offers convenience, low prices, and—if you're careful—quality. Don't hesitate to return anything you're not happy with, though.

• Compare unit prices: Which costs more—a 16 oz. bottle of juice for $2.38, or an 8 oz. bottle for $1.50? The larger bottle is a lot less expensive. Take a pocket calculator with you to the grocery store and compare unit prices on different sizes.

 • Never buy on impulse: There are many things in this world which you ought to do impulsively. [*Dorinne:* Calling your mother, for instance.] Shopping is not one of them.

ANNUAL SALES AND OFF-SEASON DISCOUNTS

Air conditioners	February
Blankets	January, May, November, December
Christmas cards	after Christmas, August
Coats (winter)	March
Cosmetics	January, February, September
Curtains	February
Electronics	January, February, July
Floor coverings	January, February, July, August
Furniture and lamps	February, August
Glassware	January, February, September
Housewares	January, February, September
Knives	January, February, September
Paint	August, September
Shirts (men's)	January, February, July
Shoes	January, July, November, December
Silverware	February
Stationery	February
Summer clothes	after the Fourth of July
White sales (linen)	January, August

CHAPTER SEVEN

Tell Mommy Where It Hurts—

Health and Hygiene

From the time you left your mother's womb until the day you graduated from college, you've probably enjoyed the luxury of having somebody else take responsibility for your health. Mom always made your dental appointments, didn't she? Old Doc Jones was always handy whenever you were really sick. And on those days when you just had a touch of the flu or a bad stomachache, your mother always knew exactly what to do.

Then you had to go and spoil it all. You grew up. You graduated. You moved to a distant city. At first there was no problem, because you were never sick. Why do you need a doctor when you're feeling fine? As a kid, you went to the dentist twice a year. Since you moved away from home, though, it's been two, three, maybe five years since you had your teeth checked. You always *meant* to find a dentist and a doctor, but you just never got around to it. Then one day, you're chewing some gum when . . . OWWWW!

Believe us, it's time.

We'll begin this chapter with some advice on how to find a

doctor and a dentist and how to get the most out of their services. We'll take a look at the confusing world of drugs, and
we'll give you some advice on stocking your medicine cabinet
and first-aid kit. For those times when you're not quite sick
enough to go to the doctor but too darn sick to go to work,
we'll give you Mom's "prescription" for colds, flu, diarrhea,
headache, and tummy ache. And we'll conclude with a brief
look at the cornerstones of preventive medicine: nutrition and
fitness.

The Hypocritical Oaf: Your Doctor

If you thought you felt alone and scared on the first night in
your own apartment, just wait until the first day you get sick. Of
course you could try calling your old family doctor long distance:
"Take two aspirin and come see me in the morning."
"I can't come in the morning, Doc. I live in Honolulu now."
"In that case, take two pineapples and go jump in a lake."
Even if you didn't move away from your hometown, you
may feel a little silly sitting in your old pediatrician's waiting
room reading the latest copy of *Jack 'n Jill.*
Don't you think it's time you found yourself a grown-up
doctor, or at least one who doesn't hand out lollipops after a
tetanus shot?
But what kind of doctor do you need? How do you find a
good one, and once you've found one, how often should you
go?

THE PRIMARY-CARE PHYSICIAN

In this age of specialization, the family doctor is a dying breed,
but the primary-care physician, as she calls herself today, still
survives under a variety of names.
As her title implies, the primary-care physician is your first

line of defense against illness. She can treat you for most of the ailments you're likely to get, and if she can't, she can refer you to someone who can. With a few exceptions (eye doctors, for example) you shouldn't go to a specialist without first consulting your primary-care physician. Let *her* decide if you need a specialist, and ask her for a referral.

Who are the primary-care doctors?

THE GENERAL PRACTITIONER This is the old family doctor of yesteryear, and if you can still find one, consider yourself lucky. The general practitioner has graduated from medical school and earned a license to practice medicine in your state; he may or may not have additional education. But what G.P.'s sometimes lack in formal training, they often make up for in real-life experience and gentle bedside manner. Marcus Welby, after all, was a general practitioner.

THE DOCTOR OF INTERNAL MEDICINE, OR INTERNIST In urban areas, the internist is the most common primary-care physician at work today. He has several years of post-medical school training, and he can recognize and treat a wide variety of illnesses.

THE FAMILY PRACTICE SPECIALIST A relatively new wrinkle in primary-care, the family practice specialist is a highly trained version of the old family doctor. In addition to medical school and a hospital internship, he has had a three-year residency in family medicine, which has trained him to deal with a wide variety of illnesses in both children and adults.

THE GYNECOLOGIST In theory, the ob-gyn is not a primary-care physician, but a specialist. In practice, many young women manage to get along very nicely with a gynecologist as their only doctor.

In addition, there are a few specialists you can see without a referral from your primary-care physician. Among them:

THE OPHTHALMOLOGIST An ophthalmologist is a medical doctor who specializes in treating all diseases of the eye. She's not to be confused with an *optometrist,* a non-medical professional who examines eyes and measures and prescribes lenses for common visual problems like nearsightedness. Neither of these professionals should be confused with an optician, a tradesman who grinds lenses and sells eyeglasses. If you notice any trouble with your eyes or your vision, we recommend you see an *ophthalmologist* first.

THE DERMATOLOGIST   A dermatologist is a physician who specializes in diseases of the skin, whether they're as minor as acne or as serious as cancer. If you notice an outbreak on your skin, it might save time to bypass your primary-care physician and make an appointment directly with a dermatologist.

THE PSYCHIATRIST   There are two major types of mental health professionals: the psychiatrist and the psychologist. The psychiatrist is a medical doctor and is therefore: 1) able to diagnose and treat any underlying physical cause of your emotional problems; and 2) legally allowed to prescribe drugs (such as tranquilizers), if necessary. A psychologist may have a master's or a doctorate in the study of human behavior, but he is not a physician. Not surprisingly, the psychiatrist usually charges more for an hour of counseling than a psychologist.

Of course, many young people don't bother to get any kind of doctor until they're sick, then they run off to the local hospital emergency room. The E.R. is an expensive way to get medical care and, in many cases, an inappropriate one. After all, emergency room doctors are specialists, too. They specialize in emergencies. If you've broken your leg, by all means limp over to your nearest emergency room. But if you've noticed a mysterious lump in your neck, see your primary-care physician first.

HOW TO CHOOSE A DOCTOR

Once you've decided what kind of doctor you want, you have to go out and find him. Here are some simple steps to take:
- Ask a friend: Ask five or ten people you trust to give you

the name of their family doctor. When you hear someone raving about how nice their doctor is, how easy he is to talk to, how sympathetic he is to their concerns, you're on the trail of a live one.

• Ask a professional: Do you have any acquaintances in the health care industry? Do you know a nurse, a social worker, a medical student, or a hospital administrator? They are likely to know the medical superstars in town, and they'll also know which doctors have better reputations than they deserve.

• Ask a pharmacist: They usually have the inside poop on all the doctors in the neighborhood.

• Ask your old doctor for a referral: If you had a trusted family doctor back home, give him a call to ask if he knows anybody in your new town.

• Check your health insurance plan at work: Maybe the decision has already been made for you. If your employer's health coverage is a Health Maintenance Organization (HMO) or a "Preferred Provider" plan (see Chapter 7), you may be required to see a specific doctor to receive the benefits of your health insurance.

Once you've narrowed your list down to four or five highly recommended doctors, it's time to check them out yourself. There are a few important items you can determine over the phone:

• Is the doctor board-certified? This may not apply to G.P.'s, because they aren't required to have advanced training, but internists, family practice specialists, and gynecologists should all be certified (or eligible for certification) by the medical board of their specialty. You can call the doctor and ask him, or you can check his listing in the *American Medical Directory* at your local library. Look for the words *board certified* or *diplomate of* _____. Board certification is no guarantee of quality, though, and a lack of certification is not necessarily a sign of incompetence. A board-certified doctor is simply one who has passed a very rigorous examination in her specialty.

• Is the doctor on the staff of a hospital? There are two reasons why hospital affiliation is important: Your doctor can personally admit you to the hospital if she thinks it's necessary; and it's a sign your doctor has attained a certain level of professional distinction. Give her extra points if she's on the staff of a hospital affiliated with a medical school, because those positions are even more prestigious.

• Is the doctor affordable? Don't be afraid to call the doctors on your list and talk money. If one doctor charges much more than the others, cross him off the list. He may be good, but you don't need Michael De Bakey to work on your dandruff. If the doctor (or his staff) refuses to talk money with you or acts like money is beneath his concern, hang up. He's not being honest with you or with himself. A willingness to talk money is a sign of professionalism and candor—fine qualities in a physician.

• Does the doctor want your business? You can obviously expect the best doctors to be among the busiest ones, but if the earliest you can get an appointment is some time in the next century, forget it. You need a doctor who can afford to spend a little time with you. It's common nowadays for doctors to have two or three patients in different examining rooms at the same time, but if the waiting room is jammed and the doctor is ricocheting from one room to the next like a pinball, you may want to ask yourself if his reputation is really worth waiting for.

Have you narrowed your list down to two or three? Good. Pick one of them at random and make an appointment. Tell the receptionist you're new in town and just want a check-up and a chance to get acquainted. If you have a minor complaint, mention it, and mention your age too.

Now you're ready to make the final and most important evaluation:

DO YOU LIKE HIM?

That's right, do you *like* him? If you don't, he's not the right doctor for you—even if he was the centerfold in last month's *New England Journal of Medicine.*

Can you see yourself phoning to ask him about the headache that just won't go away? Would he make a special effort to squeeze you in for an appointment, even on a busy day? Is he or she the kind of warm yet objective person with whom you wouldn't mind sharing the most personal details of your life? Does he *listen* to you?

If so, you've found a winner and your search is over. If not, pick the next name on your list and repeat the process in six months to a year.

HOW TO GET THE MOST FROM YOUR DOCTOR

Much has been written in recent years to foster a healthy skepticism about professional medicine. The days when patients regarded their doctors as official emissaries from God are long gone, and they should be. The practice of getting a second opinion before surgery, being fully informed about prescription drugs, and demanding plain-English explanations are all welcome developments . . . up to a point. To the extent that such an attitude creates a sense of *partnership* between you and your doctor, your health will be well served. If, however, you come to think of your doctor as an *adversary*, you're only hurting yourself.

Yes, you should always demand a full explanation from your doctor. You should insist that he spend a decent amount of time with you. You should question him about anything you don't understand. On the other hand, your doctor expects some things of *you:*

• Establish a "baseline" with your first visit: Doctors complain about patients who visit them for the first time with a minor ailment and, as they head out the door with their prescription in hand, proceed to list 100 other symptoms ranging from pain in the toenail to bleeding from the belly button for which they want a quick diagnosis and cure. Is that fair to your doctor? Even if you don't give a darn if it's fair, do you think it's likely to achieve success? Giving your doctor a laundry list of ailments should be done on your initial visit or your regular check-up. Don't wait until you're sick to find a doctor. You should go at least once to establish a baseline from which changes can be measured and dealt with as they occur.

• Follow your doctor's advice: Nothing is more irritating to a physician than the following situation:

"Well, Doc, it's been two whole weeks and I still ain't cured."

"Did you take the pills I gave you?"

"Nope."

"Why not?"

"I don't like taking no pills, Doc, but never you mind that. Just tell me how come I ain't cured."

Believe it or not, it happens all the time. People go to their doctor for medical advice and then they ignore it.

• Be honest with your doctor: Don't lie to your doctor because you're embarrassed to tell him the truth, and don't be evasive about your symptoms. Doctors can read an X ray, but they can't read your mind.

HOW OFTEN SHOULD YOU SEE YOUR DOCTOR?

Here we separate the girls from the boys. Young women should see their gynecologist at least once a year for a breast exam, a pap test, and a pelvic exam. They should go to their gynecologist at least twice a year if they use one of the more risky forms of birth control, like the pill or the IUD. And they should have their doctor show them how to perform a monthly self-examination of the breasts.

Men are (as usual) luckier. After you've chosen your doctor and visited him once to establish norms, it's really up to you how often you want to go for a check-up. Unless you're guarding against the recurrence of an earlier disease, statistics show that an annual check-up really doesn't pay off until you reach the age of forty. Until then, a check-up every three to five years would be prudent.

DO'S AND DON'TS OF DOCTORS

• *Do* telephone your doctor before you visit: If you follow our advice and find a doctor *before* you get sick, you may save money in the future by telephoning the doctor instead of visiting him. In many cases, he can give you advice—or even a prescription—over the phone, and he'll know if you're sick enough for an office visit.

• *Do* ask your doctor for generic prescriptions: If your doctor signs the prescription slip on the generic line, he can save you a bundle. Remind him. In some cases there may be a reason for choosing the brand-name drug, but he should explain why.

• *Do* make a list of questions for your doctor: Don't trust your memory to recall all your symptoms and questions in the precious moments you have with your doctor. Write them down, and cross them off one by one. If he appears impatient or uncomfortable with this process, find a new doctor.

The Tooth Fairy: Your Dentist

Remember when you were a kid and you put your little baby tooth under the pillow for the tooth fairy? The tooth fairy would take your tooth and leave money for you under the pillow, right? A dentist is a person who never quite outgrew this game. Now that he's an adult, however, he plays it with a little twist. He takes your tooth, and you give him all your money.

The process of choosing a dentist is similar to the one you followed for finding a doctor. Recommendations from trusted friends, medical professionals, the local dental society, and nearby dental schools are all ways to develop a list of four or five prospects.

Once you've reached that stage, however, money takes on even more importance with your dentist than it did in choosing a doctor. After all, you'd have to be pretty sick to spend $500 on your doctor, but you can give that much to a dentist before you know it.

Call the dentists on your list and ask them how much they charge for a routine check-up. Forget the ones who are much too high or much too low, and look for one on the low side of average. Ask the dentist (or his receptionist) if he offers extended payment plans in case you need a lot of work. Again, if he shows any hesitation about talking money, cross him off the list.

How did they treat you on this initial telephone call? Were they helpful and friendly? If so, you're on the right track. Don't put up with an interrogation about who recommended you, and don't accept an appointment any longer than a month in the future. Dentists are not that rare a commodity.

Group dental practices offer several distinct advantages over the lone practitioner. You can get a built-in second opinion. If you need a specialist (endodondist, orthodontist, oral surgeon, or periodontist), you can usually find him in the same office, instead of across town. And groups are more likely to have modern equipment, because it's easier for them to share the cost.

Since you visit your dentist more often than you do your doctor (twice a year, says the American Dental Association), you'll have more opportunity to evaluate his or her services. It's time to look for a new dentist if you notice the following:

• You don't get reminder notices in the mail about your next check-up.

• The dentist or hygienist does not take time to show you the proper way to care for your teeth at home.

• You are frequently kept waiting for hours in the reception area.

• Your dentist doesn't have the time or inclination to talk to you about problems and concerns.

• Your dentist does not follow modern procedures or use modern equipment.

• Your dentist shows an inclination toward radical rather than conservative treatment. Pulling teeth, for example, should be a therapy of last resort.

• Your dentist is unconcerned about your fear of pain. Don't put up with a dentist who says, "This won't hurt a bit," and then proceeds to torture you like a political prisoner. Modern dentistry has many ways of handling pain and fear, and your dentist should be willing to use all of them if necessary.

Finally, just as you did with your doctor, pick a dentist you *like*. Look at it this way: This guy's going to spend two or three hours every year with his fingers in your mouth; you might as well pick someone nice.

Tell Mommy Where It Hurts

Fortunately, the vast majority of the illnesses you get in your life will not require the attention of a doctor. Many, however, will require the attention of a mother. Don't worry if your mother isn't around to help; that's why you bought this book. Here's some advice on how to deal with some of the most common ailments that afflict mankind.

THE COLD

PROPER NAME: Upper respiratory infection

SYMPTOMS: Runny nose, scratchy throat, cough, aches, and . . . hell, you know the symptoms.

WHAT CAUSES IT?: No one knows for sure. The latest thinking, however, is that it is *not* caused by cold weather or wet feet, but by coming into contact with someone who has the virus or touching surfaces where the virus is present.

CAN YOU PREVENT IT?: Maybe. Try to avoid letting people sneeze in your face or slobber you with an infected kiss. Wash your hands often and avoid touching your eyes, nose and mouth, so that cold viruses picked up from doorknobs and handshaking won't find their way into your nose and throat.

SHOULD YOU STAY HOME FROM WORK?: Yes, if you can. And the sooner after the onset, the better. If you can stay home and rest on the very first day you notice the symptoms of a cold, you might prevent it from getting worse.

MOM'S PRESCRIPTION: "First, honey, take a day off from work, and make arrangements the day before. Tell your boss you won't be coming in tomorrow. Clear up your desk. Cancel your appointments, and when you get home, take the phone off the hook. Now, you can sleep nice and late in the morning. Get up around eleven or so and make yourself something to eat. Eat as much or as little as you want, but do eat *something.* Chicken noodle soup and a grilled cheese sandwich would be great. Get dressed in comfortable old clothes, but make sure they're warm. Now read or watch TV for three or four hours. Keep a glass of juice or water in your hand always. The more you drink today, the better. If you've got a sore throat, put two teaspoons of salt in a glass of piping hot tap water and gargle five or six times until all the water is gone. Do this every two or three hours. Take a nap around two or three o'clock and sleep until dinnertime. Have as much dinner as you want, then read or watch TV until about nine, and go to bed."

WHEN TO CALL THE DOCTOR: Colds can easily turn into something more serious, so don't be shy about asking your doctor for advice when you have a bad cold—*especially* if you have a fever, a severe sore throat, a persistent cough, or a cold that just won't go away.

THE FLU

PROPER NAME: Viral influenza

SYMPTOMS: Same as a cold, only worse. You'll probably also have a high fever, muscle pains, and some kind of stomach upset. You'll also feel very weak. Even doctors have trouble distinguishing the flu from a cold, but there are a few signs. Did your cold come on suddenly and ferociously? Influenza is an epidemic disease, so if you've been hearing the flu is "going around" and suddenly you get a helluva cold . . . guess what? You've got it. Flu can also attack your stomach and intestines, where the symptoms are vomiting and diarrhea. Don't trust this kind of flu to self-treatment; call your doctor.

WHAT CAUSES IT?: The flu is caused by any one of a hundred different viruses that work their way through the population in epidemics.

CAN YOU PREVENT IT?: You can try not to get close to people who have it, but even people without symptoms can be carriers. Good nutrition will help, but if a flu virus has your name on it, you're probably going to get it.

SHOULD YOU STAY HOME FROM WORK?: If you really have the flu, this question is academic. You're more likely to ask yourself: "Should I wake up this morning, or should I just lie here until I die?" The suddenness of the flu may prevent you from following our advice for planning ahead. If you *can* make arrangements to take time off work, however, do so. Only this time, make arrangements to be out for three to five days.

MOM'S PRESCRIPTION: "Follow Mom's prescription for a cold with a few minor changes. You may not want to get up at all for the first few days, so feel free to stay in bed all day if you want. Get up long enough to get something to eat, and have a glass of water or juice by your bedside at all times. If you're not hungry at all, fix yourself some soup or bouillon—and keep drinking. If your stomach is upset, eat very lightly, taking special care to avoid greasy, heavy foods. A little dry toast (or toast with jelly) and some hot tea might be nice. To keep your fever down, take aspirin according to the directions on the bottle."

WHEN TO CALL THE DOCTOR: Don't hesitate to phone your doctor for advice whenever you have the flu, *especially* if you experience any of the following symptoms: a fever of more than two degrees above your normal temperature; any fever that persists more than three days; stomach problems like vomiting or diarrhea; disorientation, dizziness, or difficulty in breathing.

DIARRHEA

PROPER NAME: Diarrhea

SYMPTOMS: Diarrhea *is* a symptom, not a disease. It's usually a symptom of gastroenteritis or stress.

WHAT CAUSES IT?: Diarrhea is your body's way of telling you there's something in your intestine that doesn't belong there. It may be a virus or just a rotten tomato, but one way or the other, your body has decided to eject it in the fastest way it knows how. Diarrhea can also be caused by emotional stress.

CAN YOU PREVENT IT?: Watch what you eat. Avoid foods that have given you trouble in the past, and make sure everything you eat is fresh. Viral diarrhea probably cannot be prevented, and chronic diarrhea caused by stress may require counseling or a new diet.

SHOULD YOU STAY HOME FROM WORK?: If you're hit with a sudden and nasty attack of diarrhea, a day at home may be a good idea. At least you'll always be close to the toilet!

MOM'S PRESCRIPTION: "Oh, you poor baby, you must feel just awful. Call in sick and go right back to bed. Try to catch a little sleep between trips to the toilet. Around noon, you should get up and fix yourself a little something to eat. Dry toast and tea would be perfect. Have some clear soup or broth, but stay away from greasy soups or dairy products. Drink a glass of ginger ale now and then, too. You might try cooking a clear vegetable soup and straining out the vegetables. (That's a meal like Jack Nicholson's chicken salad sandwich without the chicken salad!) Try to survive on a diet like that for as long as you can. When you start to get hungry again, you're ready for a bigger meal, but steer away from greasy, spicy foods for the rest of the week."

WHEN TO CALL THE DOCTOR: Always phone your doctor for advice about a bad case of diarrhea, *especially* if it's explosive or violent, if it's accompanied by vomiting or fever, or if it lasts for more than a day.

STOMACHACHE

PROPER NAME: It depends on exactly what you have, but abdominal pain is what your doctor is most likely to call it.

SYMPTOMS: Cramps or "gas pains" in the stomach. The pain may also be accompanied by the sound effects of bubbling and gurgling.

WHAT CAUSES IT?: "Musta been somethin' I ate," is the most common self-diagnosis, and it's usually accurate. Eating too fast or too much at one sitting will also cause a rebellion in your stomach. When stomach turbulence splashes digestive acids up into your esophagus, you will get the painful sensation known as heartburn. Stomach upset can also be caused by stress or worry.

CAN YOU PREVENT IT?: Sure. Eat sensibly, and don't fret.

SHOULD YOU STAY HOME FROM WORK?: There isn't much to be gained for a sour stomach by staying home from work. If a stomachache attacks during the day, however, you may want to knock off a little early, so you can go home and lie down.

MOM'S PRESCRIPTION: "Listen, sweetie, just don't eat much of anything for a while. Have a little tea and dry toast. Don't drink any coffee or alcohol. Later, if you get hungry, you can have some clear soup with rice or noodles, but stay away from stuff with fats and oils. Run out and buy yourself some ginger ale or plain seltzer water. The little bubbles will make you burp, and that'll make you feel better."

WHEN TO CALL THE DOCTOR: A stomachache can be something

very minor . . . or something very, very serious. So call your doctor about any bad stomachache, *especially* if the pain is very severe, if it lasts more than an hour, if there's swelling in your abdomen, or if it's accompanied by vomiting, perspiration, constipation, or diarrhea. Beware of *chronic* stomachaches, too—even if they're mild—because they may indicate a serious condition.

HEADACHE

PROPER NAME: Cephalgia

SYMPTOMS: A dull, steady ache across the forehead, temples, or at the back of the head are the symptoms of a normal tension headache.

WHAT CAUSES IT?: When you're under physical or psychological stress, the muscles in your back, neck, and scalp tend to contract, causing a tightness around the forehead and temples. Eventually, your muscles become sore from overwork. Muscle-contraction headaches, or "tension headaches" as they are more commonly known, can be caused by a variety of factors, from going too long without a meal to working too hard without a break.

CAN YOU PREVENT IT?: You bet. You can lead a headache-free life if you follow these precautions:

- Get a good night's sleep.
- Exercise regularly.
- Don't get drunk.
- Don't work too hard or too long without a break.
- Don't try to work in inadequate light.
- Avoid prolonged or excessive noise.
- Make sure your apartment and your office are properly ventilated.
- Don't skip meals.

SHOULD YOU STAY HOME FROM WORK?: Call in sick with a tension headache and your boss may ask you to stay home permanently. Leaving work an hour or two early, however, is probably the best cure for a headache known to medical science.

MOM'S PRESCRIPTION: "Lie down, honey, and close your eyes. Turn off all the lights in the room and massage your forehead with your fingertips. If you're at work, close your door and take a break for ten minutes. Clear your mind of business and picture yourself doing whatever makes you happy and relaxed. If you feel it's necessary, take aspirin according to the directions on the bottle. When was the last time you had something to eat, by the way? Did you skip lunch? No wonder you've got a headache. Treat yourself to a nice meal."

WHEN TO CALL THE DOCTOR: Any headache that won't respond to the recommended dosage of aspirin and a little relaxation should be brought to the attention of your doctor—*especially* if the pain is concentrated in one area of your head; if the headache is accompanied by other symptoms like nausea, dizziness, blurred vision, or vomiting; or if you have headaches (even mild ones) frequently.

Drugs

We won't comment on the recreational variety, but the medicinal kind deserves some attention. To learn more about prescription drugs and their side effects, buy a copy of *The Physician's Desk Reference* (PDR) or one of the many less expensive paperback books on prescription and non-prescription drugs. After consulting both the PDR *and* your doctor, make sure you have a satisfactory answer to each of the following questions before taking prescription medicine:

- Are there any side effects, and if so, should I be concerned about them?
- Is there a dangerous interaction between this drug and other drugs (including over-the-counter drugs) that I'm currently taking?
- Do I take this drug on an empty or a full stomach, or does it matter?

- Are there any foods to avoid while I'm taking this drug?
- Do I continue to take these pills until I feel better or until they are all gone?

We're not great believers in the usefulness of over-the-counter (OTC) medicines. Most of them are symptom relievers rather than cures—proving Voltaire's dictum that "the art of medicine consists of keeping the patient amused until nature cures the disease." Americans spend more than a billion dollars a year on patent medicine. Ever since the days of Lydia Pinkham's Vegetable Compound ("a sure cure for all female weaknesses"), we've been a nation of suckers when it comes to buying health in a bottle. We'd be hypocritical, though, if we tried to talk you out of using over-the-counter drugs, because we use them ourselves. Instead, we'll give you just a little advice:

- Read the labels and follow the directions carefully.
- Never mix two or more OTC drugs without checking with your pharmacist or doctor to learn if there's a harmful interaction.
- Favor drugs with a single active ingredient over combinations and "potions."
- Always call your doctor before you attempt to treat yourself with OTC drugs for anything but the most minor ailments.
- Don't expect miracles.

Your pharmacist knows a lot about over-the-counter drugs and will give you good advice on what to buy. Specifically, he knows which ones have active ingredients similar to what doctors prescribe for the same symptoms. Before you run off to the drug store, however, try to solve your problem with the best drug of all—food. Can't sleep? Try a glass of warm milk before you go to bed. Got a cough? Mix a little honey in your tea.

YOUR FIRST-AID KIT

We strongly recommend you keep a well-stocked first-aid kit in your home at all times. You can buy an excellent ready-made kit at the drug store or dime store or you can stock your own and put it in an old shoe box. We've made a list of all the things you should have in your home first-aid kit, but the two most important items are these: 1) your doctor's phone number; and 2) a first-aid manual.

A WELL-STOCKED FIRST-AID KIT CONTAINS . . .

adhesive bandages in a range of sizes
adhesive tape
ammonia inhalants
antiseptics (iodine, hydrogen peroxide, etc.)
aspirin
cotton
doctor's telephone number and address
emergency telephone numbers and addresses
eye pads
eye wash
first-aid manual
ice bag
ipecac (to induce vomiting after poisoning, but don't use without
    professional advice)
measuring spoons (for proper dosage)
rubbing alcohol
scissors
sterile gauze in a roll
sterile gauze pads in assorted sizes (individually wrapped)
sterile sponges
tweezers

• Keep all medical phone numbers taped to the top of your first-aid kit: This is your "second aid," so to speak, and without it, your first aid is almost useless. When you're injured, you can't waste time going through telephone books to find a phone number. If you're single, you face an added problem, since you can treat yourself for only the most minor injuries. So keep the following telephone numbers in your first-aid kit: the local emergency number (usually 911); the number and address of the nearest hospital emergency room; a private ambulance service; your dentist's number; the number and address of the nearest all-night drug store; the local poison control center; and *your doctor's phone number.*

It's also a good idea to have the number of your nearest friendly neighbor. If you think of it ahead of time, work out an agreement to call each other in emergencies because sometimes all you need is a helping hand.

• Keep a first-aid manual in your kit: Without a manual, your first-aid kit is an orchestra in search of a conductor. The American Red Cross publishes the standard first-aid booklet, and they usually give it away free or for a small contribution.

YOUR MEDICINE CHEST

Stocking the medicine cabinet is largely a matter of personal taste, but there are a few things everyone should have:

• A pain reliever: aspirin or acetiminophen (Tylenol is the best-known name brand), whichever you prefer.

- Disinfectants: For minor cuts and scrapes.
- Antacid: For heartburn and gas.
- Anti-diarrheal: For those late-night attacks of diarrhea when the nearest drug store is at least two toilet stops away.
- Adhesive strip bandages.
- Cotton-tipped swabs.
- Toothpaste and dental floss.
- A thermometer. [Take your temperature a few times when you're healthy to establish a norm, because your own normal temperature may be different from the average 98.6°F.]

Preventive Medicine

"An ounce of prevention," as the old saying goes, "is worth a pound of cure." By practicing a few simple rules of preventive medicine you can keep from getting sick in the first place, and you might even help yourself live longer. The foundation of preventive medicine rests on two large columns: nutrition and fitness. Let's take a look at each of them.

NUTRITION

How could so much confusion arise from something so simple? You've probably seen enough conflicting articles and books on nutrition to make you give up in frustration and eat all your meals at McDonald's.

We don't blame you. You shouldn't have to own a reference library, a pocket calculator, and a computer just to figure out what you want for dinner. The key to good nutrition is really very simple—so simple, it can be summed up in one sentence:

"Eat a balanced meal."

You've heard that all your life, haven't you? But perhaps you never realized what it meant. All the foods human beings consume (with the possible exception of bubblegum) can be divided into four basic groups:

> beans, grains and nuts
> fruits and vegetables
> dairy products
> poultry, fish, meats, and eggs

To have a "balanced" diet simply means you're eating a little from each group every day. Complicated, isn't it?

Despite what many believe, none of those food groups are "better for you" or "worse for you" than the others. The only bad thing is to eat too much from one group and not enough from another. Unfortunately, that's what most of us do.

You may think your next-door neighbor, a vegetarian, has a much healthier diet than you, and maybe she does. But unless she is an extremely *careful* vegetarian, she is probably not getting enough protein. She'd be much better off if she had a steak now and then.

Most Americans make the opposite mistake. They go too heavy on the meat and eggs, too light on the vegetables and grains.

Here are two simple rules to make sure you're eating right:

• Take a quick inventory before every meal: Does the plate in front of you contain one item from at least three and preferably all four of the basic food groups? If so, you're okay. Now, go ahead and pig out. You may prefer to spread the food groups throughout the day. You could have fruit and grains for breakfast (orange juice, melon, oatmeal, and whole wheat toast, for example); vegetables for lunch (a big chef's salad, let's say); and protein, dairy, and more vegetables for dinner (pork chops, baked potato, broccoli, and a glass of milk). Be sure to consider the manner in which your food was cooked, too. Vegetables that have been deep-fried in animal fat, for example, do not give you full credit toward your degree in vegetable eating.

• Listen to your body: Your body knows more about nutrition than you could find in all the books and magazine articles in the world, and if you listen carefully, it will tell you what to eat. Trouble with your bowels, for example, may mean you need more fiber in your diet. Too many head colds could be your body's way of telling you it wants more fruit.

Should you take vitamins? Sure, but if you eat enough from all the food groups, you're getting about a hundred times your daily requirement of every vitamin and mineral known to man.

Should you eat so-called health foods? If it makes you feel good, go ahead. There's no reason to run off to the nearest health food store, though, because your supermarket has all the health foods you'll ever need—if you know what to look for.

The rule is simple: *Buy foods that look the way they looked when the farmer said goodbye to them.* Don't buy the canned asparagus in the second aisle when you can buy fresh asparagus in the produce section. Don't buy potato chips when you can make yourself a baked potato. In short, avoid processed foods as much as possible.

Why?

Two things happen when food is processed: a lot of good stuff is taken out; and a lot of bad stuff is thrown in.

Take that can of asparagus, for example. The mere act of precooking and canning it has robbed it of vitamins, minerals, fiber, and many of the other nutrients your body needs. Meanwhile, all sorts of chemicals have been added to preserve its freshness, brighten its color, and enhance its taste.

Ironically, the additives in processed food that pose the greatest danger to you are not the BHT and Red Dye No. 2, but two more sinister chemicals: NaCl (salt) and $C_6H_{12}O_6$ (sugar). Salt and sugar are essential nutrients, but taken in excess, they can be harmful. Processed foods are literally "loaded" with them. It's not unusual to find more salt and sugar in a product than the item for which the product is named. Some breakfast cereals, for example, contain more sugar than cereal.

PHYSICAL FITNESS

If you're one of the millions of Americans who are into jogging, swimming, handball, karate, roller skating, or any of the other athletic fads sweeping the nation . . . then get out of here, we don't want to talk to you.

We're serious. Put the book down. Take a break. Skip to the next chapter. Just go. Get. Shoo.

There.

Are they gone?

Thank God.

Weren't they a pain? We don't miss them at all, do you?

Okay, now everyone who is still here should be people just like us—lazy bums.

Is changing channels on the TV set the most exercise you get all week? Do you get a little short of breath after brushing your teeth? Do you still call running shoes sneakers?

Good. You're our kind of people. That's why it hurts so much to tell you this:

You're killing yourself.

Yes, your lifestyle is laying you wide open to the possibility of developing high blood pressure, arterial sclerosis, bleeding ulcers, heart attack, stroke, and many other highly unpleasant diseases.

That's the bad news. The good news is you don't have to become a fitness buff in order to get healthy again.

If your greatest joy in graduating from high school was knowing you never had to take another gym class for the rest of your life, don't worry. You don't have to play a sport or do calisthenics if you don't want to. Just work a little exercise into your daily routine.

Try walking to work instead of riding the bus. Make a vow never to use an elevator when there's a stairway available. Take all your telephone calls standing up. Carry your groceries home. Use a bicycle instead of a car when you can. In short, don't *change* your lifestyle, just give it more juice.

Here's to Your Health . . . and a Word of Advice

When someone says to you, "Take care of yourself," he means it. Taking care of yourself is your job now. The people who love you are counting on you to do it well. Eat right, keep fit, and above all, get help when you need it.

One final word of advice: If you have the slightest doubt about a physical symptom, call your doctor. After all, this book wasn't intended to replace your doctor—just your mother.

CHAPTER EIGHT

Mother, Please!
I'd Rather Do It Myself—
Home Repair

RICHARD: *When I was a kid, my father would often ask me to run downstairs to our tool box to get a pair of pliers so he could perform some minor household task. Dutiful son that I am, I would dash down to our utility room, open the drawer marked tools, and gape into a bottomless pit of extension cord, nails, screws, and primitive-looking instruments. One question would invariably pop into my mind:*

"What is a pair of pliers?"

Inevitably, I would return with a wrench or a hacksaw and sheepishly hand it to my father, knowing very well it was not what he had requested.

"I SAID PLIERS, FOR HEAVEN'S SAKE," he would patiently explain to me. At which point the whole process would be repeated as many times as necessary for the law of averages to supersede my ignorance, until I finally brought back a pair of pliers.

DORINNE: *"Dutiful son?"*

There's nothing like the feeling of pride you'll get when you make your first home repair. The first time you do it, changing a fuse is as rewarding as completing an A+ term paper or impressing your boss at an important meeting. Even if it isn't the Sistine Chapel, painting a ceiling can be a satisfying aesthetic experience. And sewing a button on your shirt will make you feel wonderfully self-sufficient.

The advantages of being handy around the house are many. You'll save money on plumbers, carpenters, and painters. You'll spare yourself the aggravation of complaining to an unsympathetic landlord. Your sense of independence and self-esteem will grow. And the repairs themselves will be better because, as the saying goes, "If you want something done right, you'd better do it yourself."

We realize some people have more God-given talent for home repair than others, so we won't try to make you into something you are not. But we firmly believe you can accomplish all the tasks we've outlined in this chapter, including: fixing a toilet, unclogging a sink, changing a fuse, and mending a rip in your pants. If you're the kind of ignorant fool who can't tell a pair of pliers when you see one, we'll give you some advice on how to stock a tool box, and we'll conclude with some thoughts on how to protect your apartment from fire and theft.

Repairs: Who's Responsible? You or the Landlord?

By far the easiest way to repair anything in your apartment is to have the landlord do it for you. If you live in one of those luxury high-rises where home repair consists of leaving a note at the front desk saying, "Fix my toilet, please," you need only skim this chapter and laugh at the rest of us.

Even in more humble apartment buildings, there are certain repairs that the landlord must make himself. Among them are those that need to be made in common areas like the hallways, lobby, laundry room, or basement. If your apartment came complete with a refrigerator and a stove—as most do—these two appliances are usually the landlord's responsibility as well. So is the plumbing.

But not everything is so clear-cut. Take painting and plastering, for example. Some landlords will repaint your apartment every few years whether you like it or not. Others will gladly do it on request. Many, however, will laugh in your face when you ask them to paint, and they'll hand you a brush. The meanest landlords refuse to do it for you and refuse to let you do it yourself!

So what can you do?

First, check your lease. Before you talk to your landlord about repairs or improvements, you must know your legal rights. Of course, the lease probably gives your landlord everything except your first-born child, but don't despair. He may not know the terms of the lease any better than you do. Call him up and make a deal. But get the agreement in writing, especially if he promises to reimburse you for your own labor or expense.

Do you remember that old aspirin commercial: "Mother, please! I'd rather do it myself." Well, sometimes waiting for your landlord to perform a minor repair can give you a bigger headache than it's worth. Sure it's his responsibility to fix a leaky faucet. But if the darn thing is keeping you awake at night, you can't wait two weeks for him to call the plumber. That's when you must take the crescent wrench in your own hands and do it yourself!

But first, *what's a crescent wrench?*

Stocking the Home Tool Kit

Anthropologists have long believed it is man's use of tools that distinguishes him from the animals. If this is the case, why do so many of us look like monkeys when we use them?

Often the problem is simply a matter of choosing the right tool for the job . . . and having that tool on hand. So here is a list of the tools we recommend, with an explanation of what each is designed to do. We suggest you buy as many of these items as you can afford and store them in one spot, whether it's a steel toolbox or just an empty drawer.

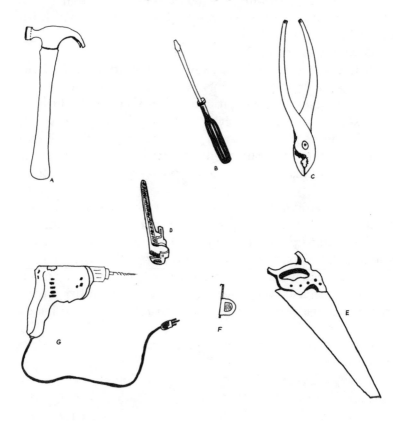

• Claw hammer (A): You may not have known its proper name before. The *claw* in claw hammer refers to that curved tail on the end that you use for pulling out nails. Buy a standard 13 oz. size.

• Screwdriver (B): Theoretically, you should have four of these devils: a large and small Phillipshead; and a large and small standard. But you can buy a 4-in-1 model with interchangeable tips. [You know what a Phillipshead screwdriver is, don't you? It's the one with the X-shaped tip that you never have when you need it.]

• Pliers (C): Ask the hardware man for a pair of slip-joint pliers with a wire-cutter jaw. This handy tool is used for getting a firm grip on something while you work on it, and as you've guessed, it also cuts wires.

• Crescent wrench (D): Wrenches are used to tighten or loosen bolts. The crescent wrench in particular has the advantage of being adjustable.

• Handsaw (E): They come in a confusing variety, but if you want an all-purpose handsaw, ask for a 20-inch crosscut blade with 7-8 points per inch. A saw, however, is seldom needed for simple repairs around the apartment, so you may want to hold off buying one until the need arises.

• Tape measure (F): You'll be surprised how handy this little item is. Get the kind that retracts into a solid metal case, and use the hook at the end to grasp the edge of whatever you're measuring so you can reach across a wide area without assistance. Tape measures are easier to work with and more convenient to store than yardsticks.

• Electric drill (G): In addition to drilling holes, your power drill also can be used for many other household jobs, including mixing paint, sanding wood, driving screws, and driving your neighbors crazy.

• Miscellaneous: Round out your tool box with a roll of masking tape and electrical tape, a bottle of white (polyvinyl) glue, an all-purpose lubricant ("3-in-1 Oil," for example) and an assortment of standard nails and screws.

Here are three more items no apartment should be without:

• Grocery cart: Don't worry. You won't look like a little old lady pulling one of these, unless of course you *are* a little old lady. Grocery carts are great for shopping, laundry . . . even picnics in the park.

• "Plumber's friend" (plunger): A plumber's friend is used to flush out blockages in the toilet or sink. It's a misnomer, actually, because owning a plumber's friend often means you won't have to call the plumber at all. "With friends like that," says the plumber, "who needs enemies?"

• Stepstool: Don't climb on furniture to reach the top shelf in your kitchen cabinet or change a lightbulb. You're likely to fall off or damage the furniture or both. A small foldable stepstool kept in the kitchen will come in handy time and again.

• Flashlight: Indispensable during power failures or when you've lost something under the bed.

Nine Household Repairs We Know You Can Do

Now that you've got your tools, you may feel all dressed up with nowhere to go. Don't worry. Just proceed with life, and sooner or later—probably sooner—the day will come when your tools will be pressed into service. Here are nine things that are bound to happen to you eventually.

A BLOWN FUSE

A fuse is a little gadget designed to protect you from your own foolishness. When the fuse senses too much electricity is being drawn on a single circuit, it "blows" and cuts off all the juice. This will happen when you have too many electrical appliances running at the same time, or when one of your appliances has a short circuit (a crossed wire, for example, that isn't making a proper electrical connection). You may be angry at the fuse for plunging you into darkness, but it really has your best interests at heart. You see, if it didn't turn off all the electricity, you might have set the apartment on fire.

Your first job is to find out exactly what caused the fuse to blow. Since a short circuit is a potentially hazardous situation, you'll want to rule out that possibility by checking carefully. Begin by totaling the wattages on all the appliances that went out when the fuse blew.

Now, locate your electrical service entrance panel, or fuse box. It's that steel-gray thing that looks like a wallsafe, and it's probably somewhere in the kitchen or, if you live in a house, the basement.

Open the box and look inside to find out if you have a 20-amp circuit or a 15-amp circuit. The amperage is often written on the fuse or circuit breaker switch itself. Now check the sum of the wattages of your appliances to see if you simply overloaded the circuit:

- A 15-amp circuit can hold only 1800 watts before it blows.
- A 20-amp circuit can hold only 2400 watts before it blows.

Is that what happened? If so, you're lucky, because a mere overload is a minor problem. Before you reset the fuse, change your extension cords so you don't have too many appliances coming out of one plug. Turn off some appliances, and try to be less greedy in the future.

But what if your wattages *don't* exceed the limit? You may have a short circuit in one of your appliances or in your internal electrical wiring. To find out which, you must turn off and unplug all the appliances and reset the fuse.

RESETTING A FUSE OR CIRCUIT BREAKER   Look inside your service entrance panel again to determine if you have a fuse system or a circuit breaker system. A fuse system has a bunch of little round things that look like bottle tops. A circuit breaker system has a panel of ordinary OFF/ON switches. Follow the directions that apply to you.

Be very careful when working in your fuse box, because you're dealing with a lot of electricity and you don't want to do your Sacco and Vanzetti impression if you can help it—especially if there's no one around to laugh. Wear rubber-soled sneakers, stand on a rubber mat, and wear gloves. Never use a screwdriver or pliers to remove the fuse. To be extra careful, turn off the switch marked MAIN. This will shut off all the power coming into your service panel.

If you have a fuse system: As you look at the row of fuses in your service entrance panel, you'll notice one fuse looks different from the others. The metal strip or spring inside it may be blackened or broken or the whole fuse may have "popped out." The odd-man fuse is the one that blew. If you have the pop-out kind, you need only push it back in. But if you have the kind with a metal strip or spring, you need to replace it.

Remove the blown fuse and take it to the hardware store. Ask the man for a box of fuses *exactly like* the one you're replacing. Don't replace a fuse with one that has a higher amperage, and never replace a fuse with a penny. (A penny may cause a fire because it can't tell when you're drawing too much electricity.) Screw in the new fuse, restore the power from the MAIN, and you're back in business.

If you have a circuit breaker system: Consider yourself lucky because circuit breakers are much easier to work with than fuses. One of the breaker switches will look different from the others. It will be in the OFF position, and it may have a little red stripe on it. All you have to do to restore power is turn it to the ON position. (With some systems, you may have to turn the switch to the RESET position and then the ON position.)

LOCATING THE SHORT CIRCUIT If the fuse blows or the circuit breaker trips immediately after you restore power—even though all your appliances and lights are turned off—then you have a short circuit in your internal wiring. You *must* call an electrician. This is a serious problem, and you can't fix it yourself.

If the fuse does not blow, check the plugs and electrical connections on each appliance for black smudge marks, frayed wires, burns, or the odor of electrical overheating. If you find such signs, you've found the culprit. Unplug the appliance and get it repaired before you use it again.

If you can't find the short circuit by visual inspection, you must play a game of electrical Russian Roulette. Turn on each appliance one at a time until you blow the fuse. The last one you turn on is the one with the short circuit. Unplug the appliance and get it fixed.

A RUNNING TOILET

Take a moment to familiarize yourself with the anatomy of a toilet. With apologies to Rube Goldberg, here's how a toilet works:

Relieved human being A pushes tank lever B, which lifts trip lever C and raises lift wire D. This pulls rubber tank ball E out of discharge opening F. When the discharge opening is clear, all the water in the tank rushes down into the bowl and down the drain. As the water drains from the tank, rubber tank ball E falls back down on

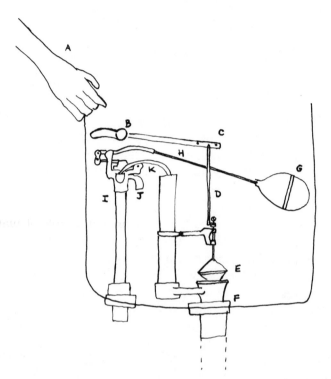

discharge opening F and float ball G descends with the water level. In doing so, float ball G pulls down float arm H, which opens supply valve I. Supply valve I refills the tank with water through discharge pipe J and refills toilet bowl through refill tube K. As the tank refills, float ball G rises with the water level, lifting float arm H until it is high enough to shut off supply valve I. At this point, the cycle is complete, and your toilet happily awaits your next command.

The most common problem you have with your toilet is when it doesn't refill properly and keeps running. There are four major causes: 1) your tank ball is worn out; 2) your lift wire is bent or misaligned; 3) your float ball is worn out; or 4) your float arm is bent. Here's how to diagnose and cure each problem:

WORN-OUT TANK BALL   After years of use, the rubber tank ball (E) will become frayed and chipped. When this happens, it cannot plug the discharge opening, and water continues to seep through, even after the flush cycle is complete. Since the water level in the tank cannot rise to its proper height, the float ball never gets high enough to shut off the supply valve. As a result, the supply valve continues to discharge water into the tank, creating a noise that eventually will cause you to take a high-powered rifle to the roof and begin firing on innocent citizens.

Here's how to fix it:

First, turn off the main water valve behind the toilet or in the basement. Now, flush the toilet to empty the tank of water. Reach down and unscrew the worn tank ball. Take it to the hardware store and buy a new one just like it. Screw on the new tank ball, restore the water supply . . . and enjoy!

BENT LIFT WIRE   If your tank ball is in good shape, the problem may be with the lift wire (D). Sometimes the lift wire is bent and will keep the tank ball from dropping squarely over the discharge opening. Jiggle the toilet lever a few times and look inside to see if the ball is falling directly onto the discharge opening. If not, you may need to buy a new lift wire (the hardware store carries them) or simply bend the old one back into shape.

WORN FLOAT BALL   If your float ball (G) has holes in it, it won't float. As a result, it won't rise high enough to shut off the supply valve. Buy a new float ball at the hardware store.

BENT FLOAT ARM   Sometimes the problem is not with the ball itself, but with the float arm (H) attached to it. If this is bent, it may keep the float ball from rising high enough to shut off the supply valve or it may allow the ball to rise *too* high, causing excess water to drain down the overflow tube (L). Straighten the arm, or buy a new one.

A BACKED-UP SINK

Haven't we warned you about pouring grease down the drain?

Well, this is what you get for not paying attention.

Unclogging a sink is like fighting an escalating war. You start out with conventional weapons and gradually move up to the serious stuff.

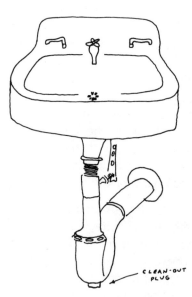

CLEAN-OUT
PLUG

• Phase one: (bayonets) Get a screwdriver and a wire coat hanger. Unwind the coat hanger until it is one long string of wire. Now remove the strainer at the bottom of the sink basin. If the clog is located directly under the strainer, you can work it out just by scraping and scouring it with the screwdriver and wire.

If that doesn't work, escalate to Phase Two.

• Phase two: (explosives) Boil a teapot full of water on the stove. Pour the boiling water down the sink, and chase it with a capful of ammonia. Take your plumber's helper and place it squarely over the drain. Plunge down vigorously four or five times. This creates an explosion of compressed air, which literally blows away the clog.

If *that* doesn't work, escalate to Phase Three.

• Phase three: (chemical warfare) Go to the grocery store and buy some commercial drain cleaners. Drano is one of the best-known names. Buy some rubber gloves while you're at it. Follow the directions explicitly, and please be careful. These chemicals will eat through your skin as easily as they'll eat through the clog. Be sure to clean the sink thoroughly when you're finished.

• Phase four: (surgical strike) Look below your sink for a U-shaped pipe located right underneath the drain. Chances are, the clog is located at the bottom of this U. Also located there is a clean-out plug. Put a bucket below the U-shaped pipe and unscrew the clean-out plug. Then use your wire and screwdriver to loosen the clog.

• Phase five: (surrender) Call the plumber.

A STOPPED-UP TOILET

Toilet bowls are somewhat more fragile than sinks, so your range of weaponry is comparatively limited. Don't use boiling water or chemicals in your toilet bowl, since they may damage the porcelain.

Take your plunger and place it squarely over the drainage opening at the bottom of the bowl. Plunge vigorously several times. When you're ready to try a test flush, be prepared to shut off the water supply quickly in case the toilet is still clogged. Repeat often.

If that doesn't work, call the plumber, because your other options are too sickening to contemplate.

A LEAKY FAUCET

If you're handy enough to try fixing a leaky faucet, you're much too handy to be reading this chapter. If not, for heaven's sake, call the plumber.

But if you can't get any sleep while you're waiting for him to arrive, try this:

Tie a string to the tip of the faucet and let it drop down into the sink. The droplets will "ride" down the string and make a soft (and quiet) landing at the bottom.

DEFROSTING THE REFRIGERATOR

The trick to defrosting your refrigerator is not to wait until it becomes a crisis situation. If you plan to do it once every two or three months, you will find it a simple and painless task. If, however, you wait until the freezer begins to look like Mt. Everest, you may have to chip away at the ice with a hammer and chisel to find your way to the thermostat.

Turn off your freezer compartment or, if necessary, unplug the entire refrigerator. Empty the freezer and put everything you wish to save in the refrigerator section or in a cooler. Boil water in a teakettle on the stove and pour it into a large roasting pan. Now, put the pan in the freezer. The heat generated from the hot water will melt the ice to the point where you can easily scrape and lift it out with your hands. Keep adding fresh boiling water every few minutes. Once you've removed all the ice, sponge down the freezer with baking soda and water. The whole process will take no longer than a half hour, and your food will still be frozen.

PAINTING

You could write an entire book on the subject of painting, so this one brief section must be limited to basic advice. Perhaps the best tip we can give you is to refrain from painting until you've tried to get your landlord to do it for you. Once you've exhausted the usual arguments, you might consider one of these:

1. Tell your landlord you've discovered a wonderful new shade of purple and you can't wait to get started on the job yourself.

2. Tell your landlord that if he won't paint the apartment, your only alternative is to buy some of that Playboy brand wallpaper you've been admiring.

3. Tell the landlord you want to do the job yourself but you have one question before you begin: "What's the difference between paint and varnish?"

If none of these approaches works, you may be forced to do your own painting. But don't worry, it isn't that difficult. In fact, if you put yourself in the right frame of mind, buy a six-pack of beer, and turn on the radio, you might even enjoy it.

For the best results, follow these tips:

BUY GOOD EQUIPMENT   People who paint infrequently are often tempted to buy the cheapest tools they can find and throw everything away when they're done. That's a mistake. Buy good equipment and keep it for the next time you paint. Go to a paint store—not a hardware store—to buy your supplies. You'll not only find a higher grade of equipment, but you'll get better advice from the sales clerks.

Here's what you need:

• Paint: Tell the sales clerk exactly what you plan to do, and ask for his advice. Generally speaking, latex paint is easier to work with than enamel. It dries fast, cleans with soap and water, and doesn't smell. Some jobs, however, *require* enamel paint—especially the bathroom, kitchen, baseboards, moldings, and any area that occasionally needs to be wiped clean. Buy the best paint you can afford, and if you buy enamel paint, be sure to get a can of solvent to clean your brush and roller afterward.

Buy *enough* paint. As a rule of thumb, one gallon of paint covers 400 square feet of wall space. But don't forget you're going to use two coats. Better to have too much paint on hand than too little, because you can always save leftover paint for next time.

• Brush: Ask the salesman for advice (based on the kind of paint you've chosen and the type of job you're going to do), and buy the best brush you can afford.

- Painting hat: Unless you want to look prematurely gray!
- Roller: Look for a sturdy roller with an extension handle for ceilings and high walls.
- Rolling pan: Buy a deep and rugged pan.
- Dropcloth: Get a professional canvas model, not the flimsy plastic kind that will drive you bonkers in minutes.
- Spackling mix: If you have chips and cracks in your wall, you may want to patch them with spackle before you paint. Just follow the directions on the label. Let it dry before you begin painting, and rub the spackled area with sandpaper for a smooth surface.
- Stepladder: We hope you already own one of these. But if not, beg, steal, or borrow one before you begin to paint.

BE PREPARED   Don't rush headlong into the job; take a moment to compose yourself and prepare your apartment before you begin. Make sure your furniture is covered with old sheets and your floor is protected by a sturdy dropcloth. Open the windows to make breathing easier and to help the paint dry faster.

FOLLOW CONVENTIONAL TECHNIQUES   We know you like to do everything in your own special way, but when it comes to painting, you'll save time and effort by following standard operating procedures:

- Paint the ceiling first, the walls second.
- Always use two coats of paint, even if the first one looks okay. Otherwise, you'll have to paint again before you know it.
- Don't overpaint or underpaint. You are overpainting if globs of congealed paint accumulate in the seams of the wall. You're underpainting if you don't brush over every area at least twice.

SEWING BUTTONS

You'll probably never miss your mother as much as you will on the first day a button pops off your shirt. But don't throw away the whole shirt in despair. Sewing on a button is easier than you think.

Go to the dime store and buy a small sewing kit. The Singer Company makes a great one, including needles, thread, scissors, and a thimble, for less than two bucks.

Now follow these steps:

1. Using thread of a matching or neutral color, cut off a piece about two feet long.

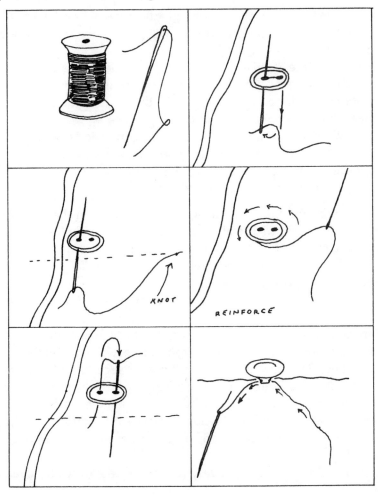

2. Thread one end through the eye of the needle.

3. Run the thread halfway through and bring the two strands together by moistening your thumb and forefinger and rolling the two strands into one. Loop the thread once around your forefinger and make a knot.

4. You're probably *replacing* a button rather than installing a new one, so you will see the holes in the material where the old thread was. If so, place the button so the holes in it correspond to the ones in the fabric.

5. Bring the needle *up* through the material and through one of the button holes. Your knot will prevent the thread from coming all the way through.

6. Bring the needle *down* through the next hole and continue this process—up and through, down and through—several times. If there are four holes in the button, for example, repeat until you've used all of them.

7. When the button feels secure, bring the needle *down and through* one last time and make a knot on the side of the fabric opposite the button, as close to the fabric as possible.

8. Cut the thread behind the knot.

If the button you're working on has an eye on the back (a little circle made of metal or plastic) instead of holes, use a similar technique: *up* through the fabric, loop through the eye, and *down* through the fabric; repeat until secure. Try to keep all your stitches close together.

If the button is going on a coat or jacket, use a heavy thread. Begin the process just as you would for an ordinary shirt button, but slip a wooden matchstick between the button and the fabric. This will prevent you from sewing the button on too tightly. Sew up and down until it feels secure, and remove the match. The button should be hanging a little loose. Bring the needle up through the fabric one last time and wrap it around and around the threads between the button and the fabric as reinforcement. Then bring the needle down through the fabric and knot it.

If you are working with very heavy material (a winter overcoat, for example), consider it money well spent to find a tailor or dry cleaner who will replace the button for you. They will use heavy nylon thread, which will keep the button on longer.

RIPS AND TEARS

Of course, losing buttons isn't the only calamity that can befall your wardrobe. Three-cornered tears and holes in the pockets are just two of the heartaches and thousand natural shocks that wool is heir to. If these things happen to you, use *iron-on fabric tape.* You can buy it at a dime store.

1. Match the color of the iron-on tape to the color of your torn garment. Bring the garment with you to the store rather than trust your memory.

2. Turn the fabric inside out.

3. Smooth out the torn threads as much as possible.

4. Cut a piece of iron-on tape in a circle or oblong shape with no sharp edges; make sure it's large enough to cover the tear.

5. Following the directions on the package, iron the tape on the *inside* of the garment. When you turn it right side out, neither the tear nor the patch should be noticeable.

There's a wonderful product on the market now called Stitch Witchery. You're sure to find many uses for it. When changing a hem length, for example, this tape eliminates the need for needle and thread. Just follow the directions on the package and iron the tape in place. Between Stitch Witchery and iron-on-patches, you can probably live your entire life without ever touching a sewing machine, and believe us, that's a blessing.

Home Security: Burglary

No matter what kind of neighborhood you live in, you face the threat of being robbed. Yet you can reduce your chances of suffering such a disaster if you take a few steps to protect yourself.

Start by considering the psychology of the typical apartment burglar. Nine times out of ten, he is not a professional. After all, why would a professional burglar be interested in your apartment? He is far too busy stealing priceless art collections to be overly concerned about your Sony Walkman.

No. The person robbing you is probably an amateur. Probably young. Probably scared. Quite possibly a junkie. He is looking for an easy job: an apartment that is easy to enter, with valuables that are easy to "fence." (He likes television sets and jewelry especially, but he's not above selecting a leather jacket for personal use.) Most important, he'd rather not have anything to do with you if he can help it. This is a robbery, after all, not a social call.

Such a burglar is like the cockroach we discussed in Chapter 6: You can't really stop him, but you *can* encourage him to bother someone else. To do so, you must deter him, delay him, and detect him.

You *deter* a burglar by giving your home the *appearance* of being secure. Burglar alarm stickers (even if you don't have a burglar alarm), crowbar guards, and lights that make it look like you're at home when you really aren't—all carry a strong subliminal message for the burglar: namely, "Try another apartment."

You *delay* the burglar by installing strong locks, strong doors, and whatever additional devices you can afford. Every minute you add to the time it takes to break into your apartment brings the thief one step closer to changing his mind about the whole deal.

And you *detect* the burglar by installing an alarm, buying a dog, installing outside lights and, most important, following the golden rule of home security:

LOVE THY NEIGHBOR.

Yes, when it comes to preventing losses from both theft and fire, the smartest thing you can do is make friends with your neighbor. Make a pact to keep an eye on each other's apartment. Offer to pick up his mail and newspaper when he's away. When you get to know him better, you might even exchange apartment keys.

In apartment buildings, good neighbors must protect each other by establishing commonsense rules. Never buzz someone through the door unless you know who it is. Don't let anyone follow you into the building unless you recognize him as another tenant. When you go through the front door, always take a moment to make sure it locks behind you. And if the hallway or foyer lights have burned out, raise a stink with the landlord.

LOCKS

The most important thing to know about locks is that they don't work very well unless you use them. Most burglars couldn't pick a lock if their life depended on it, but they seldom have to . . . because victims obligingly leave their doors and windows open. In a recent spot check by the Pittsburgh police department, no fewer than 16 apartments in one 60-unit building were found unlocked.

Next to the fellow who leaves his door unlocked, the burglar's favorite victim is the guy who puts a hundred expensive locks on his door but neglects to buy a decent door. If a door doesn't fit snugly in its frame, a simple flick of a crowbar will defeat the best locks money can buy. And if the hinges of a door are located on the outside, the burglar will ignore the locks entirely and simply remove the door! No wonder crime prevention experts often say, "A lock is only as strong as the door it's on."

If you're moving into a new apartment, change the locks

immediately. You never know who has the keys to the old locks. In most cases, you can save money by asking the lock-smith to install new cylinders instead of entirely new locks.

What kind of locks should you buy?

A jimmy-proof dead-bolt rim lock affords the best protection. This kind of lock is not built in the door but attached to the *surface* of it. It's jimmy-proof because the deadbolt drops down vertically instead of horizontally, which makes it harder to pry.

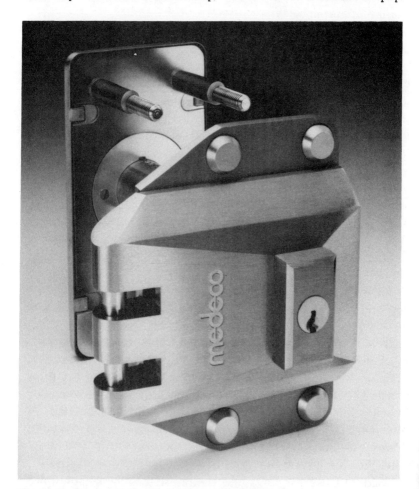

The Rolls Royce of deadbolt locks—Medeco.

The worst lock you can have on your front door is the spring-latch, or key-in-the-knob, lock. A burglar can break this lock simply by knocking off the doorknob with a good whack from his crowbar. Or if he wants to be quiet, he can "slip" the lock, using his Gold American Express card. If your front door is secured with a spring-latch lock, you won't be safe until you add at least one, preferably two, deadbolt locks.

You may want to consider buying a double-cylinder lock. They can be locked from both outside and inside. Since criminals usually enter through the window and leave through the door with their hands full of goodies, one of these locks can really spoil a burglar's day. Double-cylinder locks have one disadvantage, though. Unless you're very careful to keep keys near the door when *you* are inside the apartment, you may find yourself locked indoors someday with a blazing fire, mumbling, "Now, where the heck did I put those keys?"

There's one last type of door lock worthy of our attention: the chain lock. This lock is designed to let you crack the door to see who's on the other side before you open it all the way. But even for this modest function, the chain lock isn't very effective. Once you've released the dead-bolt locks and opened the door slightly, a big man can throw his weight against the door and send the chain lock flying. We suggest you install a peephole instead.

If you're like most people, you'll pay much attention to locking and securing your front door and little or none to locking your windows. Yet the window is the thief's favorite point of entry!

The simple twist-type sash locks on most windows are horridly ineffective. One tug with a crowbar is enough to pry them loose. Fortunately, you have an inexpensive and effective alternative. You can "pin" your windows, as we've illustrated. All you need is an electric drill and a couple of long metal eyebolts. Make sure the eyebolts slip in and out easily, so you won't have trouble getting out in a fire.

Sliding glass windows and doors are a security nightmare, but there are a few things you can do. Saw off an old

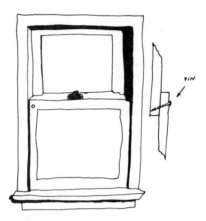

broomstick and put it in the tracks. Pin the spot where the two sliding doors meet, just as you did with your regular sash windows. Or ask your locksmith to install a key-operated dead-bolt lock designed especially for sliding glass doors and windows.

Why go to such efforts to protect your windows when all a thief has to do is break the glass and walk in? It sounds like a good question until you realize burglars don't *like* to break glass. They'd much rather go into your apartment quietly. If you present them with the choice of breaking glass or moving on to some other apartment, they're bound to choose the latter.

WHAT TO DO WHEN YOU'RE AWAY ON VACATION

The trick to protecting your home when you're away for an extended period of time is to make it look like you are *not* away. Begin by telling your most trusted neighbor when you plan to be on vacation. Give him the keys to your apartment and a phone number to reach you in an emergency. Ask him to pick up your mail and newspaper. If you haven't yet cultivated such a neighbor, file a hold-mail order with the post office and cancel your newspaper service.

Go to the hardware store and buy two or three electrical timers. You can get them for less than ten dollars each, and they offer great protection. We suggest you hook one to your radio, one to your TV, and one to a lamp. Be careful not to overload your timer with an appliance that has a higher wattage than it can handle. Check the labels on both the timer and the appliance before you connect them.

Set your timers to go off at different times. Here's a good schedule:

> Lights: dusk to 9:00 P.M.
> Television: 9:00 P.M. to 2:00 A.M.
> Radio: 6:00 A.M. to 5:00 P.M.

Tune your radio to a news or talk station and set the volume just loud enough to be heard softly from outside. It's not a bad idea to turn the radio on *any time* you leave your apartment, even for only a few hours.

WHAT TO DO IF A BURGLAR IS WAITING FOR YOU WHEN YOU GET HOME

If you come home from an evening out and notice your door ajar or any other sign of burglary, stop right there.

Go to your neighbor's or to a phone booth and call the police. Never enter an apartment that appears to have been robbed. If you surprise the burglar while he is at work, he might just turn around and shoot you.

In New York City, where people have a lot of experience with burglaries, some folks leave a $20 bill sitting within plain view of the front door whenever they're away. As soon as they open the door upon their return, they look to see if the bill is still there. If not, they close the door and call the cops.

If you have fully entered your apartment before you realize it has been robbed, call the police immediately. Don't touch anything, and don't clean up to have it nice and tidy before the cops arrive.

If the burglar is still there, look him right in the eye and say,

"Take whatever you want. I won't try to stop you." Don't make any aggressive moves, but stand passively and use the time to get a good physical description of the crook. If, however, he attacks you, you must do everything you can to protect yourself. Screaming is always a good idea, but yell "Fire" instead of "Help." Yelling "Help" turns your neighbors into cowards; yelling "Fire" attracts many eager volunteers.

Home Security: Fire

Cigarettes, grease, and electricity are the three biggest culprits when it comes to fire in the home. Yet you can protect yourself from the threat they pose by taking just a few minutes to fire-proof your apartment.

Many devastating apartment fires begin with a small grease fire in the oven or on the range. When the panicked cook tries to douse the flame with a glass of water, he is horrified to see the water spreading the grease—and the fire—further. In moments the fire is raging through the kitchen, and the apartment must be evacuated. We recommend you buy a small fire extinguisher and keep it mounted on the kitchen wall, within easy reach of the stove. Learn how it works, and don't hesitate to use it on any grease fire—no matter how minor it may seem. Believe us, ruining your T-bone steak is better than losing everything you own. If you can't afford a fire extinguisher, keep an open box of baking soda by the stove and pour it over the fire.

You can prevent electrical fires by making periodic inspections of your electrical appliances and wiring. Check the cords on your appliances from time to time to see if they are hot to the touch or if they smell like they're burning. If so, disconnect the appliance and don't use it again until it's fixed. Always use new extension cords, and never overload your electrical outlets by adding too many multiple plugs.

Cigarette fires are the easiest kind to prevent.

Quit smoking.

If you're not ready for that step, however, promise yourself you won't smoke in bed (or any other place where you have a tendency to fall asleep). Get in the habit of checking for lit cigarettes before you leave your apartment. And empty your ashtrays in the toilet, not the wastebasket.

The home smoke alarm is one of the best inventions to come along in many years. If your landlord has not given you one, go out and buy your own. It will only cost between $15 and $30, and it can literally save your life. Get the kind that gives a little warning sound when the batteries are low, and follow the instructions on installation very carefully, because a smoke alarm in the wrong spot is almost useless. Check your alarm at least once a month by blowing out a lit match a few inches beneath the alarm.

Finally, spend a few moments designing and rehearsing an escape plan to use in case of fire. You should have at least two different ways to get out of your apartment in a hurry. If your building doesn't have a fire escape, you can buy yourself a rope ladder and keep it attached to the radiator by the window. Once you've planned your escape routes, promise yourself you'll never hesitate to use them. Running from a fire and calling the fire department is almost always the smartest thing to do. Never fight a fire on your own for more than sixty seconds before you give up and get out.

How to Become a Decent Human in 7 Days or Less—
Commonsense Etiquette

It all seems so silly when you're young: the right things to say and the things you mustn't ever say; what *must* be done and what simply *isn't* done. But something changes as you grow older and take your place in the world. You are no longer just a member of a family, answering only to Mom and Dad. Now you are a member of society and must answer to every other member as a responsible adult. Etiquette may seem trivial when you're growing up. But one day, when *you* are hurt by someone's rude behavior or inconvenienced by their thoughtlessness, the importance of etiquette will become painfully clear.

One of the least fortunate legacies of the sixties and seventies is that many people grew up and reached adulthood believing the rules of etiquette and polite behavior were no longer "relevant."

"Do your own thing" was the motto of an entire generation of youngsters, many of whom are now wondering why no one seems to like them. As long as you don't care what other people think of you, this philosophy of life works well. But when the time comes to look for a job, find a mate, or meet friends, your image in the eyes of others becomes a matter of some importance.

As the hippie generation grew up, those who did not move to Maine or California for a life of pot smoking brought their boorishness with them into the business world and made it respectable. They attended "assertiveness training" seminars to learn how to be rude in a systematic way, and they read books with titles like "Get Yours," which told them it was okay to behave like venomous snakes.

In recent years, the pendulum has begun to swing back in the other direction. The importance of courtesy, etiquette, and kindness is reasserting itself. But there's one problem. The children of the sixties and seventies (and now *their* children) don't know *how* to be polite. They never learned. Growing up thinking it was irrelevant, they never bothered to read the rules of etiquette or observe the good manners of their elders.

Are you, like so many of us, getting a late start on all this? Don't worry about it. Etiquette is not the complex subject it's believed to be. The old-fashioned etiquette books were crammed full of rules, but they can all be boiled down to one: Do unto others as you would have them do unto you. Etiquette is not a matter of arbitrary rules at all, but rather a set of guidelines designed to help us avoid hurting each other. Like stoplights and traffic laws, they allow us to maneuver through social situations without crashing into another person's feelings or totalling our own ego with embarrassment.

We'll begin with a look at thank-you notes and the other kind notes that are the mark of a polite gentleman or lady. We'll discuss both formal and informal invitations and how to respond to them, and we'll show you how to be the ideal overnight guest. Finally, we'll conclude with some advice on how to have, and how to *be,* a good neighbor. Throughout this chapter, we beg the forgiveness of William Shakespeare, whose characters we've used to illustrate the finer points of how polite men and women behave.

The Thank-You Letter and Other Kind Notes

The most distinctive mark of a polite and thoughtful individual is a penchant for writing notes. All kinds of notes. Thank-you notes, condolence notes, notes of congratulations and good cheer. There is perhaps no better way to cultivate the friendship and earn the respect of the important people in your life than to shower them with notes.

Notes should be spontaneous and not studied. Sometimes it helps to speak the words aloud so the note sounds like a conversation. Sure, you could call. But the thought that you took the time to sit down, write, and mail the note means a lot to the recipient. He never has to know the truth: namely, that writing a quick thank-you note actually takes *less* time than a phone call.

And that raises an important point. Don't procrastinate on writing notes. The one-paragraph note you write and mail to-day is much better than the ten-page essay you never get around to. We're convinced the number-one cause of pro-crastination on thank-you letters is that many of us secretly be-lieve we are undiscovered literary geniuses and that all our letters are being saved for posterity, probably by some large university in the Midwest. How can we cheat generations of English Lit. students by writing, "Thanks for the bash last night. It was super." So we laboriously compose thank-you letters in our mind: "My dear friend and colleague, Jimmy. It is with a bittersweet sense of fond memory that I write to thank you for your festive and sensuous blah, blah, blah." Unfortunately, let-ters like these never quite get written, do they?

So what do you say? Well, let's look at some of the occa-sions that call for a thank-you note and give you a few sugges-tions on what to write.

THANK-YOU NOTES

In a note of thanks for a dinner party, you might mention specifically one of the foods that was served. If there were other guests, you could say how congenial they were or even single out one or two by name with whom you found a common interest. Your hostess will be delighted to learn that the "mix" worked.

Naturally, anytime you receive a gift you should write a note of thanks. Showers, weddings, or birthday and Christmas presents that are received by mail should all be acknowledged promptly. There's nothing more frustrating than to send a wedding present and never hear if the person has received it. The old etiquette books said you had a year to write these notes, but please don't take a year. If the package really has been lost along the way, it's not easy for the sender to deal with the store or the post office a year later.

Be sure to mention the gift by name in your letter and tell the giver what you intend to do with it. Even if it wasn't exactly what you were hoping for, don't write, "Thank you for the lovely gift." Instead, say, "I just adore the plastic bird cage you sent us. Until I can find the perfect bird to occupy it, I'm using it as a planter, and it looks marvelous. Thanks so much for thinking of me." You don't have to mention that you keep your new planter out by the trash.

There are many other occasions when a thank-you note is appropriate. Perhaps someone wrote a personal recommendation for you when you applied for a new job. That certainly deserves a note. Just say how much you appreciated his taking the time to write.

Was a store clerk particularly helpful when you were looking for just the right pillow for your new couch? Maybe she searched the stock room, called another one of their stores, arranged to have one especially ordered. If you feel she went out of her way to be helpful, write a note to the store. Even if you don't have her name, a brief description of her and the department in which she works will suffice. In these days of get-it-yourself shopping, where the clerk's only responsibility seems to be collecting your money, the helpful employee should be rewarded. And a thank-you note in her personnel file is a great way to do it.

The impact of a timely thank-you note can be tremendous. Think how King Lear's unhappy life would have changed if his eldest daughters had taken five minutes to write this simple thank you.

> Dear Pop,
>
> On behalf of both Goneril and myself, I want to thank you for giving us each one third of Britain. I'm sure we'll find many, many exciting uses for this land. Cornwall and I have already built a castle on our section, and we want you to know you're invited to visit anytime. In fact, we're thinking of taking the castle and going co-op, and we'd be glad to give you one of the best units at an insider's price, if you ever wanted to come live with us . . . which, of course, we would just adore! Again, thank you for your generosity. You are the greatest father ever.
>
> > Love,
> > Regan

Notice how Regan takes care to mention the gift and to tell her father exactly what she intends to do with it. Even more important, she remembers to emphasize the fine qualities of the *giver* more than those of the gift itself. She makes it clear that she loves her father and wants to see him more often. Expressing love and affection for the giver, not the gift, is the essence of a good thank-you note.

THE GET-WELL NOTE

In the cheer-up note, do just that. When writing to someone in the hospital, don't go through a long list of your own illnesses in the hope your friend will consider himself lucky to be better off than you. Instead, try a story he might have missed, or include some news of a mutual friend. There are wonderful greeting cards available for all occasions, and the humorous ones designed for hospital patients are among the best. But be sure to include a personal note as well. When sending a card to a sick friend, take into account what the problem is and choose the card accordingly. If it's a serious illness (one from which it's unlikely your friend will recover), it's best not to send cards that suggest he is fooling around with the nurses or that he will be "back on his feet in no time." Just write, "I'm thinking of you," and he'll know what you mean.

Here's how Hamlet handled the get-well note.

Ophelia
c/o St. Mary's Convent
Copenhagen, Denmark

Dear Ophelia,

Just a short note to cheer you up and to wish you a speedy recovery.

I'm so glad you took my advice to get away to a place where you could have a chance to rest and think things over. I think it's just what the doctor ordered.

Things are about the same here at Elsinore. I stabbed a rat behind a curtain the other day, and it turned out to be your father. God, did I feel like a fool! Get well soon. We miss you, babe.

Yours,
Hamlet

Hamlet's brief letter contains many of the elements of a good get-well note. Although he makes polite reference to Ophelia's disease, he does not dwell on it. Instead, he merely implies that he is confident in her quick recovery. He goes on to tell her an amusing anecdote, and he closes by saying everyone misses her and wants her back.

CONDOLENCE NOTES

Notes of sympathy to a bereaved friend are probably the most difficult to write, but if you are sincere and genuine, you can't go too far wrong. Write promptly—as soon as you hear the bad news—because you don't want to make this difficult note any more so by having to excuse yourself for tardiness. If you yourself have lost someone close to you, you might mention that in the note and let the person know you understand what he's going through. But if you haven't had this experience, don't say you know how it feels, because you don't. Better just to say how very sorry you are, adding that he or she will be in your prayers. Most important, when the busy time has passed for this friend and the loneliness has taken hold, make a point of seeing him.

Here's what King Claudius of Denmark said to his nephew Hamlet on the death of Hamlet's dad.

> Dear Hamlet,
>   I was saddened to learn of the death of your father, and I want to express my sympathy to you. I want you to know you are very much in my thoughts and my prayers at this difficult time. (In fact, I actually thought I *saw* you during my prayers last night.) If you ever need help of any kind, please feel free to call on me and my wife, er, your mother, I mean your father's widow, uh, you know who I mean, the queen, Gertie.
>
>   Your uncle,
>   Claudius
>   (acting king of Denmark)

Claudius wisely keeps his expressions of sympathy brief. Notice he does not dwell on his own grief (even though he was the brother of the deceased) but rather seeks to comfort Hamlet on *his* loss. As all good sympathy notes do, this one ends with a sincere offer to help the bereaved in any way possible.

Incidentally, if, unhappily, you are the person who is bereaved, remember that flowers and condolence letters should always be acknowledged by a personal note. Printed cards for this purpose have become common, but they will never take the place of a personal note of thanks. Even if someone has sent you a commercial sympathy card, reply with a note.

NOTES OF CONGRATULATIONS

Congratulations can be sent for a variety of reasons. You got the job; I'm proud of you. You got the girl; I'm envious. You won an award; no one deserves it more. The note of congratulations helps people savor the important moments in their lives, making them last just a little longer. Shylock would have earned a better reputation in history if he'd taken a moment to write this note.

> Dear Antonio,
>
> So, I read in the papers the other day your ships finally came in. I knew they would. You are a skilled importer, and you richly deserve the financial reward you'll reap from this success.
>
> Listen, that "pound of flesh" business was just a joke. I hope you didn't take it seriously. You can come to me for a low-interest loan anytime. I know things got a little tense in court the other day. But stop by sometime for some bagels and lox, and we'll have a good laugh about it. Again, congratulations on your success, and take your time paying me the 3,000 ducats. I know you're good for it.
>
> Your friend and colleague,
> Shylock

Shylock has used this note of congratulations to mend some fences. Not a bad idea. The third line is a masterful touch in the art of writing congratulations notes: It implies the recipient *deserves* his good fortune.

COMPLAINT LETTERS

The letter of complaint may not be the nicest note you can write, but it sure is the most satisfying. Don't take your satisfaction, however, by being rude and sarcastic. The object of a good complaint letter is to get results, and the way to do that is to be polite. "Kill 'em with kindness" is the operative phrase. Be specific about the nature of your complaint, be firm about what remedy you desire, and support your claim with as much factual evidence and documentation as you can assemble.

Here's how Theseus, duke of Athens, did it.

Mr. Nick Bottom
Bottom Productions
Athens, Greece

Dear Mr. Bottom,

On Saturday, July 2, I contracted with your firm to perform a dramatic sketch and dance for the entertainment of my guests after dinner. I paid a sum, in advance, of 250 ducats for what I was led to believe would be an elaborate production, using professional actors and sophisticated sound and light equipment. Instead, what I got was an exceedingly amateurish performance, which fell short of my expectations in several key respects:

First, instead of professional actors, the performers were clearly local tradesmen who showed very little musical or dramatic talent.

Second, instead of elaborate scenery, there was one actor who was assigned to play a wall and who held his index and middle finger in the air to indicate a chink in that wall. A second actor portrayed the moon by carrying a lantern.

Third, instead of the "high-tech sound and lights" that were mentioned in your advertisements, the entire play was lit by the moonlight showing through a casement window in my living room.

I feel I was misled by your ads and your salesman as to the exact nature of the service I contracted for, and I want my money refunded in full.

I enclose copies of your invoice and my cancelled check, plus a copy of the "guarantee of satisfaction" given to me by your employee, Mr. Peter Quince.

I look forward to hearing from you by the end of July, before I seek assistance elsewhere.

Thank you for your prompt attention to this matter.

> Sincerely,
> Theseus
> duke of Athens

Theseus has written an ideal complaint letter. It is polite but firm. Although he makes it clear how dissatisfied he was with the entertainment provided, he resists the temptation to become sarcastic and threatening. The letter begins with specifics, like the date of the performance and the amount paid. It then lists a series of particular complaints. It continues with a firm and specific request for satisfaction: "I want my money refunded in full." Theseus supports his claim with copies of relevant documents, and he politely gives Mr. Bottom a reasonable but definite deadline for resolving the problem. All things considered, a very effective note. In fact, if Bottom does not respond to this letter, he is truly an ass.

STATIONERY SUPPLIES

By now, you should be eager to begin writing notes to everyone you know, so don't use a lack of proper writing supplies as a cop-out. Except when you're replying to formal invitations, you can write a note on almost any kind of paper. If you begin to enjoy writing notes and you want to make your mark as a proper gentleman or lady, you might want to lay in a small supply of notepaper and greeting cards. If you have some money to spend, consider ordering personal stationery with an engraved monogram on the letterhead and your return address on the envelopes. If you're not quite ready for that step, go to a card shop and buy some commercially printed notepaper. Women should look for a plain white or cream-colored paper with a subtle design, while men are better off sticking to gray or tan paper without embellishment. A box of simple cards that say "Thank You" on the outside and have empty space on the inside for you to write a short note will come in very handy. If notepaper seems expensive to you, remember this: Commercially printed greeting cards sell for a dollar or more at a pop. If you write more than a few thank yous, happy birthdays, and congratulations during the year, your investment will pay off very quickly.

While you're at the stationery store, buy yourself a small engagement calendar and keep it by your telephone.

Why an engagement calendar?

Well, now that you're widely known as a nice person, you might just receive an invitation.

The Invitation and How to Respond

The golden rule of replying to invitations is to respond in the same manner and style that the invitation was issued. Today, many invitations are made casually over the telephone. If you're able to say yes or no right then, it's perfectly acceptable to leave it at that. If your answer is yes, all you have to do is mark your engagement calendar and show up at the appointed time and place. If you have to consult with another person before answering, however, try to get back as soon as possible. Another phone call is all it takes.

THE RSVP

Sometimes, though, things become more complicated. Suppose you receive a written invitation to a party and at the bottom of the card are the letters RSVP. From the French expression *répondez s'il vous plaît,* meaning "reply if you please," this notation is your cue to issue a written response. Some people prefer to write "please reply" on their invitations, which obviously means the same thing. If you've been invited to a large affair where the exact number of guests is not as important as it is, say, for a small dinner party, you may receive an invitation bearing the words *regrets only,* which means you should reply only if you *cannot* attend. If a telephone number is indicated after the RSVP, it's perfectly polite to respond by phone, but you can never go wrong by sending a note. Since most of the invitations you receive will be informal, feel free to respond in a friendly and casual manner. "Dear Jane, I can't think of a better way to spend Friday night than to have dinner with you and Joe. See you then."

FORMAL INVITATIONS

But what about those infrequent yet important occasions when you receive a *formal* invitation? This is when you should break out your good notepaper, your best pen, and write a formal response. Refer to yourself in the third person and use the wording of the invitation itself as a guide for how to phrase your response. Use your best handwriting and try to center the lines on the page. (Be sure you respond to the people who issued the invitation and not to the bridal couple themselves.)

Let's suppose you receive the following wedding invitation in the mail·

Lord Capulet and Lady Capulet
request the honor of your presence
at the marriage of their daughter
Juliet
to
Romeo (whose last name we'd rather not mention)
on Saturday, the sixteenth of June
at twelve o'clock noon
St. Mary's Church
Verona, Italy

RSVP

Here's how you respond:

Ms. Jane Smith
accepts with pleasure
the kind invitation of
Lord and Lady Capulet
for
Saturday, the sixteenth of June
at twelve o'clock noon

If you must decline, follow this format:

Ms. Jane Smith
sincerely regrets that she will be unable to accept
the kind invitation of
Lord and Lady Capulet
for
Saturday, the sixteenth of June
due to

At this point, fill in some decent excuse.

GOOD EXCUSES

- an illness in the family
- a sudden death in the family
- a European vacation

BAD EXCUSES

- the fact she is washing her hair that evening
- the fact that the final episode of *Dynasty* is on that night
- the fact that something better came up

If you must decline the formal invitation of a very close friend or relative, answer in the formal style, but include a personal note explaining in more detail why you cannot attend (and, of course, how upset you are about it).

Why all this formality? Well, a wedding is one of the most

important events in most people's lives, and because of that, they tend to save every little scrap of paper, ribbon, and matchbook cover that had anything to do with it. It's common for the bridal couple or their parents to make a book out of these formal responses and keep it forever. In fact, this may be the closest you ever get to immortality, so why not play the game?

Presents

When are you obligated to give someone a present?

Never.

Well, almost never.

If you have been invited to a wedding reception and you plan to *attend*, it is very bad form to drink the father of the bride's liquor, munch his hors d'oeuvres, and gobble his roast beef without offering some kind of tribute to his daughter and her new husband. The same applies to any such event (like a shower, birthday party, or christening) where you will partake of someone else's hospitality.

These occasions aside, however, presents should come from the heart, not from a sense of obligation. That's what makes them meaningful. No matter how many wedding invitations, birth announcements, and graduation cards you receive, don't send a present unless you love the person and have a genuine desire to show him your affection. It's perfectly polite to respond to all of the above with a congratulatory note or the proper RSVP.

Now that we've let you off the hook, however, you should know there are many times when a little gift is a thoughtful touch.

DINNER PARTIES If you're invited to a friend's home for dinner, something as simple as a bottle of inexpensive wine or a bunch of flowers from a street vendor is appropriate. You certainly don't have to take a gift every time someone suggests you stop by to share a pizza. But if a friend is going to some trouble to prepare a pleasant evening for you, a small gift is a nice way of saying thanks.

OVERNIGHT INVITATIONS   When you are invited to someone's house for the weekend, by all means take along a gift. Try some guest soap or a hardcover book that you know they'd enjoy. It doesn't have to be fancy or expensive, just thoughtful. If your budget permits, a basket with some unusual food items inside is a different kind of hospitality gift. Be careful when you buy knick-knacks or works of art that will be conspicuous by their absence when you visit your friend's home later.

"Say, Jim, where's that felt nude I bought you the last time you invited me to your beach cottage?"

"Uh, well, we have it in cold storage for the summer, Bob, but we just love it."

PARTIES   As for those occasions when you're expected to bring a gift, don't feel you have to spend a lot of money to be remembered. The mark of a good gift is the amount of thought, not the amount of cash, that goes into it. If you're invited to a friend's birthday party, for example, you might consider making a collage from old snapshots of the two of you. You can buy a frame with multiple openings at the dime store and make a memorable gift in minutes.

SHOWERS   Choosing a gift for a shower is easy, because showers are usually organized along a theme. There are wedding showers, baby showers, kitchen showers, and so on. If you've been invited to a shower, go to the appropriate department in a large store and look for something in your price range.

WEDDINGS   Your choice of wedding gift will be simplified if you ask the bride's mother where the couple is registered. Brides-to-be often fill out a long list of things they need at one or two local department stores. The store will give you a copy of this list and will note which items have already been sold. When it comes to buying china, silver, pottery, and stainless flatware, you *must* check with the store to learn what pattern the bride has chosen. But checking the registry also comes in handy in choosing towels, sheets, and even kitchen equipment. You don't want to give a purple colander, for example, to someone who is planning an entire apartment in shades of dusty rose.

Send your wedding gift ahead of time, if you can. In most cases the store will gladly send it for you. Wedding gifts should be mailed to the *bride's* home, or to the new home of the married couple. Try not to drag your gift with you to the wedding reception (although a dozen or so people always do). In the confusion at the reception, cards are sometimes lost or mixed up, and the bridal couple won't know whether you sent the microwave oven or the plastic salt and pepper shaker!

Nine Ways to Be the Ideal Overnight Guest

Ben Franklin summed it up for all time when he said that "fish and visitors begin to stink after three days." But have you ever known fish to last that long? We've noticed that unless you put them in the freezer, fish and visitors will start to smell pretty bad after about a day and a half. Fish really have no control over this, especially since they're dead, but the wise visitor knows how to keep himself fresh.

It takes an average of ten years after college to disabuse people of the notion they can drop in on their friends without notice, spread a sleeping bag on the floor, and stay for an indefinite period of time without jeopardizing the friendship. It also takes about a decade after college for some people to realize invitations to visit are often issued more out of a sense of politeness than sincerity. Just as "how are you?" is more of a greeting than it is a question, so "come and visit us" is more a sign of kindness than an invitation.

There will be times in your life, however, when business or pleasure takes you to a distant city and the thought will occur to you that it would be 1) pleasant, 2) convenient, and 3) cheap to stay with a friend. On rare occasions you might even receive a sincere and specific invitation. Follow our advice, and you won't blow it.

• Make a request, not a reservation: We think it's very rude—even among the best of friends and the closest of relatives—to simply announce your visit to a friend or relative and, in effect, demand to stay with him. But with a very good friend, you may approach it as you would asking for a special favor. Tell him you're planning a visit to his city and ask, very humbly, if it would be all right to stay with him. It wouldn't hurt to suggest that you could just as easily stay in a hotel or that you could postpone your trip to a more convenient time if necessary. In fact, the best way to ask—even though it may be a little devious—is simply to call and ask your friend if he could recommend a good hotel. If he says, "Why, the Mayfair Hotel is nice, so I'm told," you're out of luck. But if he says, "Of course not, you must stay with me, I won't hear of anything else!" make a few polite protests and pack your bags.

• Give your host lots of notice with specific arrival *and* departure times: Cushion the shock of your visit by letting your host know about it far in advance. Tell him exactly what time to expect you, and be on time. Most important, make it clear from the very beginning exactly when you plan to leave. Remember, hosts thrive on hope—the hope that you will eventually go home—so always let them see the light at the end of the tunnel.

• Be prepared: The Boy Scout motto, "be prepared," applies especially to those occasions when you've been invited to someone's beach house or weekend cabin in the mountains. Call your host ahead of time and ask him what kind of clothing to bring. He knows the territory, the climate, and the agenda better than you do. Many a weekend (and friendship, too, no doubt) has been ruined by guests who spoiled everyone's fun because they didn't have the right gear.

• Bring money: Far more important than the clothing you bring, however, is the cash you bring. A good houseguest has lots of money and is constantly looking for ways to lavish it on his hosts. You may choose to go out and buy them a week's supply of groceries, for example. Or spontaneously decide to take their children to the movies. You should never be unable to pursue an activity that your host suggests because you don't have the money.

• Remember: *You're* the one on vacation. You, on the other hand, should never be the one to suggest an expensive activity unless you're prepared to treat. Remember, your host is not on vacation. He doesn't have a wad of traveler's checks burning a hole in his pocket. In fact, he probably has to squeeze your visit into his normal weekly budget, even though he'll be buying more groceries, eating out more often, and paying for more entertainment than he normally would. You may think your arrival calls for a celebration in which all sober thoughts about life as usual should be temporarily set aside, but your host may not agree.

• Take your host to dinner: If you do nothing else for your hosts all weekend, at least take them out to dinner. But don't start one of those embarrassing tug-of-wars for the check at the end of a meal. Instead, make it clear *before* you arrive that you intend to treat your hosts to dinner during your visit. You may have to do a little research, but it's best if *you* suggest the restaurant so you won't put your host in the uncomfortable position of deciding how much you will spend. When you make the invitation, be clear and specific. "Well, Todd and Karen, I certainly am looking forward to seeing you, and to thank you, I want you both to be *my guests* for dinner at La Fleur on Sunday night." Don't take no for an answer.

• Help around the house: Always ask your host what you can do to help. When it comes to some tasks, however, don't even bother to ask, just jump in and do them. You should always make your own bed, for example, keep your bedroom and bathroom tidy, and clear the dinner table. Offer to wash the dishes, but if your host declines, don't protest too much. He may think it's easier to do them without you.

• Give your host a break: It is not at all rude to entertain yourself alone away from the house now and then, especially if your visit lasts longer than a weekend. Go for a walk. Spend the afternoon shopping. It gives your host the chance to belch, nap, walk around with his clothes off, clean his ears, and do all the other things that you can only do at home, alone. You may wish to visit other friends in the same city. That's fine. Invite your host along, but don't insist. Under no circumstances should you invite your other friends to your host's home, no matter how certain you are they'll like each other. That's an abomination.

• Write a thank-you letter: The thank-you letter written after you've been an overnight guest is so obligatory that it even has its own name—a bread-and-butter note. The good bread-and-butter note cannot be too extravagant in its praise of the host, too humble in its gratitude for the hospitality, or too enthusiastic about the pleasures of the visit. It's not a bad idea to send along a little gift as well. (Even if you arrived with one.) Be sure to mention one or two highlights from your stay just to show you didn't sleepwalk through the whole weekend. As shown by the following example of a bread-and-butter note, you should extend these courtesies no matter how bad a time you really had.

My dear Thane of Cawdor, Thane of Glamis, and soon (if I don't start feeling better) King of Scotland, Macbeth:

Thank you very much for letting me stay in your castle on Tuesday night. Dinner was great. I'm afraid I overindulged myself a bit, though, because I noticed some pains in my stomach during the night. But it was well worth it. My compliments to the chef.

I'm so sorry my injuries prevented me from enjoying

breakfast with you. The doctor says I should be out of the hospital soon. My best to your charming wife, and regarding those spots, may I suggest she read Chapter 5 of a new book, *Leaving the Nest,* which I'm enclosing as a small token of my gratitude.

Your friend,
Duncan

A Good Neighbor Policy

As we've mentioned on more than one occasion in this book, a good neighbor can be a very handy thing to have. A solid relationship with your neighbors plays an important role in keeping your apartment safe from crime and fire. It can give you added bargaining power in disputes with the landlord. And it can even rescue your baked chicken on a day when you forgot to buy butter.

It's easy to get to know your neighbors, because no matter how different you may turn out to be, you always start off with something in common—your building (or your neighborhood). It's especially easy to get to know your neighbors when you're new. Just stick out your hand, and say "Hi, I'm your new neighbor." Only about one out of twenty people will fail to respond positively to this approach, and they tend to be the same ones who are locked up in their rooms torturing puppies anyway, so it's no great loss.

Once you've established a "hi-how-ya-doing" relationship with your neighbors, however, it's important to remember that good neighbors do not necessarily have to be good friends. Unless you find more things in common than just your address, don't feel you have to become special chums with every neighbor. A good neighbor relationship is more like a marriage of convenience than one of love, because it is based mostly on mutual needs. As strange as it sounds, many a good neighbor relationship has been spoiled because one person wanted to become friends and the other did not.

The best way to have good neighbors is to be one yourself. Keep an eye on your neighbor's place, even if he hasn't asked you to, and let him know if you notice anything wrong. Offer to help when you see him lugging a new piece of furniture up the stairs. Sign for his packages when he's not in and make sure he gets them later.

Are you bucking for sainthood? No. Just the opposite. You're scratching your neighbor's back because someday you may need him to scratch yours.

When the day comes when you must ask a favor of your neighbor, don't overdo it. Replace whatever consumable items you borrow and don't make a habit of borrowing things that you really should buy yourself. The person who borrows a vacuum cleaner because his own broke down is simply availing himself of a neighborly relationship. But the person who borrows a vacuum cleaner from his neighbor once a week because he is too poor or too lazy to go out and buy one is a pest.

Don't exploit your neighbors, either. If you must sell chocolate bars to raise money for your favorite charity, have the decency to do it to strangers, not your neighbors. Another good way to ruin your relationship with your neighbors is to sell them laundry products. As far as we know, there is no Amway distributor in America whose neighbors don't hold their breath every time he walks by.

The worst way to get to know your neighbors is to have them come to the door when you're having a party and threaten to call the police if you don't shut up. We know a little trick for preventing this situation. First, invite your neighbors to the party. But if you don't want to do that (and as we've said, you certainly needn't feel obligated to), just warn them in advance. Write a note: "Dear Jim, I just wanted you to know I'm going to have some friends over for a little party tonight. If it gets too loud, please let me know. Thanks, Susan." Having been treated with such respect, it will take a thermonuclear blast for Jim to complain.

But what if Jim has a bash and he wrote you no such note? How do you handle a noisy neighbor? Your first inclination will be to bang on the walls or stamp your foot on the floor. Don't do that. You're combating rudeness with rudeness, and we hope we've made it clear by now that you should never do that. Don't fall for the illusion of anonymity that you have in these situations. One stamp of your foot on the floor and your neighbor will know exactly who is complaining, just as you know exactly who is playing his stereo too loud. Once you and your neighbor have communicated by blasting and banging at each other, it will be very hard to face one another in the halls tomorrow, much less borrow a cup of sugar. Instead, we recommend you put on a robe (the more tired and bedraggled you look, the better) and trudge barefoot over to his apartment, knock gently on the door, and politely ask him to turn down his stereo.

The Lord's admonition to "love thy neighbor as thyself" really covers all the bases when it comes to dealing with your neighbors and dealing with other people in general. Why some people consider etiquette irrelevant is a mystery to us. The way in which we treat others may be the *most* relevant and important subject in the world; certainly it's the most important subject covered in this book. After all, they don't call it the golden rule for nothing.

Epilogue:
The Secret of Life

Well, there it is. We've told you everything we know. From here on out, you're on your own. But there's one thing we *haven't* told you. Because up until now it's been a secret.

When it comes to balancing your checkbook, cleaning house, cooking your own meals, and all the little mundane tasks we've talked about in this book, you'll never hear anyone do anything but whine and complain.

They'll never tell you the truth:

IT FEELS GOOD.

Yes, it feels good. No, not as good as sex, or even as good as hugging a puppy. But there is an undeniably pleasant sensation about being in charge of your own life, managing your affairs with intelligence and skill.

When you can sew your own button and scramble your own egg, unclog your own toilet and change your own fuse, you're acting like an adult. And because of that, you can enjoy all the fun of being one, too.

Of course life won't always be easy, but we know you can make it.

Just remember, your mother loves you.

And if things don't work out, you can always come home.

Because home is the place where they *have* to take you in . . . even if they'd really rather not!

Bibliography and Sources

The following books were particularly helpful to us in compiling the information for *Leaving the Nest*, and we thought you might find them helpful, too. Many times we were forced by the limitations of space to merely scratch the surface of complex subjects—especially money, nutrition and health; interior decoration; and home repair. If you'd like to learn more about such topics, we recommend you start with these fine books:

Almeida, Philip. *How to Decorate a Dump.* Secaucus, New Jersey: Lyle Stuart, Inc., 1983. An amusing, lavishly illustrated and very useful book on how to take a slummy-looking apartment and turn it into a palace.

Ardman, Harvey, and Perri Ardman. *The Complete Apartment Guide.* New York: Macmillan Publishing Company, 1982. Is there any aspect of living in an apartment which isn't covered in this book? We don't think so.

Aslett, Don. *Is There Life After Housework?* Cincinnati: Writer's Digest Books, 1981. The best book on cleaning we've ever seen.

Bingham, Joan. *The Handbook for Apartment Living.* Radnor, Pennsylvania: Chilton Books, 1981. Good advice on all aspects of apartment life, especially furnishing and decorating.

Cook, John, and Robert Wool. *All You Need to Know about Banks.* New York: Bantam Books, 1983. An insider's look at the world of banking that will keep you laughing even as you find yourself getting angrier and angrier. Excellent information about how to establish credit, too.

Estrella, Manuel M., and Martin L. Forst. *The Family Guide to Crime Prevention.* New York: Pinnacle Books, Inc. (paperbound ed.), 1983. Helpful hints on protecting yourself against crime, both inside the apartment and out.

Grady, Tom, and Amy Rood. *The Household Handbook.* Deephaven, Minnesota: Meadowbrook Press, 1981. Packed with useful information (most of it in handy chart form) on everything from frying fish to fixing a toilet.

Martin, Judith. *Miss Manners' Guide to Excruciatingly Correct Behavior.* New York: Warner Books (paperbound ed.), 1983. The best of the new wave of etiquette books, Miss Manners offers modern advice in a charmingly antiquated style of writing.

Morehouse, Lawrence E., and Leonard Gross. *Total Fitness in 30 Minutes a Week.* New York: Pocket Books (paperbound ed.), 1976. A commonsense book on a subject in which the experts often tend to be quacks, fanatics, faddists, or just plain jerks.

Porter, Sylvia. *Sylvia Porter's Your Own Money.* New York: Avon Books, 1983. All about money, from the young person's point of view. Ms. Porter also wrote the definitive book for grown-ups on personal finance, *Sylvia Porter's New Money Book for the 80's.* Don't go through life without it.

Tobias, Andrew. *The Only Investment Guide You'll Ever Need.* New York: Bantam Books, rev. ed. 1983. A witty, easy-to-understand, and unconventional book on investing that debunks a lot of the nonsense you'll hear at cocktail parties.

Wood, Jacqueline, and Joelyn Scott Gilchrist. *The Campus Survival Cookbook #1 and #2.* New York: William Morrow & Company, 1981. Once you're sick of our recipes, try the ones in these books.

INDEX

Accent lighting, 88
Accessories (as decoration), 92–93
Aluminum foil, 46
Aluminum pans, disposable, 51
Annual sales, list of, 227
Antique shops, buying furniture
    from, 69
Ants, getting rid of, 192–194, 196
Apartment comparison chart, 40–42
Apartment hunting, 19–42
  apartment comparison chart,
    40–42
  classified ads and, 29–34
  friends' aid in, 34
  leases and, 38–40
  making the rounds, 34–36
  offering rewards, 36
  qualities to look for in
    neighborhood, 20–23
  rental agent and, 27–29
  rent guidelines for, 25

security deposit and, 37–38
  size of apartment, 23–25
  style of apartment, 25–26
  utilities and, 38
Apartment sales, buying furniture at,
    72
Apple corer, 49
Apples, 155, 157
  fried slices, 147, 149–150
Applesauce, hot, 128, 130
Appliances (kitchen), 56–57
Apron, 48
Artichoke, 155, 156, 157
Artificial plants, 92
Asparagus with cheese, 133, 134,
    135
Auctions, buying furniture at, 72

Balanced diet, 250
Banks (banking), 206–212
  balancing the checkbook,

Banks (banking) (cont.)
207–211
checking accounts, 207
savings accounts, 211
Basement apartments, 24
Bath mats, 57–58
Bathroom
cleaning plan for, 185–186
essential equipment for, 57–59
Bathtub, cleaning, 185
Bedroom
cleaning plan for, 187–189
linens for, 59
Beef
hamburger, 158–159
stuffed peppers with, 162–164
liver and bacon, 142–145
meat loaf, 130–132
pot roast, 117–120, 124–126
steak, 155–157
Bibb lettuce, 101
Blender, 56
Board-certified doctor, 233
Boston lettuce, 101–102
Bread, French, 117, 120, 150, 151
Bridal showers, gifts for, 297
Broccoli, 121, 122, 123, 124
soup, 126–128
Broiling pan, 50
Brooms, 174
electric, 177
Brussels sprouts with water
chestnuts, 160, 161
Budgets, 200–206
Burglary, home security against,
274–280
Buttons, sewing, 270–273

Cabbage
boiled, 135, 136–137
cole slaw, 133, 134, 135
Canisters, 49

Can opener, electric, 46
Carol's carrots, 162, 163, 164
Carpeting, 85–87
Carrots, Carol's, 162, 163, 164
Casserole dish, 51
Ceiling decoration, 84
Certificates of deposit (CDs), 224
Chain stores, buying furniture from,
68
Charity thrift shops, buying furniture
from, 72–73
Checkbook, balancing, 207–211
Checking accounts, 207
Cheese
asparagus with, 133, 134, 135
Cheddar, 155, 157
Cheese grater, 48
Chicken
oven-fried, 121–124
roast, 137–140
salad, 141–142
Chicory, 102
Chopping board, 46
Church bazaars, buying furniture at,
70–71
Cigarette fires, 280–281
Circuit breaker, resetting, 262–263
Classified advertising
abbreviations and phrases used in,
32–34
apartment hunting and, 29–34
buying furniture from, 72
Claw hammer, 259
Cleaning schedules, 171–173
for the bathroom, 185–186
for the kitchen, 180–185
for the living room/dining
room/bedroom, 187–189
Cleaning tool caddy, 177
Cleaning utensils, 53
Cleansers, 177–179
Closets, organization of, 80–81
Colander, 46

Colds, 240–241
Cole slaw, 133, 134, 135
Commuting facilities, proximity to, 21
Complaint letters, 291–292
Condolence notes, 289–290
Congratulatory notes, 290
Cookie sheet, 51
Cooking fork, 49
Cooking guide, 95–168
  chopping vegetables, 103–104
  conversion table for liquid measurements, 106–107
  cooking terms, glossary of, 109–111
  eggs, 98–101
  leftovers, 107–109
  measurements, 106–107
  safety measures in the kitchen, 105–106
  salad dressing, 103
  salads, 101–103
  seasoning, 106
  serving sizes, 106
  temperatures, 104–105
  weekly shopping lists, 111–116
  See also Meal plans (and recipes)
Cooking utensils, 45–50
  important, 48–49
  useful, 49–50
  vital, 46–48
Corkscrew, 49
Cottage cheese and pineapple salad, 145, 146
Cream-cheese and peach salad, 126, 127, 128
Crescent wrench, 259
Crostini alla Napolitana, 164–166
Cucumber and onion, 166, 167, 168
Cupboards
  cleaning, 182–183
  staple foods for, 53–55
Curly endive (chicory), 102

Daily cleaning schedule, 171
Decorating, 82–93
  accessories and, 92–93
  floors and, 85–87
  guidelines for, 82–84
  lamps and lighting and, 87–88
  pictures and, 88–89
  plants and, 89–92
  walls and ceilings and, 84
  windows and, 84–85
Defrosting the refrigerator, 268
Dental insurance, 219
Dentists, guidelines for selecting, 237–239
Department stores
  buying furniture from, 68
  for essential equipment, 62
  list of annual sales and off-season discounts, 227
Dermatologist, 232
Detergents, 177–179
Deviled eggs, 166, 167–168
Diarrhea, 242–243
Diets, balanced, 250
Dime stores for essential equipment, 61
Dining room, cleaning plan for, 187–189
Dinner parties, gifts for, 296–297
Dinnerware, 44–45
Disability insurance, 219
Discarded furniture, 75
Discount stores for essential equipment, 61
Dishwashing, 180–181
  aids for, 177
Doctors, guidelines for selecting, 230–237
Door locks, 275–277
Drapes, 85
Drugs (for medication), 245–246
Dual-functional furniture, 78
Dusting, 187–188

Dust mop, 175
Dust-mopping, 187
Dustpan, 174
Dustrag, 175

Eating utensils, 44–45
Efficiency apartments, 23–24
Egg beater, 48
Eggs, 98–101
  deviled, 166, 167–168
  fried, 99–100
  frittata, 150–152
  hard-boiled, 100–101
  scrambled, 99
  soft-boiled, 100
Electrical fires, 280
Electric broom, 177
Electric can opener, 46
Electric drill, 259
Electric frying pan, 56
Electric hand mixer, 56
Electric knife, 56
Escarole, 102
Etiquette, 283–304
  complaint letters, 291–292
  condolence notes, 289–290
  get-well notes, 287–288
  invitations, 293–296
  toward neighbors, 302–304
  notes of congratulations, 290
  overnight guests and, 298–302
  presents and, 296–298
  thank-you notes, 286–287,
    301–302

Factory outlets, buying furniture
    from, 69
Family practice specialist, 231
Faucets, leaky, 267–268
Fire extinguishers, 290
Fire prevention, 280–281
First-aid kit, 247–248
Fish, broiled, 133–135

Five-year plan for buying furniture,
    65–67
Fixed expenses, 200
Flashlight, 260
Flatware, 45
Flea markets, buying furniture at,
    71–72
Floors, 85–87
Flu, the, 241–242
Food processor, 56–57
Formal invitations, responding to,
    294–296
Freestanding closets, 81–82
French bread, 117, 120, 150, 151
Fried egg, 99–100
Frittata, 150–152
Fruits (staples), 55
Frying pans, 51
  electric, 56
Furniture, 65–78
  buying high-quality pieces, 67–70
  buying low-priced pieces, 70–74
  five-year purchase plan for, 65–67
  free furniture, 74–75
  layout and space for, 75–78
Fuses
  blown, 261–263
  resetting, 262

Garage sales
  buying furniture at, 70–71
  for essential equipment, 61
Garbage bags, 46
Garbage cans, 46, 176
Garden apartments, 24
General practitioner (G.P.), 231
Get-well notes, 287–288
Glassware, 45
  for the bathroom, 58
Glossary of cooking terms, 109–111
Grapes, white, 164, 166
Grease cans, 46
Green beans, 142, 144, 145

Green peppers, stuffed, 162–164
Green salad, 101–103, 117, 124, 164, 165
Grocery cart, 260
Group insurance plans, 221
Gynecologist, 231

Ham, broiled, 145–147
Hamburger, 158–159
    stuffed peppers with, 162–164
Hammer, claw, 259
Hand-me-down furniture, 74–75
Hand mixer, electric, 56
Handsaw, 259
Hard-boiled egg, 100–101
Headache, 244–245
Health and hygiene, 229–253
    colds, 240–241
    dentists, guidelines for selecting, 237–239
    diarrhea, 242–243
    doctors, guidelines for selecting, 230–237
    drugs (for medication), 245–246
    first-aid kit, 247–248
    the flu, 241–242
    headache, 244–245
    medicine chest, 248–249
    nutrition and, 249–252
    physical fitness and, 252–253
    stomachache, 243–244
Health foods, 251
Health insurance, 217–219
Health Maintenance Organizations (HMOs), 218, 233
High-quality furniture, 67–70
Homemade furniture, 73–74
Home repairs, 255–273
    backed-up sink, 266–267
    blown fuse, 261–263
    defrosting the refrigerator, 268
    the landlord and, 256–257
    leaky faucet, 267–268

painting, 268–270
rips and tears (in clothing), 273
running toilet, 263–265
sewing buttons, 270–273
stopped-up toilet, 267
tool kit for, 258–260
Home security, 274–281
    burglary and, 274–280
    fire and, 280–281
Hospitalization insurance, 217–218
House sales, buying furniture at, 70–71
Housewarming party, 61

Iceberg lettuce, 102
Ice cream sundae, 158, 159
Ice cube trays, 46
Independent furniture stores, 68
Individual retirement account (IRA), 224–225
Insurance, 217–221
    dental insurance, 219
    health insurance, 217–219
    life insurance, 220
    tenant's insurance, 220
Internist, 231
Investments, 221–225
    certificates of deposit (CDs), 224
    individual retirement account (IRA), 224–225
    mutual funds, 223–224
    stocks, 222–223
Invitations, responding to, 293–296
Ironing, 191–192

Kitchen, cleaning plan for, 180–185
Kitchen boutiques, 62
Kitchen equipment (essential), 44–57
    appliances, 56–57
    cleaning utensils, 53
    cooking utensils, 45–50
    eating utensils, 44–45

Kitchen equipment (cont.)
    pots and pans, 50–53
    staple foods, 53–56
Kitchen floor, cleaning, 183–185
Knife sharpener, 48
Knives, 46
    electric, 56

Lamb chops, 160–161
Lamps, 87–88
Landlord, home repairs and, 256–257
Laundry, 189–192
Laundry hamper, 59
Leaf lettuce, 102
Leaky faucets, 267–268
Leases for apartments, 38–40
Leftovers, 107–109
Lettuce, 101–102
Life insurance, 220
Lighting, 87–88
    plants and, 90
Liquid measurements, conversion table for, 106–107
Liver and bacon, 142–145
Living room, cleaning plan for, 187–189
Loaf pan, 51
Locks, 275–278
Loft apartments, 24–25
Long-term lease, 39
Low-priced furniture, 70–74

Mail-order furniture, 69–70
Major medical insurance, 217, 218–219
Meal plans (and recipes), 96–97, 117–168
    baked squash with sausage, fried apple slices, watercress and mushroom salad, 147–150
    braised pork chops, buttered rice, hot applesauce, 128–130

broccoli soup, cold fried chicken, peach and cream-cheese salad, 126–128
broiled fish, cold stewed tomatoes, asparagus with cheese, cole slaw, 133–135
broiled ham slice, baked sweet potato, pineapple and cottage cheese salad, 145–147
chicken salad, potato sticks, minted peas, 141–142
cold sliced meat loaf with hot tomato sauce, quick fried potatoes, boiled cabbage, 135–137
crostini alla Napolitana, green salad, white grapes, 164–166
frittata, green salad, French bread, 150–152
hamburger with fried onions on a toasted bun, "salad-bar" salad, ice cream sundae, 158–159
lamb chops, mint jelly, baked potato, Brussels sprouts with water chestnuts, 160–161
liver and bacon, green beans, potato cakes, 142–145
meat loaf, parsley potatoes, stewed tomatoes, spinach salad, 130–132
oven-fried chicken, pasta burro, broccoli, 121–124
pot roast encore, home fries, scalloped tomatoes, green salad, 124–126
pot roast with vegetables, French bread, green salad, 117–120
roast chicken, mashed potatoes, peas, Waldorf salad, 137–140
steak, artichoke, lettuce wedge with Thousand Island dressing, apple and Cheddar

cheese, 155–157
stuffed peppers, Carol's carrots,
  orange and onion salad,
  162–164
tuna fish salad, deviled eggs,
  cucumber and onion, potato
  chips, 166–168
veal picata, pasta Fulvia, 152–155
Measurements for cooking, 106–107
Measuring cups, 46–47
  for cleaning, 176
Measuring spoons, 47
Meat loaf, 130–132
Medicine chest, 248–249
Mice, getting rid of, 192–194, 195
Microwave oven, 57
Mirrors, 80
Mixing bowl, 48–49
Money management, 199–227
  balancing the checkbook,
    207–211
  banks (banking), 206–212
  budgets, 200–206
  checking accounts, 207
  insurance, 217–221
    dental insurance, 219
    health insurance, 217–219
    life insurance, 220
    tenant's insurance, 220
  investments, 221–225
    certificates of deposit (CDs), 224
    individual retirement account
      (IRA), 224–225
    mutual funds, 223–224
    stocks, 222–223
  savings accounts, 211
  savings strategies, 225–227
  taxes, 212–217
Monthly cleaning schedule, 171
Mop pail, 175
Mushroom and watercress salad,
  147, 149, 150
Mutual funds, 223–224

Napkins, 45
Neighbors, establishing good
  relations with, 302–304
Nutrition, 249–252

Off-season discounts, list of, 227
One-bedroom apartments, 23
Onions
  chopping, 104
  and cucumber, 166, 167, 168
  and orange salad, 162, 164
Ophthalmologist, 231–232
Optometrist, 232
Orange and onion salad, 162, 164
Oven
  cleaning, 181–182
  microwave, 57
  temperatures of, 105
Overnight guests
  etiquette for, 298–302
  gifts from, 297
Over-the-counter (OTC) medicines,
  246

Padding, carpet, 85–87
Painting, 268–270
  of walls and ceilings, 84
Pancake turner, 48
Pans, 50–53
Paper towels, 47, 176
Parties, gifts for, 297
Passbook savings, 211
Pasta
  burro, 121–124
  Fulvia, 152–155
Pastry brush, 49
Peach and cream-cheese salad, 126,
  127, 128
Peas, 137, 139
  minted, 141, 142
Pepper mill, 47–48
Peppers, green, stuffed, 162–164

Pets in apartments, 39
Physical fitness, 252–253
Physician's Desk Reference, The
    (PDR), 245
Pictures, 88–89
Pineapple and cottage cheese salad,
    145, 146
Pizza, crostini alla Napolitana,
    164–166
Placemats, 45
Plants, 89–92
    watering instructions for, 91
    windows and, 85
Plastic wrap, 49
Pliers, 259
Plumber's friend (plunger), 260
Polishing, 187–188
Pork
    chops, braised, 128–130
    ham, broiled, 145–147
    sausage, baked squash with,
        147–150
Potatoes
    baked, 160, 161
    cakes, 142, 144
    home fries, 125–126
    mashed, 137, 138–139, 140
    parsley, 130, 132
    quick fried, 135, 136
    sweet, baked, 145, 146, 147
Potato masher, 49
Potholders, 47
Pot roast, 117–120, 124–126
Pots, 50–53
Preferred Provider plan, 218–219,
    233
Prescription drugs, 245–246
Presents, guidelines for giving,
    296–298
Primary-care physicians, 230–232
Psychiatrist, 232
Psychologist, 232
Public services, 22–23

Rats, getting rid of, 192–194, 197
Recipes, *see* Meal plans (and
    recipes)
Refrigerator
    cleaning, 182
    defrosting, 268
    staple foods for, 55
Regular checking accounts, 207
Renewal of apartment lease, 39
Rental agencies, 27–29
Rent-controlled apartments, 39–40
Renting furniture, 70
Restaurant-supply houses, 62
Rice, buttered, 128, 129–130
Rips (in clothing), 273
Roaches, getting rid of, 192–194,
    196–197
Roasting pan, 50
Rolling pin, 49–50
Romaine, 102
RSVP invitation, responding to,
    293–294
Rubber gloves, 176
Rubber spatula, 50
Rugs, 85–87

Safety
    measures in the kitchen, 105–106
    See also Home security
Salad dressing, 103
    Thousand Island, 157
Salads
    chicken, 141–142
    green, 101–103, 117, 124, 164,
        165
    orange and onion, 162, 164
    peach and cream-cheese, 126,
        127, 128
    pineapple and cottage cheese,
        145, 146
    "salad-bar," 158, 159
    spinach, 130, 132
    tuna fish, 166–168

Waldorf, 137, 139, 140
watercress and mushroom, 147, 149, 150
Salad spinner, 50
Salt and pepper shakers, 47–48
Saucepans, 53
Sausage, baked squash with, 147–150
Savings
  investments and, 222
  list of annual sales and off-season discounts, 227
  strategies for, 225–227
Savings accounts, 211
Scissors, 50
Scrambled eggs, 99
Screwdriver, 259
Scrub pad, 176
Seasoning, 106
Second-hand shops, buying furniture from, 72–73
Security deposit, 37–38
Serving sizes, 106
Sewing buttons, 270–273
Sheets and pillowcases, 59
Shelving, 80
Shirts, ironing, 192
Shoe racks, 81
Shopping strategy
  for essential equipment, 61–62
  list of annual sales and off-season discounts, 227
  weekly shopping lists for food, 111–116
Short circuit, locating, 263
Short-term lease, 38–39
Shower, cleaning, 185–186
Shower caddy, 58
Shower curtain, 57
Sink
  cleaning, 186
  unclogging, 266–267
6-quart pot, 53

Slotted spoon, 48
Smoke alarm, 281
Soap dish, 58
Soft-boiled egg, 100
Soup, broccoli, 126–128
Spatula, 48
Special checking accounts, 207
Specialty stores, buying furniture from, 68
Spices, 55–56
Spinach, 102
  salad, 130, 132
Sponge mop, 174–175
Sponges, 175
Spray-waxing, 187–188
Squash, baked, with sausage, 147–150
Stains, removing, 191
Standing lamps, 87
Staple foods, 53–56
  for the cupboard, 53–55
  fruits and vegetables, 55
  for the refrigerator, 55
  spices, 55–56
Statement savings, 211
State tax forms, 216
Stationery supplies, 292–293
Steak, 155–157
Steam iron, 191
Stepstool, 260
Stocks, 222–223
Stomachache, 243–244
Storage space, 78–82
Studio apartments, 24
Sublets, 39
Sugar bowl, 48
Sweet potato, baked, 145, 146, 147

Table lamps, 87
Table linen, 45
Tape measure, 259
Taxes, 212–217
Tax forms, 213–216

Tea kettle, 49
Tears (in clothing), 273
Telephone installation, 60
Temperatures for cooking, 104–105
Tenant's insurance, 220
1040 tax form, 215–216
1040A tax form, 215
1040EZ tax form, 214–215
Term insurance, 220
Thank-you notes, 286–287
    overnight guests and, 301–302
Thousand Island salad dressing, 157
Thrift shops, 61
Timer, 48
Toaster, 57
Toilet bowl brush, 175–176
Toilets
    cleaning, 186
    running, 263–265
    stopped-up, 267
Tomatoes
    scalloped, 124, 125, 126
    stewed, 130, 132, 133, 134
Tongs, 50
Tool kit, 258–260
Tools (essential), 258–260
Towels, 57
Track lighting, 88
Tuna fish salad, 166–168
Two-bedroom apartments, 23

Unpainted-furniture stores, 69
Upholstery, cleaning, 187
Utilities
    paying for, 38
    turning on, 59–60

Vacations, home security during,
    278–279
Vacuum cleaner, 177
Vacuuming, 188
Variable expenses, 200

Veal picata, 152–155
Vegetable peeler, 48
Vegetables
    chopping, 103–104
    staples, 55
Vitamins, 251

W-2 tax form, 213–214
W-4 tax form, 213
Walls
    cleaning, 189
    decorating, 84
Wall space, 80
Wardrobes, 82
Warehouse sales, buying furniture at,
    69
Washing and drying laundry,
    189–190
Wastebasket, 176
Water chestnuts, Brussels sprouts
    with, 160, 161
Watercress and mushroom salad,
    147, 149, 150
Watering instructions for plants, 91
Waxing, 187–188
Wedding presents, 297–298
Weekly cleaning schedule, 171
Whisk broom, 174
White grapes, 164, 166
Whole life insurance, 220
Windows, 84–85
    locks for, 277–278
    washing, 188
Window shades, 85
Window squeegee, 176
Wire whisk, 50
Wooden spoons, 49
Wrecking-ball sales, buying furniture
    at, 73
Wrench, crescent, 259

Yearly cleaning schedule, 172

Also available from Quill

The Campus Survival Cookbook
Jacqueline Wood and Joelyn Gilchrist

This is the book to get it all together in the kitchen for the students who've made it to the with-kitchen apartments, on or off campus.

0-688-05030-1

The Campus Survival Cookbook 2
Jacqueline Wood and Joelyn Gilchrist

Here is the successor to *The Campus Survival Cookbook,* which kept thousands of college students alive and well in the seventies. Just as basic, just as useful, but with all-new, more sophisticated recipes.

0-688-00568-3

The Virgin Homeowner's Handbook
Hap Hatton and Laura Torbet

The what-to book first-time homeowners need before the how-to books—complete with 150 hands-on illustrations.

0-688-03700-3

At your local bookstore